THE COMPLETE
ALL-COLOUR

MEAT

COOKBOOK

THE COMPLETE
ALL-COLOUR

MEAT

COOKBOOK

Compiled by a team of
home economists and dieticians

Edited by Alison Leach

NEW
HOLLAND

First published in the UK in 1993 by
New Holland (Publishers) Ltd
37 Connaught Street, London W2 2AZ

ISBN 1 85368 252 7

Australian Consultant: Tess Mallos
Editors: Linda de Villiers and Alison Leach
Designers: Janice Evans and Joan Sutton
Design assistant: Tracey Carstens
Cover design: Janice Evans
Photographer: Willie van Heerden
Stylists: Gay Mitchell and Ria Esterhuizen
Illustrator: Marianne Saddington

Typeset by Hewer Text Composition Services, Edinburgh
Reproduction by Unifoto (Pty) Ltd
Printed and bound in Singapore by Tien Wah Press (Pte) Ltd

CONTENTS

FOREWORD

The Complete Meat Cookbook serves to illustrate once again that red meat is the most popular form of protein for many people. With its versatility and exceptional nutritional value, meat is a boon for everyone planning a balanced diet and healthy lifestyle. It is satisfying, sustaining and convenient as well as being a traditional favourite with all ages. A balanced diet, which includes meat, is as important today as it ever was. Nowadays most people acknowledge that meat has a role to play as the most important source of protein, as well as providing many vitamins and minerals which are vital to our wellbeing.

In this book, the basic information relating to red meat has been carefullly compiled for use by food experts, students, butchers . . . and above all, by consumers. In addition to mouthwatering recipes for beef, mutton, lamb, pork, kid and veal dishes, provision is made for the gourmet who is constantly in search of new taste experiences – an exciting collection of recipes ranging from everyday dishes to ethnic recipes and impressive party fare!

Background information about the preparation of meat before it reaches the shops is also provided. This may perhaps be of passing interest to the average consumer, but will be an invaluable source of reference for professionals.

Practical advice on storing and freezing meat is also given, as well as hints on expert carving of cooked meat. To add that extra touch of flavour, there is also a section on the use of herbs and spices, as well as a chapter on marinades, bastes and butters.

The belief that the microwave oven does not do justice to the flavour and aroma of meat dishes is effectively dispelled in the special chapter on microwave meals. A comprehensive glossary which defines lesser known cookery terms (especially those pertaining to the preparation of special dishes) is also included.

The Complete Meat Cookbook is the most up to date book available on the subject. Filled with inspiring, tasty, nutritious dishes it will appeal to meat lovers everywhere.

INTRODUCTION

Red meat is one of the most popular items on the menu in many homes. There is little doubt about its tastiness and succulence but its nutritional value may be less well known. Lean red meat is often referred to as nutrient rich because it is loaded with nutrients for relatively few calories. This characteristic of red meat confirms its position in a healthy lifestyle.

The protein content of red meat is special because it contains all the essential amino acids in the correct proportions – all this in only a moderate serving. These proteins are used for a wide variety of important functions – from growth during childhood to tissue maintenance.

There is much controversy about the role of fat in coronary heart disease. Although red meat contains fat, a large proportion is visible and can be trimmed off without much difficulty. The fat in red meat is, like most fats in nature, a combination of saturated, polyunsaturated and monounsaturated fatty acids in varying amounts. Red meat, however, contains less than fifty per cent saturated fatty acids – while the rest is mono- and polyunsaturated. By keeping servings moderate and by trimming off excess fat, only nutritious lean meat is retained without increasing fat consumption unnecessarily.

CHOLESTEROL

All animal protein contains cholesterol because it is a component of the cell walls. Health experts recommend that the intake of cholesterol should not exceed 300 mg per day. A 100 g serving of red meat contributes only about a third of the daily recommendation as it contains between 70 and 110 mg of cholesterol per 100 g. It should be remembered, however, that cholesterol is not obtained from dietary sources alone, as the body manufactures its own cholesterol in the liver.

Red meat not only consists of protein but is also a generous source of B complex vitamins such as vitamin B_1, B_2, B_3, B_6, B_{12}, folic acid and pantothenic acid. These vitamins have very important metabolic roles to fulfil in the body, one of which is the energy-releasing function from a carbohydrate source. There is no doubt that red meat is an excellent source of mineral salts. The contribution that red meat makes here is in its zinc, iron, copper, magnesium, manganese, phosphorus and potassium content. Because the human body cannot produce mineral salts by itself, it is obvious that a product such as red meat will assist in boosting a mineral deficient diet considerably.

RED MEAT COOKING METHODS AND HEALTHY EATING PRINCIPLES

☐ Choose red meat with little visible fat. Trim all visible fat to a thickness of 5 mm ($\frac{1}{4}$ inch) or less before cooking.

☐ Use as little cooking oil and fat as possible during the cooking process. Non-stick cookware and sprays are available which make the addition of fat unnecessary.

☐ Limit deep- and shallow-frying because these methods load fat and calories unnecessarily. Rather use the following:
Moist-heat cooking methods: Stewing, braising, casseroling, cooking in a cooking bag and foil.
Dry-heat cooking methods: Grilling, pan grilling, barbecuing, stir-frying and oven-roasting.

☐ Heated liquids used in red meat dishes should add to the nutritional value and taste of the dish but should not add too many additional calories. Use liquids such as fruit juices, meat stock and vegetable purées for interesting variations.

☐ Add a variety of vegetables to red meat stews and braised dishes. The recommended proportion of vegetables to red meat is two to one.

☐ Make use of dried or fresh fruit to create exotic red meat dishes. Not only is this a wonderful way of adding colour, but it also increases the nutritional value of the dish.

☐ Reap all the nutritional wealth from red meat by including a moderate, cooked serving of 125 g (4 oz) in your eating plan two to three times a week.

☐ Limit the use of salt. A better alternative is fresh or dried herbs.

☐ Cream and soured cream have a high fat content and can be substituted in sauces and soups by low-fat yoghurt and fromage frais. It is important, however, not to allow the yoghurt or fromage frais to come to the boil as it will curdle and spoil the appearance of the dish.

☐ Use low-fat cheeses such as Edam and mozzarella. Skimmed milk can successfully replace whole milk.

☐ When deciding on an accompaniment to a red meat dish, it is advisable to concentrate on high-fibre products such as brown rice, wholemeal bread and cracked wheat rather than their refined equivalents.

☐ The use of cooking oil or fat is usually unnecessary when browning meat which has enough fat of its own.

☐ After browning meat and sautéing vegetables, excess fat can be discarded before adding the liquid.

☐ Leave casseroles and stews to cool after cooking, then skim off the excess fat that sets on top.

☐ Once visible fat has been trimmed, pork contains only 1.5 per cent intramuscular fat. This makes pork an ideal food for slimmers.

☐ Cook schnitzels under a pre-heated grill instead of shallow-frying.

A healthy lifestyle includes exercise and a healthy eating plan which should include a variety of foodstuffs to ensure an adequate intake of nutrients. In moderate servings, red meat occupies a valuable position as a nutrient-rich foodstuff which, above all, has unbeatable taste appeal.

The box on page 9 offers a few hints on how to keep a serving of red meat low in fat and delicious.

BUYING MEAT

Tender, succulent and tasty – these are the most important characteristics to aim for when buying meat. Optimal tenderness, however, is only achieved after correct slaughtering, handling, chilling, freezing and thawing.

HANGING OR AGEING

Hanging or ageing meat is a natural process during which the muscle protein is broken down by enzyme action, resulting in meat that is more tender. The thin outer layer of the meat will dry out slightly because of the loss of moisture during this process, but this is amply compensated for by the extra flavour, tenderness and succulence. As enzyme action is halted by freezing, hanging or ageing should take place before freezing.

A quarter or half a carcase or the primary cuts may be hung or aged. Smaller cuts, such as steaks, cubed meat and mince, are not hung or aged because they would dry out too much due to the large surface area which would be exposed.

Beef should be ripened for 5 to 6 days, while lamb and goat's meat sould be hung or aged for 2 to 3 days, at a temperature of 0 to 4 °C (32 to 39 °F). Generally, the temperature in a butcher's cold-room is kept at a constant 0 °C (32 °F) so that the carcase can then be hung for 10 to 12 days. Normally pork and veal are not hung as there is little improvement in quality and the fat tends to become rancid quickly.

VACUUM-PACKING

Vacuum-packing involves the exclusion of oxygen combined with careful temperature control. This serves to inhibit the growth of certain bacteria, but enzyme action is not interrupted and ageing continues to take place. Beef can be stored in vacuum-packing for up to 2 weeks, provided the temperature is kept constant at 0 to 4 °C (32 to 39 °F) and the wrapping is not damaged. The wrapping material should be airtight. Boned cuts such as sirloin and fillet which are cooked using dry-heat cooking methods, are usually vacuum-packed. Vacuum-packed meat has a purplish red colour and a slightly unpleasant smell is noticed when the package is opened. On exposure to air, however, the meat regains its healthy red colour and the smell disappears.

ADVANTAGES OF VACUUM-PACKING

☆ Short-term freezing and drip loss from thawing are eliminated.
☆ Boned meat takes up less freezer space and packages can be placed on top of each other for ageing.
☆ Meat aged in vacuum-packing has less drip loss and the cut surfaces do not dry out.

REFRIGERATION AND FREEZING

Refrigeration and freezing are two simple yet highly effective methods of preserving perishable food. The nutritional value, appearance and taste of meat are retained by refrigeration and freezing, provided the meat is correctly packed and sealed. The packing material, such as plastic containers and bags, should be airtight, moisture proof,

odourless, colourless and easy to clean. Force all air from the package, then seal and mark each package with the date, amount and kind of meat.

HINTS

☆ Work as rapidly as possible to ensure that the meat remains cold.
☆ Prepare meat so that it can be thawed and used immediately:
  ● bone it beforehand
  ● slash the fat edges of steaks and chops
  ● prepare meat rolls.
☆ Remove all traces of bone dust and blood.
☆ Saw away sharp pieces of bone or cover with waxed paper to prevent the plastic wrapping from being damaged.
☆ Keep the packages square and flat in order to save freezer space and to allow them to freeze more quickly.
☆ Pack meat in family-sized portions.
☆ For rapid refrigeration, meat should be placed on the rack nearest the freezing compartment.

STORAGE TIMES FOR REFRIGERATION AND FREEZING

The storage times indicated in the box below are for meat which has been correctly packed and sealed airtight. Should the temperature rise above the given temperatures, the meat should be stored for shorter periods.

THAWING

If meat is cooked from frozen, large amounts of meat juices are lost. Meat therefore has to be thawed before being cooked. The best method is to thaw meat in the refrigerator in the wrap-

ping. Thick cuts, such as a roll, require 8 to 9 hours per 500 g (1 lb) while thin cuts, such as steaks, require 6 to 8 hours per 500 g (1 lb) to thaw. The microwave oven may be used to thaw meat quickly. Meat should be removed from the wrapping and thawed uncovered in the microwave oven – large cuts, such as a roll, for 10 minutes per 500 g (1 lb) on 30% and small cuts, such as steaks, for 5 minutes per 500 g (1 lb) on 30%. Other methods, such as thawing at room temperature, in hot water or in the sun, are not recommended as they cause the loss of large quantities of meat juices.

LARDING AND BARDING MEAT

Certain meat cuts such as topside, silverside and fillet are not well marbled. In other words they have little intramuscular fat and, therefore, these cuts should be larded or barded for extra juiciness and flavour.

LARDING

Pork fat is generally used for larding. Cut it into thin strips and put them in the freezer until firm. Lard the meat with a larding needle or a knife with a narrow blade, following the grain of the meat as far as possible.

Strips of vegetables such as celery, carrot or garlic may be used for extra flavour and to enhance the appearance of the meat cut.

MEAT	COLD STORAGE (4 °C/39 °F)	FREEZING (−18 °C/−2 °F)
Beef	2 to 4 days	6 to 12 months
Veal	2 to 4 days	6 to 9 months
Pork	2 to 4 days	3 to 6 months
Mutton and lamb	2 to 4 days	6 to 9 months
Mince	1 day	1 to 3 months
Offal	1 day	3 months
Cured and smoked meat	5 to 7 days	2 to 3 weeks*
Sausages	2 to 3 days	3 weeks
Larded and stuffed meat	2 days	1 month
Ready-frozen packages of meat	2 days	1 to 2 months
Cooked meat	–	1 month
*Not recommended since the salty flavour is intensified		

BARDING

This is the method of wrapping caul fat, pork fat or bacon around a lean meat cut, such as the fillet, and securing it by tying it with string. Bacon may also be placed on top of a meat cut, thus basting the meat automatically and making it more juicy. Barding also enhances the appearance of meat.

BONING MEAT

Most people shy away from the mere thought of boning meat, yet it is in fact very simple because no set rules are involved. If you don't the time or the inclination, however, you could ask your butcher to do it for you.

Boned meat has the advantages of saving freezer space and of facilitating and speeding up carving. A further advantage is that there are no bones to damage the freezer wrapping. Better use is also made of the less popular cuts such as the flank which can be transformed into a delicious belly roll pot-roast, for instance, with a ginger and orange stuffing.

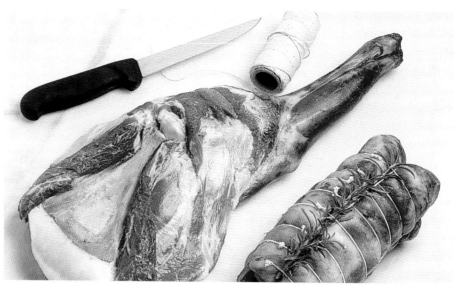
Boning of a shoulder of lamb

CUTS SUITABLE FOR BONING		
BEEF	LAMB	PORK
Chuck	Shoulder	Blade
Flat rib	Thick rib	Rib
Brisket	Rib	Loin
Prime rib	Loin	Chump
Sirloin	Chump	Leg
Rump	Leg	

HINTS

☆ *Use fresh meat for boning. Meat that has been frozen and thawed is not as firm and will not bone easily.*

☆ *Refrigerated meat is boned more easily than meat at room temperature. The fat of warm meat makes the hands oily and slippery.*

☆ *Small cuts such as scrag of lamb and shank are not worth boning because the proportion of meat to bone is very small.*

☆ *The boning knife must have a narrow, firm blade with a sharp point, and must be razor-sharp and easy to handle.*

☆ *Hold the handle of the knife between your four fingers, with your thumb on top to keep your hand from sliding. In this position the blade forms*

a right angle with the fore-arm, allowing free wrist movement for easy control of the cutting direction.

☆ *Work on a wooden surface. Marble or steel surfaces tend to blunt the cutting edge of the knife.*

☆ *Use a sharpening steel to keep knives sharp.*

☆ *Start boning where bone is visible. Work mainly with the point of the knife and try to leave as little meat on the bone as possible.*

☆ *Skewers and string are needed to prepare rolls once the meat has been boned. The skewer serves to keep the roll in position while it is being tied. Use strong natural fibre such as cotton string that will not melt when heated.*

COOKING METHODS

There are different methods for cooking meat. Some methods improve the flavour of the meat while others ensure that tougher cuts become tender and succulent. It is very important to use the correct cooking method as good quality meat can be ruined if it is cooked incorrectly. The methods commonly used to cook meat are divided into two categories, namely moist-heat and

dry-heat. These terms refer to the medium that surrounds the meat, whether it is heated liquid, oil or hot air.

DRY-HEAT COOKING METHODS

Oven-roasting, grilling, frying and stir-frying are dry-heat cooking methods. No liquid is added and the meat is cooked by direct exposure to heat (for example cooking oil) or by the circulation of hot air. Tender cuts such as veal, lamb and pork and well-hung or aged beef and mutton cuts are suitable for dry-heat cooking and ideally should be cooked until rare or medium since well-done meat tends to be dry.

Oven-roasting

A whole tender, well-hung or aged meat cut weighing 1.5 kg (3 lb) or more is recommended for oven-roasting. If the meat weighs less than 1.5 kg (3 lb), shrinkage may be disproportionately high and too much weight loss will occur.

Place the meat uncovered with the fat side uppermost on the rack of a roasting tin. For an accurate reading, insert a meat thermometer into the thickest part of the meat, ensuring that it does not touch the bone or fat.

Cooking times are as indicated below:

Rare Beef and veal	15 to 20 minutes per 500 g (1 lb) plus 15 minutes or roast to an internal temperatue of 60 °C (140 °F)
Medium Beef, veal, pork and lamb	20 to 25 minutes per 500 g (1 lb) plus 20 minutes or roast to an internal temperature of 65 °C (150 °F)
Well-done Pork and lamb	25 to 30 minutes per 500 g (1 lb) plus 25 minutes or roast to an internal temperature of 70 °C (160 °F)

To ensure extra succulence and flavour, baste the meat with a basting mixture (page 151) while roasting. Before carving, place the meat in the warming drawer for approximately 10 minutes to allow the meat juices to be reabsorbed and to facilitate carving.

Grilling

Chops, noisettes, steaks, sausages, bacon and kebabs, among others, are suitable for grilling. Slash the fat edges of steak and chops at 2.5 cm (1 inch) intervals to prevent the meat from curling during grilling. It is best to season meat with salt and pepper after grilling as to do so prior to grilling will cause loss of meat juices, with the result that the meat will be dry. Serve immediately after grilling.

There are three ways of grilling meat:

Under the grill: Preheat the grill until red hot. Place the meat uncovered on the rack of a grill pan 10 cm (4 inches) under the heat and grill beef for 5 to 7 minutes in total (rare); veal, beef, lamb and pork for 7 to 10 minutes in total (medium) and pork and lamb for 10 to 12 minutes in total (well-done).

Pan-grilling: Use a ridged pan (or greased frying pan) to grill steaks, chops, sausages, bacon and noisettes. Heat the pan without adding water or fat. Using meat tongs, place the meat in the heated pan. At first the meat will stick to the bottom of the pan but do not pull it away as this will damage the meat fibres and cause loss of meat juices. The meat will be ready to be turned when it no longer sticks to the pan. Cook the meat for the same time as for under the grill.

Sausages and bacon should be placed on the cooker in a cold pan. Set the heat on medium until the meat begins to sizzle and then turn the heat down to low. Grill the meat on both sides until cooked. Use meat tongs to turn sausages so as not to damage the meat and to retain the meat juices.

Barbecuing: Grill the meat 10 cm (4 inches) above moderate coals, using the same times as above. Meat tongs should be used to turn the meat so as not to damage it.

Frying

Minute steaks, schnitzels, fritters and croquettes are suitable for frying. Deep- and shallow-frying are the two cooking methods used. To protect the meat from the high temperature of the oil, the meat is usually covered with batter or with an egg and crumb coating.

Roll minute and thin fillet steaks lightly in plain flour, and then fry in butter. Roll schnitzels, chops and croquettes in plain flour, to dry the surface, then in egg and lastly in breadcrumbs. Place the crumbed meat in the refrigerator for 20 to 30 minutes to allow the crumbs to adhere to the surface.

Shallow-frying: Heat cooking oil, 3 mm ($\frac{1}{8}$ inch) deep, in a heavy-based frying pan. Protect the meat as described above and fry the meat until golden brown. Remove the meat and place it on paper towels to absorb excess oil.

Deep-frying: Heat oil, 10 cm (4 inches) deep, in a heavy-based saucepan. Place the meat in a wire basket and fry until golden brown. Fry croquettes prepared from leftover meat at 200 °C (400 °F) and uncooked meat at 180 °C (350 °F). The temperature of the oil can be gauged by frying a cube of bread. It will take 40 seconds at 200 °C (400 °F) and 60 seconds at 180 °C (350 °F) to turn golden brown. Drain on paper towels and serve immediately with lemon slices.

Stir-frying: A wok or frying pan is ideal for stir-frying. The round base of the pan ensures even heat distribution and only a small amount of oil is needed. Heat the oil in the frying pan or wok. Rapidly fry thin strips of meat while stirring constantly. Add the prepared vegetables, adding the faster cooking vegetables last. Add a small amount of heated liquid and seasoning and simmer uncovered for approximately 2 minutes.

MOIST-HEAT COOKING METHODS

Stewing, braising, pot-roasting, cooking in a casserole, a cooking bag or foil and boiling are all moist-heat cooking methods.

With stews, braised dishes, pot-roasts and casseroles, the meat is simmered slowly in heated liquid which may be meat stock, wine, beer or fruit juice. It is best not to use water as it does not add to the flavour or nutritional value of the dish. Heat the liquid before adding it to

the browned meat as cold liquid tends to draw out the meat juices. For best results, use a heavy-based saucepan with a tightly fitting lid.

Less tender cuts with a large proportion of connective tissue are suitable for moist-heat cooking. The moisture and the long, slow cooking convert the connective tissue into gelatine, thereby tenderizing the meat. When cooking in a cooking bag and foil, steam provides the moisture required for moist-heat cooking.

Stewing

Cubes (2.5 cm/1 inch square), slices (2 cm/$\frac{3}{4}$ inch), strips or portions may be used for stewing. Brown the meat in a mixture of heated butter and cooking oil as this improves the flavour and gives the food an appetizing appearance.

If a recipe calls for onion, garlic and curry powder, remember to fry these ingredients for one minute before adding the heated liquid.

Add the remaining seasoning and cover the saucepan with a tightly fitting lid. Reduce the heat and simmer until the meat is tender. Vegetables may be added 30 minutes before the end of the cooking time.

Braising

Slices (2 cm/$\frac{3}{4}$ inch thick) and chops (2.5 cm/1 inch thick) may be cooked using this method which is very similar to stewing. Brown the meat in a mixture of heated butter and cooking oil. Place the meat on a bed of sautéed vegetables and add only a small amount of heated liquid. Cover the saucepan with a tightly fitting lid before reducing the heat and simmering until the meat is tender.

Pot-roasting

Meat cuts weighing 1.5 kg (3 lb) or more are used. With meat cuts weighing less than 1.5 kg (3 lb), the shrinkage will be disproportionately high.

Tie the meat with string to retain its shape during cooking. As for stewing, brown the meat all over in heated butter and cooking oil. Add a small amount of heated liquid, cover the saucepan with a tightly fitting lid and simmer until the meat is tender. If desired, baste or turn the meat while pot-roasting for added succulence. Vegetables may be added approximately 30 minutes before the end of the cooking time.

Casserole cooking

Meat cubes, slices, chops, portions or whole cuts weighing 1.5 kg (3 lb) or more are suitable for this method. Brown the meat in heated butter and cooking oil in a casserole. Add heated liquid and seasoning. Cover and bake in a pre-heated oven at 160 °C (325 °F/gas 3) for 40 to 45 minutes per 500 g (1 lb) plus 40 minutes extra.

HINTS

☆ If the meat contains enough fat, it is not necessary to add butter or cooking oil.

☆ If the liquid boils away, replenish with heated liquid.

☆ If there is too much liquid left once the meat is cooked, remove the lid and reduce the liquid over high heat or thicken the sauce with a flour and water paste.

Using a cooking bag

A whole meat cut weighing 1.5 kg (3 lb) or more is used. Lard (page 11) lean meat cuts for succulence and flavour. Sprinkle seasoning over the meat or rub it in. Place the meat inside the cooking bag, tie the bag loosely and pierce a few holes in the top for the steam to escape. Place the bag in a roasting tin and bake in a pre-heated oven at 160 °C (325 °F/gas 3) for 40 to 45 minutes per 500 g (1 lb) plus 40 minutes.

Baking in foil

A whole meat cut weighing 1.5 kg (3 lb) or more may also be cooked in foil. Sprinkle the seasoning over the meat or rub it in, then place the meat on the shiny side of the foil. Wrap the meat in the foil, sealing it tightly to retain the steam. Place the meat in an oven dish and bake at 160 °C (325 °F/gas 3) for 40 to 45 minutes per 500 g (1 lb) plus 40 minutes. Open the foil during the last 30 minutes of cooking time to allow the meat to brown.

Boiling

Cured or smoked meats and meat stocks are prepared by boiling. Cover the meat or bones with cold water. Add bay leaves, cloves, peppercorns, celery, carrots, onion and a bouquet garni for added flavour. Bring to the boil, reduce the heat, cover with lid and simmer until the meat is tender and cooked. Replenish the cooking liquid with boiling water if necessary.

CARVING MEAT

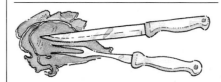

Considering the time and trouble involved in the preparation of meat cuts, it is important that the cooked meat is carved correctly. Carving is an art which is perfected with experience. The person doing the carving (the carver) should know where the bone is situated, the direction of the grain of the meat and how thick the slices should be cut. The accompanying sketches illustrate the different meat cuts, the position of the bone and the direction of the grain of the meat.

HINTS

☆ The two-pronged fork plays an important role in carving since it helps to keep the meat in position.

☆ After being cooked, the meat should be left to stand for at least 10 minutes to facilitate carving.

☆ With the exception of porterhouse steaks, meat is always carved across the grain.

☆ Carve on a flat surface, such as a wooden board, that will not slip.

☆ Beef is usually carved into very thin slices, while lamb and pork may be carved according to taste. Use the full length of the blade to cut slices of equal thickness.

☆ Keep the carving knife sharp. The blade should be long and firm. It should not be serrated as this tears the meat.

☆ Cut through the meat, using long strokes. Do not press on the meat as this will cause loss of meat juices.

CARVING IN THE KITCHEN

Before you start to carve the meat, ensure that everything is ready so that you are able to serve the meat and the rest of the food while it's still warm. Using a carving board, carve the meat quickly and arrange the slices neatly on a warm serving platter.

CARVING AT THE TABLE

Place the meat on a warm serving platter in front of the carver, with the warm dinner plates within easy reach. The serving platter should be large enough to hold the meat and the carved portions. Although garnishing is attractive, it should be kept to a minimum so that it does not get in the way. The carver, who may stand or sit as preferred, should ensure that enough meat is carved before serving each guest.

BEEF WING RIB, PRIME RIB AND SIRLOIN

Wing rib and prime rib

Ask your butcher to saw through the backbone section approximately 2.5 cm (1 inch) above the backbone and to remove the triangular backbone along the length of the meat cut ('chine' page 154).

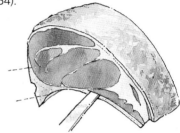

1. Before bringing the meat to the table, first cut and remove the dorsal vertebrae from the meat. Slip the knife between the meat and the dorsal vertebrae and remove the bones along the entire length of the meat.

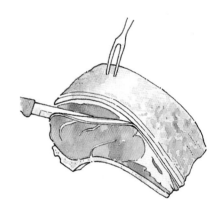

2. Place the meat in front of the carver with the ribs pointing away as shown. Insert the fork 7.5 cm (3 inches) from the right side of the meat. Start carving from the right, cutting 5 mm ($\frac{1}{4}$ inch) thick slices across the grain.

3. Slip the knife between the ribs and the meat and loosen the slices.

Sirloin

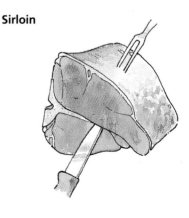

Slip the knife between the meat and the T-shaped bone and cut the meat loose from the bone. Remove the bone and set it aside. Now carve the eye muscle and the fillet across the grain and serve each person with a portion from both sections.

LOIN AND RIB OF LAMB, MUTTON AND PORK

Ask your butcher to chine (page 154) the backbone and to saw through the backbone between the ribs. This will facilitate carving at the table. Pork rind should always be scored before cooking in order to facilitate carving.

Place the cut on a meat platter so that it stands on the backbone and the fat side faces the guests. Insert the carving fork between two ribs and carve from the right-hand side between the ribs to provide one or two chops for each person. If the cut is prepared with a topping, such as a rack of lamb, place it on a meat platter with the topping uppermost and carve as described above.

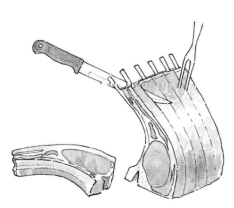

An alternative method is to carve the meat into thin slices across the grain, starting on the right-hand side of the meat cut. Slip the knife between the ribs and the meat, then cut the slices from the rib bones. The slices may either be returned to the bone or arranged neatly on a serving platter.

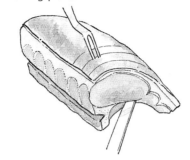

CROWN ROAST

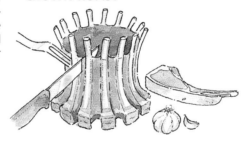

Ask your butcher to saw through the backbone between the rib bones to facilitate carving. A crown roast is made from two sets of ribs of lamb or pork. First remove any garnish or stuffing which will hamper carving. Hold the roast firmly by inserting the fork between the ribs. Start carving at the point where the two sets of ribs have been joined together. Cut downwards between the two ribs to the backbone, which has already been sawn through, and serve one or more chop to each person.

SADDLE OF LAMB, MUTTON OR PORK

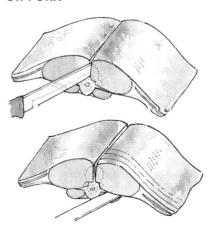

Loosen the meat by cutting on either side of the backbone. Starting on the right-hand side, carve the eye muscle into slices. Cut between the bone and the meat to remove the slices. After the eye muscles have been removed, turn the saddle over, remove both fillets completely and cut them into slices. Serve each person with a portion of eye muscle and fillet.

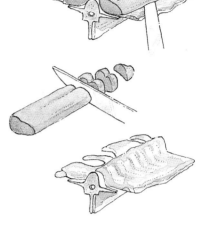

SHOULDER OF LAMB OR MUTTON

1. To facilitate carving, loosen the meat by cutting around the blade bone before cooking. Leave the bone in position. After cooking, twist the bone loose and remove it.

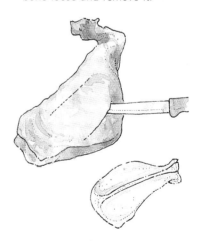

2. Hold the meat firmly by inserting the fork into the shank or by holding it with a napkin. Turn the meat so that the thickest part is uppermost. Begin by making a downward cut from the centre, then cut slices on either side of the cut. Turn the meat over and carve the shank side horizontally into slices until all the meat has been removed.

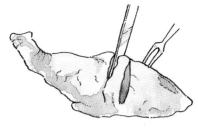

LEG OF LAMB

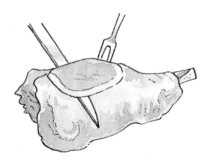

Place the leg of lamb or mutton on the serving platter with the shank bone to the carver's right-hand side and the shank side pointing up. Cut two or three slices on the underside of the meat so that it will stand level and form a firm base. Use the carving fork to turn the meat over in order to position it firmly.

Start where the shank bone is joined to the marrowbone and carve the meat at a slight angle. Make a second cut down to the bone in the direction of the shank side. Continue to the end of the shank bone. Continue to cut from the right-hand side in the direction of the pelvic joint, cutting straight down towards the bone. Continue until all the meat has been cut on that side.

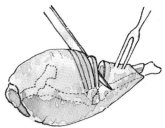

Loosen the slices by cutting along and as close to the bone as possible. Lift the slices and arrange on the serving platter. Remove the pelvic bone.

Turn the meat over. Starting from the shank side, cut around the bone with a circular movement. Loosen the slices by cutting along the length of the bone and arrange on the serving platter.

An alternative method is to remove the bone and cut the meat into slices across the grain. If it is difficult to hold the leg in position with a fork, hold the shank with a napkin or clean cloth.

LEG OF PORK, HAM

Carve a leg of pork in the same way as you would a leg of lamb or mutton. To carve a boned ham, simply carve it into thin slices across the grain.

AITCHBONE, SILVERSIDE, BLADE AND TOPSIDE

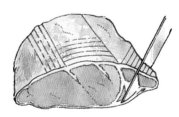

Cut the meat into thin slices across the grain. When a meat cut consists of several muscles with the grains running in different directions (the silverside, for example, contains three muscles), it is advisable to carve the muscles separately.

ROLLED MEAT

Insert the fork 7.5 cm (3 inches) from the right-hand side of the meat roll. Starting from the right, carve into thin slices, removing skewers or string as they occur.

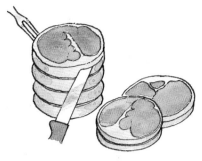

An alternative method, if the meat roll is not too long, is to place the meat roll upright. Insert the fork on the left-hand side of the meat roll and carve thin slices horizontally, starting from the right and cutting towards the fork.

OX TONGUE

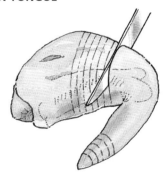

Carve the tongue downwards into thin slices. Each slice should be uniformly thin and parallel.

T-BONE OR PORTERHOUSE STEAK

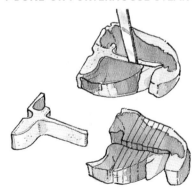

Loosen the meat from the T-shaped bone and set the bone aside.

Holding the knife at right angles to the original position of the bone, cut thin slices through the eye muscle and the fillet, following the grain. Serve each person with a portion of both.

HERBS AND SPICES

Herbs and spices with red meat are like bread and butter – they belong together – and a pinch of herbs or a sprinkling of spice accentuates the natural flavour of the meat.

The use of herbs and spices has been an integral part of our cookery heritage since the earliest times. Herbs were also used for medicinal purposes. As well as growing fruit and vegetables, virtually every family therefore had a small herb garden.

The cultivation of culinary herbs and certain spices is a simple task and it has become fashionable to have and enjoy a herb garden – even if it is only a tiny patch accommodating the most common herbs, or a kitchen window-sill garden of parsley and mint.

HERBS

Herbs are the fresh or dried leaves, flowers and sometimes stalks of aromatic plants.

GENERAL HINTS FOR HERBS

☆ *Use herbs discreetly so as to enhance but not overpower the flavour of the meat.*

☆ *Do not use too many different herbs in one dish as they may affect the natural flavour of the meat.*

☆ *Store dried herbs in jars with tightly fitting lids in a cool, dark place in the kitchen.*

☆ *Buy dried herbs in small quantities as the flavours tend to lose their intensity in time.*

☆ *The flavour of a herb intensifies when dried and, therefore, dried herbs have a stronger flavour than fresh. The proportion of dried to fresh herbs is generally 1 to 3, for example 1 tsp dried or 3 tsp chopped fresh thyme.*

☆ *The volatile oils which give the herb its flavour are encapsulated in tiny cells in the leaves. To release the oils, therefore, chop or bruise fresh herbs before use. Dried herbs may be crushed with the thumb in the palm of the hand to improve their flavour.*

☆ *Use a sprig of a fresh herb such as rosemary or thyme instead of a basting brush to apply a basting mixture to roast or grilled meat.*

☆ *For added flavour, place a sprig of fresh herbs on a meat roll before roasting it.*

☆ *Because herbs contain almost no salt or calories, slimmers may use them freely to flavour meat.*

☆ *The flavour of herbs intensifies with freezing. It is advisable therefore to limit the quantity if the meat dish is to be frozen for some time.*

MEAT MIXTURES FOR MEAT

Herbs may be used separately or in combination. The following is an example of a well-known herb mixture.

Bouquet garni

This is a French term for a small bunch of herbs used to flavour stews, casseroles and soups. A basic bouquet garni usually consists of:

2 bay leaves
1 sprig thyme
2 sprigs parsley (parsley stalks impart a stronger flavour)

OR

1 bay leaf
$\frac{1}{2}$ tsp dried thyme
1 tsp dried parsley

If using fresh herbs, tie them into a bunch or, if using dried herbs, wrap them in a piece of muslin before adding them to the dish.

Herbs such as rosemary, sage and oregano, and spices such as peppercorns and cloves may be added accordingly to taste.

HINT

☆ *Use a long piece of string when tying a bouquet garni so that the ends can be tied to the handle of the saucepan during cooking for easy removal afterwards.*

PRESERVING FRESH HERBS

Seasonal herbs may be dried for future use. This can be done by hanging sprigs of fresh herbs upside down in a shady, warm, airy place. When thoroughly dried, strip the leaves from the stems, pack them in airtight containers and store in a cool, dark place for use in meat dishes. Alternatively, dry fresh herbs in the microwave oven as follows:

Microwave drying: Rinse herbs, remove stalks and dry gently. Spread herbs over paper towels and cover with more paper towels. Microwave on 10% to 30% until dry. Rearrange herbs from time to time. As their volatile oils differ, the drying times will vary according to the quantity and type of herb. Watch constantly. Once dry, crush the leaves and store in an airtight container.

Freezing: Herbs freeze extremely well. Pack fresh herbs tightly into ice-trays, then cover with water and freeze for up to two months. For longer storage, first blanch the herbs, then cool and freeze them in airtight containers. Thaw and drain in a sieve, then pat dry and use like fresh herbs.

SPICES

A spice is the aromatic part of a woody plant and may comprise the seed, bark, buds or root. These parts are generally dried and used whole or in ground form.

GENERAL HINTS FOR SPICES

☆ *Buy spices whole as they remain fresh longer, and grind as required.*
☆ *Toast spices by roasting or frying them before grinding. When heated, the volatile oils contained in the outer layer of the seeds release the aroma and flavour of the spice.*
☆ *Take care not to burn spices or they become bitter.*
☆ *After toasting spices, allow them to cool before grinding them.*
☆ *Grind spices in a blender, coffee mill or with a pestle and mortar.*
☆ *The flavour of a spice intensifies the longer it is simmered. Use spices discreetly so as to enhance but not overpower the flavour of the meat.*
☆ *If using whole spices, use the Indian method to release the full flavour of the spice. Heat ghee (clarified butter) or cooking oil in a heavy-based saucepan over medium heat, add the whole spices and stir-fry for about 1 minute. Then proceed with the preparation of the dish.*

ROASTING SPICES

In the oven: Preheat the oven to 110 °C (225 °F/gas ¼). Spread spices on a baking tray and roast for 30 minutes.

In a pan: Preheat a frying pan. Add spices and stir constantly for approximately 5 to 10 minutes.

STORING SPICES

☆ *Store spices in glass jars with screw or cork tops in a cool, dark place.*
☆ *Avoid having spice racks above the cooker or oven – the heat and light cause the aroma of the spices to fade rapidly.*
☆ *Spices have a shelf life of only 6 months so it is best to buy them in small quantities.*

SPICE MIXTURES FOR MEAT

Spices too may be used separately or in combination. The following recipes illustrate just a few of the myriad mixtures that can be created.

Curry Powder

This consists of a variety of spices such as cumin, coriander and chilli pepper, blended and ground to achieve a delicate flavour combination. It is the chilli pepper that determines the hotness of the curry.

Use the following recipe to prepare your own curry mixture:

BASIC MILD CURRY POWDER

125 g (4 oz) ground turmeric
125 g (4 oz) whole coriander
125 g (4 oz) cumin seeds
90 g (3 oz) dried ginger root
(optional)
2 black peppercorns
1 cardamom pod
1 dried red chilli
30 g (1 oz) saffron (optional)
4 tsp mustard seeds

Combine all the ingredients and grind them in a coffee mill or blender, or with a pestle and mortar. Store in an airtight container in a cool, dry place.
Makes about 500 g (1 lb)

BASIC HOT CURRY POWDER

125 g (4 oz) ground turmeric
125 g (4 oz) whole coriander
125 g (4 oz) cumin seeds
60 g (2 oz) dried ginger root
(optional)
2 black peppercorns
30 g (1 oz) cardamom pods
30 g (1 oz) fennel seeds
30 g (1 oz) dried red chilli
30 g (1 oz) blades mace
30 g (1 oz) mustard seeds
30 g (1 oz) poppy seeds

Combine all the ingredients and grind them in a coffee mill or blender, or with a pestle and mortar. Store in an airtight container in a cool, dry place.
Makes about 625 g (1¼ lb)

> **NOTE**
> ☐ To prevent a floury taste in curries, always remember to fry the curry powder for about a minute before adding the liquid.

TRADITIONAL COMBINATIONS OF HERBS AND SPICES WITH RED MEAT

	Herbs and spices
Beef Any of the herbs indicated alongside are popular, especially if a dash of wine is also added.	Basil, savory, tarragon, bay leaf, marjoram, rosemary, sage
Veal Marjoram and thyme are particularly popular with veal and complement its rather bland flavour	Star anise, basil, dill, tarragon, chervil, coriander, marjoram, rosemary, sage, lemon balm, lemon thyme, fennel
Lamb and mutton Rosemary is a traditional favourite with lamb. Try basil and marjoram for delicious results with roasts.	Basil, savory, tarragon, bay leaf, marjoram, rosemary, sage. Mint in the form of mint sauce is particularly delicious with lamb.
Pork Sage is the most popular herb to use with pork. Use sparingly as the flavour can be overwhelming	Star anise, basil, savory, dill, tarragon, chervil, coriander, mint, marjoram, rosemary, sage, lemon balm, thyme, fennel

GARAM MASALA

Garam masala is not a curry powder in the strict sense of the word although some of the spices are also used in curry powder. Garam masala is added at the end of cooking time, not at the beginning as with curry powder.

250 g (8 oz) whole coriander
125 g (4 oz) cumin seeds
125 g (4 oz) caradmom pods
60 g (2 oz) whole cloves
125 g (4 oz) black peppercorns
1 tsp grated nutmeg

Roast coriander and cumin seeds in separate containers in the oven for 2 to 3 minutes. Do not allow the seeds to burn. Remove the husks of the cardamom pods. Grind the ingredients in a blender or in a mortar.
Makes about 700 g (22 oz)

HINT
☆ *To save time, add the following spices (see box below) to commercially prepared curry powder for added flavour.*

BEEF	LAMB	PORK
2 white cardamom pods, crushed	2 white cardamom pods, crushed	2 white cardamom pods, crushed
star anise	cumin seeds	bay leaf
bay leaf	whole cloves	cassia

NOTE
☐ *Cassia* is the dried bark of the cassia tree, a relative of the cinnamon tree. It is thicker and coarser than cinnamon with a harsher flavour. Although also sold in tight scrolls, it is usually sold in flat pieces or in ground form. Cassia is used in highly spiced dishes such as curries.
☐ *Cinnamon*, the dried aromatic bark of the cinnamon tree, has a sweet, warm taste and spicy flavour. It is sold in ground form and in the form of cinnamon sticks.

MIXED SPICE

This mixture of sweet spices is generally used in puddings, cakes, biscuits and milk- and custard-based dishes. It can also be added with delicious results to many meat dishes.

2 tbsp whole cloves
2 tbsp whole allspice
2 cinnamon sticks
1 tsp black peppercorns
3 tbsp ground ginger
3 tbsp grated nutmeg

Grind the whole spices together and add the ginger and nutmeg. Mix and store in an airtight container. Use sparingly in meat dishes.
Makes about 75 g (2$\frac{1}{2}$ oz)

HERB VINEGAR, OIL AND BUTTER

The following recipes may serve as an inspiration to use these versatile seasonings more frequently. Presented in attractive labelled containers, herb vinegars, oils and butters make wonderful gifts for friends and family.

Herb Vinegar
It is important to use a good quality white or red wine vinegar and young fresh herbs to flavour it.

Place a few sprigs of herbs in a bottle and pour heated vinegar over. Cork the bottle tightly and leave it in a cool, dry place for approximately 6 weeks. Strain the vinegar through muslin. Pour it into a bottle and seal it with an airtight, rust-resistant top.

A whole herb sprig may be placed inside the bottle to identify the kind of vinegar. Use in salad dressing or in a marinade for beef, lamb or pork.

Herb Oil
Herb oil may be brushed over meat before grilling. Use sunflower or olive oil and fresh herbs, such as rosemary, thyme, tarragon, marjoram, fennel, savory, sage and basil.

Lightly crush enough herbs to half fill a bottle. Cover the herbs with oil and seal the bottle with a rust-resistant top. Leave it in a warm place for 2 weeks; shake once a day. Strain oil through muslin, then return it to the bottle and seal. Repeat the process if the flavour is not strong enough.

Herb Butter
Cream soft, unsalted butter with finely chopped fresh herbs. Add other ingredients such as grated orange or lemon rind, crushed garlic, lemon juice, crushed green peppercorns, freshly ground black pepper and salt if desired. Shape into a roll by wrapping it in foil or waxed paper and chill until firm. Cut into slices and serve on top of grilled meat such as steak.

Herb butter may also be used together with heated cooking oil when browning meat to be cooked using moist-heat cooking methods.

BEEF

QUALITY CHARACTERISTICS OF BEEF

Few people realize how versatile the forequarter really is. There are various cuts to choose from – from tender cuts for roasting and grilling, such as the prime rib, to cuts that are less tender but perfect for a variety of stews and braised dishes.

The forequarter contains only 2% to 4% more bone as well as more white connective tissue (collagen) than the hindquarter but it wins hands down when it comes to taste. With a little imagination and the use of the correct cooking methods, cheaper forequarter cuts can be transformed into a variety of delicious dishes.

The hindquarter is and always will be popular for meat cuts ranging from steaks to pot-roasts. By using the correct cooking method for a chosen cut, you can be sure that your family and friends will always enjoy tender and succulent meat. With the great variety of meat cuts available from the hindquarter (sausage, kebabs, roasts, mince, steak, minute steaks, pot-roasts), you can prepare delicious meat dishes every day.

Colour
Fresh beef can vary from bright red to cherry-red, depending on the degree of exposure to oxygen. Where the meat on a carcase has been cut through, the meat often assumes a brownish red colour, which is the result of exposure to oxygen during the few days the carcase is being ripened. The cut surface is also slightly dried out. A dark plum-red appearance can be an indication that the meat comes from an older animal.

Texture
The meat should be firm but not dry and should have a smooth and fine texture.

Fat
The outer layer of fat should be firm and evenly distributed. An oily appearance can be an indication that the meat comes from an older animal. The type of fodder given to the animal can influence the colour of the fat. For instance, yellow maize produces bright yellow fat.

Bones
The surface of sawn-through bones should be red and porous in very young animals and whiter and harder in older animals. In young animals red flecks will be visible on the ribs on the inside of the carcase while fewer or no red flecks will be apparent in older animals.

The cartilage between the vertebrae should be white and jelly-like. The absence of cartilage is an indication of an older animal.

THE FOREQUARTER

SHIN
The shin consists of a large proportion of bone and a lot of white connective tissue (collagen), which makes this a tough but tasty cut.

USES
☆ Slices:....................................Braised dishes or soups
☆ Cubes: ....Stews
☆ Bones:...................................Meat stock

☆ This kind of stewing beef requires long, slow, moist cooking. Sometimes pork fat or bacon fat is added to add extra moisture and prevent the meat from drying out.
☆ Any meat labelled for stewing will require longer cooking than for braising.
☆ Meat for stewing is often sold cubed or sliced.
☆ This cut of beef can always be used in recipes for casseroles.

Opposite clockwise from top: Beef olives (**page 37**); Beef pie (**page 27**); and Rolled sirloin basted with sherry (**page 34**)

CLOD, STICK IN OR CHUCK (NECK END)

The clod consists of neck vertebrae surrounded by a large amount of meat. It contains a large proportion of white connective tissue, which makes the clod one of the most flavoursome cuts. The yellow connective tissue (elastin) present must be removed before cooking as it is not made tender by heat.

USES
☆ Slices:.......................................Braised dishes or casseroles
☆ Cubes: ....Stews and pies
☆ Bones:.....................................Meat stock
☆ Trimmings:..............................Mince

BLADE

The blade is characterized by the bright red muscle layer (red fleck on fat layer) on top. It is a boneless cut with a coarse texture and consists of several muscle layers which run in different directions. The blade contains very little intramuscular fat. The different muscle layers can be separated by following the natural seams.

USES
☆ Whole (over 1.5 kg/3 lb): ....Roast, pot-roast
☆ Thin slices:................................Beef olives, stew
  Minute steaks, shallow-fry
☆ Thicker slices:...........................Braised dishes
☆ Strips:.......................................Stir-fry
☆ Cubes: ....Stews
☆ Trimmings:..............................Mince

CHUCK (RIB END)

The chuck consists of six backbone vertebrae sawn through, six to seven ribs, the shoulder blade, dorsal vertebrae, yellow connective tissue (elastin) and several smaller muscles which run in different directions. The texture varies from coarse to fine and so does the degree of tenderness.

USES
☆ Bones and rolled: ....Pot-roast or cook in a cooking bag or foil
☆ Rib-eye steaks: ....Grill
☆ Slices:.......................................Braised dishes
☆ Cubes: ....Stews
☆ Bones:.....................................Soup
☆ Trimmings:..............................Mince

BRISKET

This flavoursome cut with a coarse texture contains the breastbone and a few ribs. The brisket can be divided into the point brisket, middle cut and plate.

USES
☆ Boned and rolled:.....................Pot-roast, cook in cooking bag or foil
☆ Boned, rolled and cured:...........Corned (salt) beef
☆ Portions: ....Stews
☆ Slices:.......................................Braised dishes

FLAT, TOP OR SHORT RIB
This cut contains ribs with two thin muscle layers separated by a layer of connective tissue and fat.

USES
☆ Boned and rolled:......................Pot-roast, cook in cooking bag or foil
☆ Bones:.....................................Meat stock
☆ Portions:..................................Stews
☆ After boning, some tender
meat will remain between the ribs.
Cut into portions, then marinate
and grill.

PRIME OR FORE RIB
The prime rib consists of the dorsal vertebrae, backbone vertebrae, three ribs, the large eye muscle, smaller muscle layers and an even outer fat layer of fat.

USES
☆ Whole: ....Roast (chine)
☆ Boned and rolled:.....................Roast
☆ Club (rib) steaks: ....Grill
☆ Rib-eye steaks: ....Grill

THE HINDQUARTER

FLANK
The flank consists of a boneless section and a few ribs known as short rib. The whole cut is covered with a thick layer of connective tissue (elastin) which must be removed before cooking.

USES
☆ Thin flank (skirt) steak
(removed from inner section of
flank): ....Marinate and grill
☆ Boned and rolled:.....................Pot-roast
☆ Short rib:.................................Cured and simmered
☆ Portions:..................................Braised dishes
☆ Cubes: ....Stews
☆ Trimmings:..............................Mince

SILVERSIDE
The silverside consists of three parallel muscles: a round muscle, which is covered with a silvery layer of connective tissue, a rectangular muscle and a small triangular muscle. The meat of the silverside has a coarse texture with little intramuscular fat.

USES
☆ Whole:.....................................Pot-roast
☆ Remove muscle layers along
natural seams:...............................Pot-roast (preferably larded)
☆ Cured and smoked (round
muscle):..Smoked beef
☆ Cured:.....................................Corned beef
☆ Slices:.....................................Beef olives
☆ Cubes: ....Stews

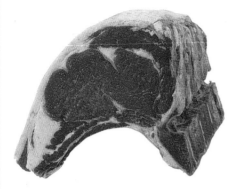

WING RIB

As in the case of the prime rib, the wing rib consists of the backbone, three or four ribs, the large eye muscle and an even covering of fat.

USES

☆ Whole: .... Roast (chine)
☆ Club (rib) steaks: .... Grill
☆ Boned and rolled:...................... Roast
☆ Boned Scotch fillet (sirloin): .... Roast
☆ Scotch fillet (boneless sirloin)
steaks:.. Grill

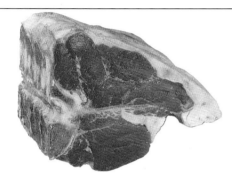

SIRLOIN

A characteristic feature of the sirloin is the backbone vertebrae with the T-bone. The T-bone is flanked on one side by the eye muscle with its even fat covering and on the other by the fillet. The sirloin contains no ribs.

USES

☆ Whole: .... Roast
☆ Boned and rolled:...................... Roast
☆ T-bone steaks: .... Grill
☆ Porterhouse steaks:................... Grill

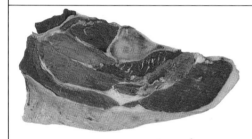

RUMP

The rump consists of several loose muscle layers and the large pelvic bone. A section of the fillet is also situated in the rump. Also sold boneless with fillet removed.

USES

☆ Boned and tied: .... Roast
☆ Rump steak: .... Grill
☆ Cubes: .... Kebabs, grill

FILLET

The fillet, situated inside the carcase alongside the backbone and protected by the layer of kidney fat, runs from the sirloin to the rump. The fillet becomes larger towards the rump. This meat cut is boneless, almost without fat and the most tender cut in the carcase.

USES

☆ Whole: .... Roast (preferably barded or basted)
☆ Fillet steaks:............................ Grill
☆ Tournedos: .... Grill
☆ Châteaubriand: .... Roast

AITCHBONE

The aitchbone forms part of the silverside and contains the tail-bone. It has a coarse texture with little intramuscular fat (marbling).

USES

☆ Whole: .... Pot-roast
☆ Cured:..................................... Corned (salt) beef or pastrami
☆ Slices:..................................... Beef olives

TOPSIDE

A characteristic feature of this cut is the thick half moon-shaped fat layer. Just below the fat layer is a thin flat muscle and below that two thicker muscle layers. The topside is boneless, has a coarse texture and is tasty.

USES
☆ Corner cut: .... Roast
☆ Outer muscle layer rolled: .... Pot-roast
☆ Thicker muscle layer: .... Pot-roast
☆ Slices: .... Beef olives
　　　　　　　　　　　　　　　 Minute steaks, shallow-fry
☆ Cubes: .... Stews
☆ Trimmings: .... Mince

THICK FLANK OR ROUND

The thick flank consists of three muscles. The inner muscle, also known as the mock fillet, is the most tender.

USES
☆ Whole: .... Pot-roast
☆ Cubes: .... Stews
☆ Steaks: .... Fry
☆ Slices: .... Braised dishes

MOCK FILLET STEW

4 thick flank (round) slices
1 tbsp cooking oil
2 onions, chopped
$\frac{1}{2}$ tsp curry powder
125 ml (4 fl oz) meat stock (page 133)
5 tbsp tomato purée
2 tsp dried or 2 tbsp chopped mixed fresh herbs
1 tsp salt
freshly ground black pepper to taste

Brown meat in heated cooking oil in a heavy-based saucepan. Add onion and sauté until translucent. Add curry powder and fry for another minute. Heat meat stock and remaining ingredients and add to meat. Cover with lid, reduce heat and simmer for $1\frac{1}{2}$ to 2 hours or until meat is tender.
(4 servings)

VARIATION
☆ *Substitute 400 g (14 oz) canned whole, peeled tomatoes for the tomato purée and meat stock.*

SUGGESTED SIDE DISHES
Brown rice
Vegetable fritters

Mock fillet stew

LARDED BLADE WITH PRUNE AND PISTACHIO TOPPING

1.75 kg (3½ lb) blade of beef
90 g (3 oz) pork fat, cut into strips
1 tbsp cooking oil
15 g (½ oz) butter
1 large onion, chopped
2 tsp salt
freshly ground black pepper to taste
1 tsp dried or 1 tbsp chopped fresh oregano
1 tbsp soy sauce
2 tbsp wine vinegar
250 ml (8 fl oz) meat stock (page 133)
1 tbsp fruit chutney

TOPPING

10 pitted prunes, chopped
60 g (2 oz) pistachio nuts, chopped

Lard (page 11) meat with pork fat. Secure meat with string to retain its shape during cooking. Brown meat in heated cooking oil and butter in a heavy-based saucepan. Add onion and sauté until translucent. Add seasoning. Heat soy sauce, wine vinegar, meat stock and chutney and add to meat. Cover with lid, reduce heat and simmer for 1½ to 2 hours or until meat is tender. Remove meat from saucepan.

To prepare the topping, mix the ingredients together. Mix approximately 3 tbsp of the liquid in which meat was cooked with the prune and nut mixture and press firmly onto top of meat. Place meat on the rack of a roasting tin and cook under a pre-heated grill for approximately 2 minutes. If desired, boil the remaining cooking liquid until reduced and slightly thickened and serve separately.

(8 servings)

VARIATIONS

☆ Substitute marrowbone fat for the pork fat.
☆ Substitute almonds for the pistachio nuts.
☆ Substitute 60 g (2 oz) seedless raisins for the prunes.

SUGGESTED SIDE DISHES

New potatoes
Sautéed courgettes

COUNTRY CASSEROLE

1 kg (2 lb) boned clod or chuck (neck end), thickly sliced
2 tbsp cooking oil
4 lamb's kidneys, membranes and cores removed, and sliced
2 large onions, sliced
2 cloves garlic, crushed
250 g (8 oz) mushrooms, wiped and sliced (optional)
8 potatoes, peeled and quartered
2 tsp salt
freshly ground black pepper to taste
1 tsp dried or 1 tbsp chopped fresh thyme
350 ml (12 fl oz) meat stock (page 133)
1 tbsp plain flour

Brown meat in heated cooking oil in a heavy-based saucepan. Add kidneys and fry lightly. Add onion, garlic and mushrooms and sauté until onion is translucent. Place potatoes in an oven dish and sprinkle half the salt over. Spoon meat, kidneys and vegetables on top of potatoes and sprinkle with remaining salt and seasoning. Add heated meat stock, cover with lid and bake at 160 °C (325 °F/gas 3) for 2 to 2½ hours. Thicken sauce with a flour and water paste if necessary.

(8 servings)

VARIATIONS

☆ Substitute neck of lamb for the boned neck of beef.
☆ Substitute 220 g (7 oz) canned smoked oysters for the lamb's kidneys, but add them only during the last 20 minutes of the cooking time.
☆ Substitute washed and sliced courgettes for the mushrooms.

SUGGESTED SIDE DISHES

Buttered carrots with celery
Mixed green salad

Larded blade with prune and pistachio topping

MEXICAN BEEF

1 kg (2 lb) shin of beef, thickly sliced
125 g (4 oz) dried kidney beans
125 g (4 oz) dried haricot beans
1 litre (1¾ pints) water
2 tbsp cooking oil
1 onion, chopped
1 clove garlic, crushed
410 g (13 oz) canned whole
tomatoes, chopped
2 tsp salt
½ tsp dried or 2 tsp chopped fresh
oregano
freshly ground black pepper to
taste
½ tsp cayenne pepper or chilli powder
½ tsp dried or 2 tsp chopped fresh
parsley
250 ml (8 fl oz) meat stock (page 133)
3 tbsp tomato purée
2 tsp granulated sugar
1 red pepper, seeded and cut into
julienne strips
1 green pepper, seeded and cut into
julienne strips

Soak beans in water overnight, rinse and place in a saucepan. Cover with cold water, bring to the boil and boil rapidly for 10 minutes. Drain. Brown meat in heated cooking oil in a heavy-based saucepan. Add onion and garlic and sauté until onion is translucent. Add drained beans, tomatoes and seasoning to meat. Heat meat stock, tomato purée and sugar and add to meat. Cover with lid, reduce heat and simmer for 1½ to 2 hours or until meat and beans are tender. Add red and green peppers and simmer for another 15 minutes.
(8 servings)

VARIATIONS
☆ *Instead of haricot and kidney beans, use 250 g (8 oz) fresh green beans and add them 25 minutes before the end of the cooking time.*
☆ *Substitute canned beans for the dried haricot and kidney beans and add with the green and red pepper.*

HINT
☆ *Alternatively, the dried beans can be boiled for 5 minutes and then soaked for 1 hour before use.*

SUGGESTED SIDE DISHES
Tacos
Cucumber and yoghurt salad

Mexican beef

BEEF PIE

1 kg (2 lb) boned clod or chuck (neck end), cut into 2.5 cm (1 inch) cubes
2 tbsp cooking oil
3 onions, chopped
2 carrots, grated
2 tsp salt
freshly ground black pepper to taste
½ tsp ground cloves
1 tbsp ground coriander
1 tbsp Worcestershire sauce
2 tbsp wine vinegar
250 ml (8 fl oz) meat stock (page 133)
2 tbsp plain flour

BUTTERMILK PASTRY
185 g (6 oz) plain flour
1 tsp salt
125 g (4 oz) butter
125 ml (4 fl oz) buttermilk
2 tbsp milk

Brown meat in heated cooking oil. Add onion and carrot and sauté until onion is translucent. Sprinkle seasoning over. Heat Worcestershire sauce, wine vinegar and meat stock and add to meat. Cover with lid, reduce heat and simmer for 2 to 2½ hours or until meat is tender. Thicken liquid with a flour and water paste. Transfer meat to a pie dish and leave to cool. Place pie funnel in centre of dish.

To prepare the pastry, sift flour and salt together. Cut butter into small pieces and rub it into the flour mixture until it resembles breadcrumbs. Stir in buttermilk and mix to a soft dough. Place in a plastic bag and chill in refrigerator for 20 minutes. Roll out pastry thinly and cover meat. Seal edges and brush pastry with milk. Bake pie at 200 °C (400 °F/gas 6) for 15 minutes or until golden brown and cooked.
(6 servings)

VARIATION
☆ *Sprinkle sesame seeds and/or crushed poppy seeds over pastry before baking.*

SUGGESTED SIDE DISHES
Stir-fried vegetables
Stewed dried fruit

POT-ROASTED TOPSIDE WITH BRANDY SAUCE

1.5 kg (3 lb) topside
3 cloves garlic, slivered
2 tbsp cooking oil
2 onions, chopped
3 tbsp brandy
2 tsp salt
freshly ground black pepper to taste
1 tsp each dried or 1 tbsp each chopped fresh parsley, thyme and rosemary
125 ml (4 fl oz) dry red wine
125 ml (4 fl oz) meat stock (page 133)
410 g (13 oz) whole tomatoes, chopped
4 celery stalks, cut into julienne strips
4 carrots, sliced
1 tbsp plain flour

Make small incisions in meat and insert garlic. Secure meat with string to retain its shape during cooking. Brown meat in heated cooking oil in a heavy-based saucepan. Add onion and sauté until translucent. Heat brandy in a small saucepan, pour over meat and ignite. Shake to and fro until flames are extinguished. Add seasoning, heated wine, meat stock and tomatoes. Cover with lid, reduce heat and simmer for 1½ to 2 hours or until meat is tender. Add celery and carrots 15 minutes before end of cooking time. Thicken liquid with a flour and water paste.

(8 servings)

VARIATIONS

☆ Substitute 1.5 kg (3 lb) blade for the topside. As blade has very little intramuscular fat, lard the meat with either marrowbone or pork fat to keep the meat succulent.
☆ Substitute courgettes and red and green peppers for the celery and carrots.

SUGGESTED SIDE DISHES

Potato rosettes and a green salad or Parsley noodles and a mixed salad

Quick stir-fry

GREEK BEEF OLIVES

8 thin slices of topside
1 tbsp olive or cooking oil
15 g (½ oz) butter
1 onion, chopped
½ tsp each dried or 2 tsp each chopped fresh oregano and basil
2 tsp dried or 2 tbsp chopped fresh parsley
freshly ground black pepper to taste
5 tbsp tomato purée
150 ml (¼ pint) meat stock (page 133)
150 ml (¼ pint) dry white wine
1 tsp granulated sugar
8 black olives, stoned (optional)
1 tbsp plain flour

STUFFING

200 g (6½ oz) feta cheese, crumbled
8 chives, chopped

First prepare the stuffing by mixing the ingredients together.

To prepare the meat, place each slice between two layers of cling film and flatten slightly with the palm of the hand. Spoon a little stuffing onto each slice, roll up and secure with string or cocktail sticks. Brown meat in heated oil and butter. Add onion and sauté until translucent. Add seasoning. Heat tomato purée, wine, meat stock and sugar and add to meat. Cover with lid, reduce heat and simmer for 1 to 1½ hours or until meat is tender. Add olives and heat through.

Thicken liquid with a flour and water paste if necessary.

(4 servings)

SUGGESTED SIDE DISHES

Parsley rice
Glazed carrots

QUICK STIR-FRY

500 g (1 lb) boned blade or rump, cut into thin strips
2 tbsp cooking oil
2 carrots, cut into julienne strips
1 onion, sliced
1 green pepper, seeded and cut into julienne strips
200 g (6½ oz) courgettes, sliced
315 g (10 oz) mushrooms, sliced
90 g (3 oz) bean sprouts

Beef stew with asparagus

SAUCE

250 ml (8 fl oz) mango juice
5 tbsp wine vinegar
1 tsp soy sauce
5 tsp soft brown sugar
$\frac{1}{2}$ tsp salt
good pinch ground ginger (optional)
freshly ground black pepper
to taste
2 tbsp cornflour

Brown meat in heated cooking oil in a wok or a heavy-based saucepan. Add vegetables in the order listed above and stir-fry until vegetables are just cooked but still crisp.

In the meantime, mix sauce ingredients together, bring to the boil and simmer for 3 minutes, stirring constantly. Add sauce to stir-fried vegetables and stir to combine.

(6 servings)

VARIATIONS

☆ Substitute canned pineapple juice for the mango juice and add the pineapple pieces to the stir-fry.
☆ Substitute 315 g (10 oz) frankfurters or Vienna sausages for the meat strips.

HINT

☆ All the preparation may be done in advance and the ingredients kept in airtight containers in the refrigerator.

SUGGESTED SIDE DISHES
Wild rice or flavoured rice
Noodles

BEEF STEW WITH ASPARAGUS

1 kg (2 lb) boned chuck, cut into 2.5 cm (1 inch) cubes
4 rashers rindless streaky bacon, chopped
2 tsp cooking oil
2 cloves garlic, crushed
3 leeks, sliced
1 tsp salt
freshly ground black pepper
to taste
250 ml (8 fl oz) meat stock (page 133)
410 g (13 oz) canned asparagus pieces, drained
1 tbsp plain flour
125 g (4 oz) Gruyère cheese, grated

Fry bacon until crisp in a heavy-based saucepan. Remove bacon and set aside. Add cooking oil to rendered fat and brown meat. Add garlic and leeks and sauté. Season meat with salt and pepper. Heat meat stock and add to meat. Cover with lid, reduce heat and simmer for 1$\frac{1}{2}$ to 2 hours or until meat is tender. Add asparagus and heat through. Thicken liquid with a flour and water paste if necessary. Spoon into an oven-proof dish, sprinkle cheese and reserved bacon over meat and cook under a pre-heated grill until cheese has melted.

(6 servings)

VARIATIONS

☆ Substitute canned artichokes or fresh asparagus for the canned asparagus pieces.
☆ Substitute Cheddar cheese for the Gruyère cheese.
☆ Substitute 4 tbsp dried breadcrumbs for the bacon.

SUGGESTED SIDE DISHES
Parsley rice
Patty pan squash

Marinated cocktail kebabs with mustard yoghurt

MARINATED COCKTAIL KEBABS WITH MUSTARD YOGHURT

1.5 to 2 kg (3 to 4 lb) flat rib
1 tsp salt
freshly ground black pepper to taste

MARINADE
4 tbsp cooking oil
250 ml (8 fl oz) meat stock (page 133)
1 tsp whole coriander seeds
2 tsp fennel seeds
$\frac{1}{2}$ tsp ground cardamom
4 whole allspice
2 tsp garam masala or medium curry powder
1 tbsp grated lemon rind
2 tbsp lemon juice
1 tsp dried or 1 tbsp chopped fresh rosemary

MUSTARD YOGHURT
$\frac{1}{2}$ onion, finely chopped
1 clove garlic, crushed
1 tsp butter
$\frac{1}{2}$ dried red chilli, finely chopped (optional)
1 tsp Pommery mustard
salt and pepper to taste
250 ml (8 fl oz) plain low-fat yoghurt

Prepare the meat by cutting the meat from the bone as illustrated below.

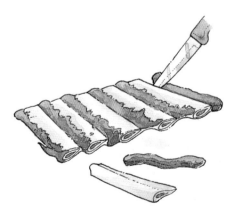

Prepare the marinade by mixing all the ingredients together. Place meat in a glass or ceramic container, pour marinade over and marinate for 3 to 4 hours.

Meanwhile prepare the mustard yoghurt. Sauté onion and garlic in heated butter until onion is translucent. Reduce heat and add remaining ingredients except yoghurt. Fry for 1 minute and remove from heat. Allow

Rolled flat rib with spinach stuffing

to cool, then stir in yoghurt. Mix well and refrigerate.

Remove meat from marinade and reserve marinade for later use. Thread meat concertinawise onto cocktail sticks, place meat on the rack of a roasting tin and grill for 5 minutes in total (rare) or / minutes in total (medium-done), basting frequently with the marinade. Season with salt and pepper. Serve warm with the chilled mustard yoghurt.
(6 servings)

VARIATION
☆ Substitute 500 g (1 lb) boned shoulder of lamb for the flat rib. Cut the lamb into 2.5 cm (1 inch) cubes and marinate in the above marinade for 3 to 4 hours. Thread cubes of meat, red and green peppers, fresh pickling onions and cherry tomatoes alternately onto metal, wooden or bamboo skewers and grill for 7 to 10 minutes.

ROLLED FLAT RIB WITH SPINACH STUFFING

1.5 kg (3 lb) boned flat rib
1 tsp salt
freshly ground black pepper to taste
1 tbsp plain flour

STUFFING
3 rashers rindless bacon, chopped
2 leeks, sliced
1 clove garlic, crushed
125 g (4 oz) spinach, chopped
freshly ground black pepper to taste
$\frac{1}{2}$ tsp dried or 2 tsp chopped fresh thyme
5 tbsp fresh breadcrumbs
2 tbsp crumbled blue cheese

First prepare the stuffing. Fry bacon lightly, add leeks and garlic and sauté until translucent. Add spinach and stir-fry for 1 minute. Allow to cool, then add seasoning, breadcrumbs and cheese.

To prepare the meat, spread stuffing over the inside, leaving 2 cm ($\frac{3}{4}$ inch) clear around the edges. Roll meat and secure with string. Mix salt, pepper and flour and sprinkle over meat. Place meat in a cooking bag, secure the bag and place in a roasting tin. Pierce a few holes in the top of the bag and bake at 160 °C (325 °F/gas 3) for $1\frac{1}{2}$ to 2 hours or until tender.
(6 servings)

VARIATION
☆ Substitute Parmesan cheese to taste for the blue cheese.

HINT
☆ After boning the flat rib, there is still meat remaining between the ribs which is very tender and may be marinated and grilled.

SUGGESTED SIDE DISHES
Baked sweet potatoes
Pumpkin fritters

PRIME RIB STEAKS WITH CREAMY TARRAGON AND CAPER BASTING MIXTURE

4 prime rib steaks, 2 cm ($\frac{3}{4}$ inch) thick
1 tsp salt
freshly ground black pepper
to taste

BASTING MIXTURE
200 ml ($6\frac{1}{2}$ fl oz) soured cream
good pinch salt
2 tsp Dijon mustard
1 tsp dried or 1 tbsp chopped fresh
tarragon
1 tbsp drained and chopped capers
(optional)
2 tsp dried or 2 tbsp chopped fresh
parsley
fresh ground black pepper to taste

First prepare the basting mixture by combining all the ingredients.

To prepare the meat, slash the fat edges at 2.5 cm (1 inch) intervals to prevent curling. Place meat on the rack of a grill pan and cook 10 cm (4 inches) under a pre-heated grill for 5 to 7 minutes in total (rare) or 7 to 10 minutes in total (medium), basting the meat frequently with the basting mixture. Season with salt and pepper and serve immediately.

(4 servings)

VARIATION
☆ Substitute 1 tbsp crushed Madagascar green peppercorns for the capers.

SUGGESTED SIDE DISHES
Rice timbales
Buttered vegetables

STUFFED BRISKET WITH ORANGE-AND-SHERRY SAUCE

1.5 kg (3 lb) boned brisket
$1\frac{1}{2}$ tsp salt
freshly ground black pepper
to taste
1 tbsp marmalade
1 tbsp cooking oil
125 ml (4 fl oz) meat stock
(page 133)
juice of 1 orange
3 tbsp medium cream sherry
3 to 4 ginger snaps, crumbed
(optional)

STUFFING
$\frac{1}{2}$ pineapple, peeled and grated
90 g (3 oz) cooked brown rice
30 g (1 oz) fresh wholemeal
breadcrumbs
3 tbsp chopped almonds (optional)

First prepare the stuffing by mixing all the ingredients together.

To prepare the meat, sprinkle half the salt and pepper over the inside of the meat. Spread marmalade over meat, followed by stuffing, leaving 2 cm ($\frac{3}{4}$ inch) clear around the edges. Roll and secure meat with string and sprinkle with remaining salt and pepper. Brown meat in heated cooking oil in a heavy-based saucepan. Heat meat stock, orange juice and sherry and add. Cover with lid, reduce heat and simmer for 2 to $2\frac{1}{2}$ hours or until meat is tender. If necessary, thicken liquid by stirring in the ginger snap crumbs.

(8 servings)

VARIATIONS
☆ Substitute boned flat rib for the brisket.
☆ Substitute 90 g (3 oz) dried apricots, finely chopped and soaked in sherry, for the pineapple.

SUGGESTED SIDE DISHES
Baked potatoes
Broccoli soufflé
Carrots julienne

RIB-EYE STEAKS WITH RED WINE SAUCE

4 rib-eye steaks, 2.5 cm (1 inch) thick
30 g (1 oz) butter
5 juniper berries (optional)
250 ml (8 fl oz) single cream
1 tsp salt
freshly ground black pepper
to taste

MARINADE
375 ml (12 fl oz) dry red wine
4 leeks, sliced
1 tbsp lemon juice
2 tsp lime juice
2 tsp dried or 2 tbsp chopped fresh
parsley

To prepare the meat, slash the fat edges at 2.5 cm (1 inch) intervals to prevent curling. Mix marinade ingredients together. Place meat in a glass or ceramic container and pour marinade over. Marinate in refrigerator for 4 hours, turning regularly. Remove meat from marinade and pat dry with kitchen paper. Reserve marinade. Heat butter in a heavy-based frying pan and add steaks one at a time to prevent the pan from cooling down too rapidly. Fry for 5 to 7 minutes in total (rare) or 7 to 10 minutes in total (medium). Transfer steaks to a heated meat platter.

To prepare the wine sauce, add the reserved marinade to the pan juices and boil rapidly for a few minutes to reduce. Remove from heat and add juniper berries and cream. Season steaks with salt and pepper, pour sauce over and serve immediately.

(4 servings)

VARIATIONS
☆ Substitute 3 tbsp orange juice and 1 tsp grated orange rind for the lemon and lime juice.

SUGGESTED SIDE DISHES
Baked jacket potatoes
Broccoli salad

AVOCADO MEAT SALAD

1 thin flank steak, connective tissue
removed
cooking oil
1 avocado, cubed
2 tsp lemon juice
5 tsp plain yoghurt
5 tsp French salad dressing
1 medium tomato, skinned and
cubed
freshly ground black pepper
to taste

Brush meat with cooking oil. Heat a ridged pan to smoking hot and grill meat for 5 to 7 minutes in total (rare) or 7 to 10 minutes in total (well-done). Leave meat to cool, then cut at a 45° angle into thin slices. Combine remaining ingredients and toss gently with meat.

(4 to 6 servings)

VARIATION
☆ Substitute any leftover meat for the flank steak.

SUGGESTED SIDE DISHES
Pitta bread, tacos or wholemeal bread

Top: Avocado meat salad. Bottom: Rib-eye steaks with red wine sauce

ROAST BEEF WITH CHEESE AND LEMON TOPPING

1 whole wing rib, approximately
1.25 to 1.5 kg (2½ to 3 lb)
1½ tsp salt
freshly ground black pepper to taste

CHEESE AND LEMON TOPPING
2 tbsp lemon juice
125 g (4 oz) Cheddar, Gruyère or
mozzarella cheese, grated
2 tbsp chopped chives
1 tsp French mustard
freshly ground black pepper to taste
½ tsp grated lemon rind

Season meat with salt and pepper, then place fat side uppermost on the rack of a roasting tin and roast at 160 °C (325 °F/gas 3) for 15 to 20 minutes per 500 g (1 lb) plus 15 minutes (rare) or 20 to 25 minutes per 500 g (1 lb) plus 20 minutes (medium).

To prepare the topping, mix all the ingredients together and spread topping over the meat 20 to 30 minutes before the end of the cooking time. Return meat to oven and continue roasting. Allow to rest in warming drawer for 10 minutes before carving and serving.

(4 to 6 servings)

SUGGESTED SIDE DISHES
Broccoli with almonds
Carrot timbales
Fried potato slices

ORANGE KEBABS

500 g (1 lb) rump, cut into 2.5 cm
(1 inch) cubes
8 fresh pickling onions
8 orange or lemon leaves
(optional)

MARINADE
3 tbsp orange liqueur
250 ml (8 fl oz) orange juice
2 tsp lemon juice
½ tsp salt
freshly ground black pepper to taste
1 tbsp cornflour

Thread meat, pickling onions and orange or lemon leaves alternately onto skewers. Mix marinade ingredients, except cornflour, and marinate kebabs for 4 hours or overnight. Remove meat form marinade and pat dry with kitchen paper. Cook kebabs under a preheated grill while basting frequently with remaining marinade. Heat remaining marinade and thicken with a paste of cornflour and water. Serve as a sauce with kebabs.

(4 servings)

VARIATIONS
☆ *Substitute chunks of courgettes or whole mushrooms for the pickling onions.*
☆ *Substitute apricot juice for the orange juice and thread dried apricots alternately with the meat onto skewers.*

HINT
☆ *Blanch the pickling onions before threading onto the skewers.*

SUGGESTED SIDE DISHES
Wholemeal bread rolls
Spinach salad

RUMP WITH GREEN PEPPERCORN SAUCE

1.5 kg (3 lb) whole rump
2 tsp cooking oil
5 tsp dried green peppercorns, crushed
2 tsp salt

GREEN PEPPERCORN SAUCE
3 chives, chopped
15 g (½ oz) butter
1 tbsp cooking oil
5 tsp plain flour
½ tsp salt
1 tsp French mustard
200 ml (6½ fl oz) white meat stock
(page 133)
5 tsp medium cream sherry
3 tbsp drained Madagascar green peppercorns, crushed
185 ml (6 fl oz) double cream

Brush meat with oil. Sprinkle with crushed peppercorns and gently press onto meat. Season with salt. Place meat on the rack of a roasting tin and roast at 160 °C (325 °F/gas 3) for 15 to 20 minutes per 500 g (1 lb) plus 15 minutes (rare) or 20 to 25 minutes per 500 g (1 lb) plus 20 minutes (medium). Allow to rest for 10 to 15 minutes in warming drawer before carving.

To prepare the sauce, sauté chives in heated butter and oil. Add plain flour, salt and mustard and stir for 1 minute. Add heated meat stock and stir until sauce is thick. Simmer for 3 minutes, then stir in sherry, crushed green peppercorns and cream and heat through.

(8 servings)

VARIATION
☆ *Low-fat variation: Substitute 185 ml (6 fl oz) plain low-fat yoghurt for the cream.*

SUGGESTED SIDE DISHES
Vegetable stir-fry and Rösti or Pumpkin bread

ROLLED SIRLOIN BASTED WITH SHERRY

1 rolled sirloin, approximately 1.5 kg
(3 lb)
1 tsp salt
freshly ground black pepper to taste

BASTING MIXTURE
1½ tsp paprika
good pinch ground coriander
3 tbsp dry sherry
3 tbsp apple juice
3 cloves garlic, crushed
1 tsp salt
freshly ground black pepper to taste

Rub salt and pepper onto fat side of meat. Place meat on the rack of a roasting tin and roast at 160 °C (325 °F/gas 3) for 15 to 20 minutes per 500 g (1 lb) plus 15 minutes (rare) or 20 to 25 minutes per 500 g (1 lb) plus 20 minutes (medium). Mix basting ingredients and baste meat regularly during the last 30 minutes of cooking time. Allow meat to rest for 10 minutes before removing string and carving meat into thin slices.

(8 servings)

VARIATION
☆ *Substitute brandy and orange juice for the sherry and apple juice.*

HINT
☆ *Use any leftover meat in a meat salad or for sandwiches.*

SUGGESTED SIDE DISHES
Boiled potatoes
Green peas with bacon

Fillet with pepper stuffing

FILLET WITH PEPPER STUFFING

1.5 kg (3 lb) whole fillet

STUFFING

125 g (4 oz) mozzarella cheese, grated (optional)
$\frac{1}{2}$ red pepper, seeded and cut into julienne strips
$\frac{1}{2}$ green pepper, seeded and cut into julienne strips
2 cloves garlic, crushed

BASTING MIXTURE

3 tbsp melted butter
5 tsp lemon juice
2 lemon leaves, crushed
2 tsp salt
freshly ground black pepper to taste

First prepare the stuffing by mixing all the ingredients together.

Prepare the basting mixture by mixing all the ingredients together.

To prepare the meat, make a lengthwise incision in the fillet without cutting through. Fold open and flatten meat slightly with the palm of the hand. Spread stuffing over one half of fillet, fold over and secure with string at 2.5 cm (1 inch) intervals. Place meat on the rack of a roasting tin and roast at 160 °C (325 °F/gas 3) for 15 to 20 minutes per 500 g (1 lb) plus 15 minutes (rare) or 20 to 25 minutes per 500 g (1 lb) plus 20 minutes (medium), basting the meat regularly with the basting mixture. Allow fillet to rest for approximately 10 minutes before removing string and carving.

(8 servings)

HINT

☆ *Serve with a sweet wine sauce (page 102) or a herb butter (page 152).*

SUGGESTED SIDE DISHES

Duchess potatoes
Brussels sprouts

Aitchbone with vegetables

CURRIED MEAT WITH PEARS

500 g (1 lb) thick flank, cut into
2.5 cm (1 inch) cubes
4 tsp cooking oil
1 onion, chopped
4 tsp mild curry powder
meat stock (page 133)
410 g (13 oz) canned pears in juice,
drained and juice reserved
1 tsp salt
freshly ground black pepper
to taste

Brown meat in heated cooking oil in a heavy-based saucepan. Add onion and sauté until translucent. Add curry powder and fry for 1 minute.

Add sufficient meat stock to reserved pear juice to make up 250 ml (8 fl oz), season with salt and pepper and heat. Add to meat, cover with lid, reduce heat and simmer for $1\frac{1}{2}$ to 2 hours or until meat is tender.

Cut pears into thin slices and add to meat approximately 10 minutes before the end of the cooking time.

(4 servings)

VARIATIONS

☆ Substitute 1 sliced cooking apple and 200 ml ($6\frac{1}{2}$ fl oz) apple juice for the pears.

☆ Substitute mangoes in fruit juice for the pears.

☆ Substitute either chuck or clod of beef for the thick flank.

SUGGESTED SIDE DISHES
Poppadums
Tomato sambal
Cucumber raita
Toasted coconut

POT-ROASTED SILVERSIDE WITH HAM

1.5 kg (3 lb) silverside
6 tsp prepared mustard
200 g (6½ oz) smoked ham, sliced
2 tbsp cooking oil
1 tsp salt
good pinch cayenne pepper
2 tbsp chutney
200 ml (6½ fl oz) meat stock
(page 133)
5 tsp plain flour
125 ml (4 fl oz) plain yoghurt

Spread 2 tsp of the mustard over ham slices and freeze until firm. Cut into 5 mm (¼ inch) strips and lard (page 11) silverside. Brown meat in heated cooking oil in a heavy-based saucepan. Add salt, cayenne pepper, chutney and remaining mustard to meat stock and heat. Add to meat, cover with lid, reduce heat and simmer for 1½ to 2 hours or until meat is tender. Thicken sauce with a flour and water paste, then remove from heat and stir in yoghurt. Carve meat and serve with the sauce.
(8 servings)

VARIATIONS
☆ Substitute marrowbone or pork fat for the ham and omit the mustard.
☆ For extra flavour and a more attractive appearance, lard the silverside with carrot and celery stalks as well.

HINT
☆ Use a larding needle to insert the strips of ham into the meat.

SUGGESTED SIDE DISHES
Pearl barley
French green beans

BEEF OLIVES

12 thin slices topside
1 tsp salt
freshly ground black pepper
to taste
15 g (½ oz) butter
1 tbsp cooking oil
2 onions, sliced
2 cloves garlic, crushed
345 ml (11 fl oz) meat stock
(page 133)
1 tbsp plain flour

SPINACH STUFFING
250 g (8 oz) fresh spinach, stalks removed, blanched and chopped
6 spring onions, chopped
2 cloves garlic, crushed
15 g (½ oz) butter
pinch grated nutmeg
3 tbsp curd cheese
4 tsp dried or 3 tbsp chopped fresh parsley

MUSHROOM STUFFING
125 g (4 oz) mushrooms, chopped
1 onion, chopped
30 g (1 oz) butter
75 g (2½ oz) ham, coarsely chopped
2 tsp dried or 2 tbsp chopped fresh parsley

Place meat between two layers of cling film and flatten slightly with the palm of the hand. Season meat with half the salt and pepper.

To prepare the spinach stuffing, fry spinach, spring onions and garlic in butter. Combine the mixture with the remaining ingredients.

To prepare the mushroom stuffing, fry mushrooms and onion in butter until onion is translucent. Combine mixture with remaining ingredients.

Spoon a little stuffing of your choice onto each meat slice, then roll up and secure with string or a cocktail stick. Brown meat in heated butter and cooking oil. Add onoin and garlic and sauté until onion is translucent. Add heated meat stock and simmer for 1 to 1½ hours or until meat is tender. Thicken sauce with a flour and water paste. Remove string or cocktail sticks and serve.
(6 servings)

VARIATIONS
☆ Substitute red wine for half the meat stock. Thicken sauce with a paste of soured cream and plain flour at the end of the cooking time.
☆ For a quick and easy stuffing, use the following:
● Mozzarella cheese and chopped gherkins
● Pitted prunes filled with cottage cheese or nuts
● Chutney, apple and banana
● Rashers of bacon with chopped celery or slices of banana.

SUGGESTED SIDE DISHES
Vegetables and rice

AITCHBONE WITH VEGETABLES

1.5 kg (3 lb) aitchbone (silverside)
2 cloves garlic, crushed
2 tsp dried or 2 tbsp chopped fresh parsley
30 g (1 oz) soft butter
2 tbsp cooking oil
10 fresh pickling onions
2 celery stalks, cut into 2.5 cm (1 inch) pieces
16 baby carrots
250 ml (8 fl oz) meat stock (page 133)
125 ml (4 fl oz) dry white wine
1 tsp dried or 1 tbsp chopped fresh rosemary
2 tsp plain flour
125 ml (4 fl oz) crème fraîche (page 154) or soured cream
1 tbsp lemon juice
1 tbsp French mustard

Mix garlic, parsley and butter into a paste. Make small incisions along the grain of the meat and stuff with butter mixture. Brown meat in heated cooking oil. Add onions, celery and carrots and fry until onion is translucent. Add heated meat stock, wine and rosemary. Cover with lid, reduce heat and simmer for 1½ to 2 hours or until meat is tender. Mix flour, crème fraîche or soured cream, lemon juice and mustard and add. Heat through.
(8 servings)

HINT
☆ Tie the meat with string to retain its shape.

SUGGESTED SIDE DISHES
Brown rice
Beetroot salad

LAMB AND MUTTON

References from the Bible show that lamb and mutton were man's earliest sources of protein. Today they still play an important role in several food traditions throughout the world. Because of its versatility, lamb has become one of the most popular meats in many different countries.

The difference between lamb and mutton is that lamb comes from an animal slaughtered at a young age (younger than 6 months). The meat is very tender as little connective tissue has developed. Mutton, on the other hand, has more connective tissue and is, therefore, less tender than lamb. During cooking, however, the white connective tissue (collagen) is converted into gelatine which makes mutton as tender and tasty as lamb.

THE QUALITY CHARACTERISTICS OF MUTTON AND LAMB

Colour
Good quality lamb is bright pink whereas mutton is slightly darker in colour.

Texture
The meat of lamb and mutton should feel firm to the touch, have a smooth appearance and a fine texture. Lamb has a finer texture than mutton.

Fat
The fat of good quality lamb and mutton is firm and evenly distributed throughout the carcase.

Bones
In lamb the sawn-through bones are red and porous and red flecks occur on the ribs. In mutton the bones are usually less red and harder while the ribs are a greyish white.

Cartilage
The cartilage found between the vertebrae of the lamb carcase is white and gelatinous, whereas in a mutton carcase the cartilage is hard.

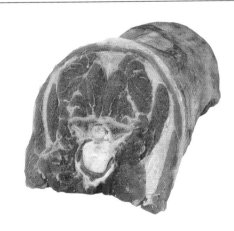

SCRAG OR NECK
The scrag consists of the neck vertebrae and coarse-textured meat containing a large amount of white connective tissue (collagen). Long, slow cooking will convert this connective tissue into gelatine and make the meat tender. The yellow connective tissue (elastin) is not affected by heat and should therefore be removed prior to cooking.

USES
☆ Whole: .... Pot-roast or cook in cooking bag
☆ Boned and rolled: .... Pot-roast
☆ Slices: .... Braised dishes
☆ Cubes: .... Stews and casseroles
☆ Bones: .... Meat stock

SHOULDER
The shoulder blade, marrowbone and shank bone are situated in the shoulder, which is covered with an even layer of fat. Attached to the shoulder blade is the softer cartilage section. If the shoulder is removed round, the upper portion of the thick rib is included.

USES
☆ Boned and rolled: .... Roast (lamb), pot-roast (mutton)
☆ Boned and butterflied: .... Roast or grill over the coals
☆ Cubes: .... Kebabs, grill
☆ Shank slices: .... Stews or braised dishes

Opposite Top: Gerhard's coriander rib (page 45). Bottom: Lamb and aubergine meal-in-a-pot (page 42)

FLANK AND BREAST

The breast is sawn off with the flank for convenience. The cut contains the breastbone and ribs in a triangular shape where the flank joins the breast. A large proportion of white connective tissue occurs in the flank and the meat has a coarse texture.

USES

☆ Boned, rolled and tied: ....Pot-roast or cook in cooking bag or foil
☆ Cubes: ....Casseroles and stews
☆ Portions:................................Stews
☆ Strips:....................................Concertina kebabs, grill

THICK RIB OR FOREQUARTER

The thick rib consists of a few vertebrae, 5 to 6 ribs, part of the shoulder blade and an even layer of fat. If the shoulder is removed round, the upper muscle layer and fat layer of the thick rib are removed with the shoulder blade.

USES

☆ Chops: ....Grill (lamb), braised dishes (mutton)
☆ Boned and stuffed if shoulder has not been removed round (cushion): Roast (lamb), pot-roast (mutton)
☆ Cubes: ....Kebabs (lamb), grill
Stews (mutton)
☆ Trimmings:...............................Mince

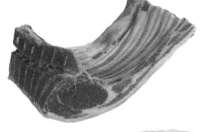

RIB OR BEST END

The best end consists of vertebrae, ribs, a single eye muscle and an uneven fat layer. The meat has a fine texture.

USES

☆ Rack of lamb (8 ribs, chined and frenched): ....Roast
☆ Chops: ....Grill
☆ Boned and rolled:.....................Roast
☆ Cutlets: ....Grill, shallow fry
☆ Noisettes: ....Grill

LOIN

A feature of the loin is the T-shaped vertebrae flanked by the very tender fillet on the one side and the eye muscle on the other. If removed before the carcase is halved, this cut is known as a saddle.

USES

☆ Whole saddle:..........................Roast
☆ Whole loin:..............................Roast
☆ Boned and rolled:.....................Roast
☆ Saddle chops: ....Grill
☆ Loin chops: ....Grill
☆ Noisettes: ....Grill

CHUMP

The chump contains the pelvic bone and a large proportion of meat. The chump can be left on the leg.

USES

☆ Whole: .... Roast
☆ Boned: .... Roast
☆ Chops: .... Grill

LEG

The leg contains the pelvic bone, marrowbone and shank bone and is possibly the most popular cut.

USES

☆ Whole: .... Roast (lamb), pot-roast (mutton)
☆ Boned and rolled: .... Roast (lamb), pot-roast (mutton)
☆ Cured and smoked: .... Boil
☆ Slices: .... Schnitzels, shallow-fry
☆ Cubes: .... Stews (mutton)
Kebabs (lamb), grill

SHANK

The shank contains the shank bone, meat with a coarse texture and a large proportion of white connective tissue.

USES

☆ Slices: .... Braised dishes

MUTTON PIE

500 g (1 lb) boned thick rib of lamb or mutton, cut into 2.5 cm (1 inch) cubes
500 g (1 lb) shank of mutton slices, 2 cm ($\frac{3}{4}$ inch) thick
4 rashers rindless streaky bacon, coarsely chopped
15 g ($\frac{1}{2}$ oz) butter
2 onions, chopped
1 tsp salt
freshly ground black pepper to taste
200 ml ($6\frac{1}{2}$ fl oz) meat stock (page 133)
1 tsp prepared mustard
1 tbsp lemon juice
5 tbsp medium cream sherry
2 tsp dried or 2 tbsp chopped fresh parsley

CREAM CHEESE PASTRY

250 g (8 oz) plain flour
good pinch salt
125 g (4 oz) butter
250 g (8 oz) cream cheese
beaten egg for glazing

To prepare the meat, fry bacon lightly in a heavy based saucepan. Add butter and meat and brown. Add onion and sauté until translucent. Season meat with salt and pepper. Heat meat stock, mustard, lemon juice and sherry and add to meat. Cover with lid, reduce heat and simmer until meat falls from the bone. Remove bones and flake meat. Add parsley and mix. Spoon meat into a pie dish, place pastry funnel in centre and allow to cool.

Heat oven to 200 °C (400 °F/gas 6). Prepare the cream cheese pastry by sifting flour and salt together. Cut butter into small pieces and rub into flour until it resembles breadcrumbs. Add cream cheese and mix to a firm dough. Wrap pastry in cling film and chill in refrigerator for at least 30 minutes. Roll out pastry thinly and cover meat. Trim edges and brush pastry with egg. Cut a cross in the pastry on top of the funnel and bake for 20 to 30 minutes or until golden brown and cooked.

(6 servings)

VARIATIONS

☆ Substitute prepared rolled-out flaky pastry for the cream cheese pastry.

Crumb herb crust: Mix together 125 g (4 oz) fresh breadcrumbs, 1 small onion, chopped, 1 clove garlic, crushed, 1 tbsp dried or 3 tbsp chopped mixed fresh herbs, 125 g (4 oz) butter, melted, and 60 g (2 oz) Cheddar cheese, grated. Spoon the mixture on top of the meat in a pie dish and bake at 160 °C (325 °F/gas 3) for 20 minutes or until the crust is cooked and golden brown.

HINTS

☆ Meat should be cold before covering it with pastry.
☆ A marble slab is an ideal surface on which to handle pastry.

SUGGESTED SIDE DISHES

Creamy spinach or
Sautéed courgettes
Brandied dried fruit

BASIC RECIPE FOR A LAMB STEW

1 kg (2 lb) scrag (neck) of lamb,
thickly sliced
2 tsp butter
2 tsp cooking oil
1 onion, chopped
1½ tsp salt
freshly ground black pepper to taste
250 ml (8 fl oz) meat stock (page 133)
1 tbsp plain flour

Brown meat in heated butter and cooking oil in a heavy-based saucepan. Add onion and sauté until translucent. Add seasoning and heated meat stock. Cover with lid, reduce heat and simmer for 1½ to 2 hours or until tender. Thicken liquid with a flour and water paste.
(6 servings)

VARIATIONS
☆ *Substitute cubes or portions for the neck of lamb slices.*

Dried fruit stew: Add 125 g (4 oz) mixed dried fruit, ½ tsp ground ginger, 2 whole cloves, good pinch grated nutmeg, 1 cinnammon stick, 2 tbsp port and 2 tbsp lemon juice to the basic lamb stew 30 minutes before the end of cooking time. Remove cinnamon before serving.
Lamb stew with dumplings: *Heat 410 g (13 oz) canned tomatoes, coarsely chopped, 1 tsp sugar and 2 bay leaves with the meat sotck from the lamb stew and add to meat. Prepare the dumplings by sifting together 125 g (4 oz) plain flour, 2 tsp baking powder and ½ tsp salt. Rub in 15 g (½ oz) butter, add enough milk to form a soft dough. When meat is cooked, remove bay leaves and top with spoonfuls of dough. Cover with lid, reduce heat and simmer for 15 to 20 minutes.*

HINT
☆ *The flavour of stews and casseroles improves if prepared the day before they are served.*

SUGGESTED SIDE DISHES
Brown rice
Crisp summer salad
Creamy spinach

LAMB CURRY WITH GINGER AND PAWPAW

750 g (1½ lb) breast of lamb, sawn
into portions
750 g flank of lamb, cut into portions
1 large onion, chopped
2 cloves garlic, crushed
1 tbsp mild curry powder
1 tbsp ground coriander
1 cinnamon stick
2 bay leaves
2 whole cloves
2 tbsp chopped fresh ginger root
2 tsp salt
1 to 2 chillies, seeded and chopped
375 ml (12 fl oz) meat stock (page
133)
2 tbsp lemon juice
500 g (1 lb) pawpaw, peeled and
cubed

Brown meat in a heated heavy-based saucepan. Add onion and garlic and sauté until onion is translucent. Add curry powder and fry for 1 minute. Add remaining spices, ginger, salt and chillies. Heat meat stock and lemon juice and add to meat. Cover with lid, reduce heat and simmer for 1½ to 2 hours or until meat is almost tender. Place pawpaw on top of meat and simmer for a further 30 minutes. Remove cinnamon and bay leaves.
(8 servings)

VARIATIONS
☆ *Substitute thick rib, shank or neck for the breast and flank.*
☆ *Substitute sliced cooking apple, pears or cubed sweet melon for the pawpaw. Dried fruit may also be used.*

HINT
☆ *Experiment by making your own curry mixture (page 18).*

SUGGESTED SIDE DISHES
Rice and chutney and/or coconut
Poppadums and sambals

SAMBALS AND RAITA
Tomato sambal: Mix together 1 large ripe tomato, diced, 1 onion, diced and 1 green pepper, seeded and diced.

Banana and coconut sambal: Slice 3 bananas, toss in 1 tbsp lemon juice, then roll in 2 tbsp desiccated coconut.
Cucumber and yoghurt raita: Grate 1 cucumber and drain thoroughly. Mix cucumber with 250 ml (8 fl oz) plain yoghurt and ½ tsp dried or 1 tsp chopped fresh mint.

LAMB AND AUBERGINE MEAL-IN-A-POT

1.5 kg (3 lb) shank of lamb, thickly
sliced
3 medium aubergines
15 g (½ oz) butter
1 tbsp cooking oil
1 green pepper, seeded and cut into
julienne strips
1 onion, sliced
2 cloves garlic, crushed
250 ml (8 fl oz) meat stock (page 133)
410 g (13 oz) canned whole
tomatoes, coarsely chopped
2 tsp salt
1 tsp soft brown sugar
freshly ground black pepper to taste
1 tsp dried or 1 tbsp chopped fresh
rosemary
½ tsp dried or 2 tsp chopped fresh
thyme
1 bay leaf

Slice aubergines, sprinkle with salt and leave for 30 minutes. Rinse under cold water and pat dry with paper towels. Fry aubergines in heated butter and cooking oil until light brown. Add more cooking oil if necessary. Add green pepper, onion and garlic and fry until onion is translucent. Add heated meat stock, tomatoes and seasoning and simmer for 5 minutes.

In a separate saucepan, brown the meat in additional cooking oil. Spoon meat into aubergine and tomato mixture, cover with lid, reduce heat and simmer for 1½ to 2 hours or until meat is tender. Remove bay leaf.
(6 servings)

VARIATION
☆ *Substitute carrots, potatoes or leeks and potatoes for the aubergines.*

HINT
☆ *Cook aubergines under a pre-heated grill instead of frying them.*

SUGGESTED SIDE DISH
Boiled wheat

Butterfield leg of lamb basted with tomato (page 44)

BUTTERFIELD LEG OF LAMB BASTED WITH TOMATO

1 boned leg of lamb,
approximately 1.5 kg (3 lb)

TOMATO BASTE
4 tbsp tomato paste
4 tbsp cooking oil
200 ml (6½ fl oz) dry white wine
3 tbsp honey
½ tsp each dried or 2 tsp each
chopped fresh rosemary and
oregano
2 cloves garlic, crushed
1 tsp salt
freshly ground black pepper
to taste
1-2 tsp plain flour

First prepare the basting mixture by mixing all the ingredients together.

To prepare the meat, cut the boned leg open and flatten slightly with the palm of your hand. Place meat on the rack of a roasting tin and roast at 160 °C (325 °F/gas 3) for 20 to 25 minutes per 500 g (1 lb) plus 20 minutes (medium) or 25 to 30 minutes per 500 g (1 lb) plus 25 minutes (well-done). Baste the meat frequently with the tomato basting mixture during the last 30 minutes of cooking time. Allow meat to rest in warming drawer for 10 minutes. This will facilitate carving and the meat juices will be reabsorbed.

Thicken remaining tomato basting mixture with a flour and water paste and serve as a sauce.

(8 servings)

VARIATIONS
☆ Substitute basil for rosemary.
☆ Make shallow incisions with the grain of the meat and stuff with a mixture of chopped bacon, parsley and crushed garlic.

HINTS
☆ Use a sprig of crushed rosemary to apply the basting mixture.
☆ Grill the meat slowly over hot coals, basting the meat frequently with the tomato baste. Lower the grid during the last 30 minutes of cooking time.

SUGGESTED SIDE DISHES
Jacket potatoes
Buttered mushrooms
Green salad

Tasty neck of mutton (page 45)

TASTY NECK OF MUTTON

750g (1½ lb) whole neck of mutton
4 tsp plain flour
1 tsp salt
freshly ground black pepper
to taste
155 g (5 oz) baby carrots
2 celery stalks, cut into chunks
10 fresh pickling onions
2 large potatoes, peeled and
quartered
3 tbsp dry white wine
3 tbsp meat stock (page 133)

Mix flour, salt and black pepper and rub well into meat. Place meat, vegetables and liquid in a cooking bag. Secure the bag and place it in an oven dish. Pierce a few small holes in the top to allow steam to escape, then bake at 160 °C (325 °F/gas 3) for 45 minutes per 500 g (1 lb) plus 40 minutes. Serve whole.
(4 servings)

HINTS
☆ *Use a casserole instead of a cooking bag.*
☆ *To serve, loosen meat from bone using two forks.*

SUGGESTED SIDE DISH
Brown rice

GERHARD'S CORIANDER RIB

1 kg (2 lb) breast of lamb
1 tsp salt
1 tbsp ground coriander
3 tbsp lemon juice

Mix salt, coriander and lemon juice and brush rib with half the mixture. Cook rib over moderate coals or under a preheated grill for approximately 20 minutes or until cooked, turning occasionally and brushing with remaining mixture.
(6 servings)

VARIATION
☆ *Substitute a mixture of coarse salt, garlic and chopped parsley for the coriander. Omit the fine salt.*

SUGGESTED SIDE DISH
Mixed salad

RACK OF LAMB WITH LEMON SAUCE AND ASPARAGUS

1 rack of lamb (8 ribs)
3 tbsp chopped chives
5 tsp cooking oil
5 tsp medium cream sherry
½ tsp salt
freshly ground black pepper to taste
1 tsp dried or 1 tbsp chopped fresh
rosemary
2 to 3 asparagus spears per person

LEMON SAUCE
60 g (2 oz) butter
4 large eggs
3 tbsp dry white wine
3 tbsp lemon juice
125 ml (4 fl oz) single cream
½ tsp salt
1 tsp grated lemon rind

To prepare the meat, french (page 154) rib ends for 2.5 cm (1 inch). Ask your butcher to chine the rack and saw through the backbone to facilitate carving. Stuff natural separation between the upper fat layer and the eye muscle with chives. Brush meat with oil and sherry, then season meat on fat side with salt, pepper and rosemary. Place meat fat side uppermost on the rack of a roasting tin and roast at 160 °C (325 °F/gas 3) for 20 to 25 minutes per 500 g (1 lb) plus 20 minutes (medium) or 25 to 30 minutes per 500 g (1 lb) plus 25 minutes (well-done), basting frequently. Allow meat to rest for 10 minutes before cutting into chops and serving with the asparagus and lemon sauce.

Meanwhile prepare the asparagus. Remove hard ends of asparagus spears, rinse under cold water and tie into bundles. Boil for 7 to 10 minutes with the stalk section immersed in hot salted water. Drain thoroughly.

To prepare the lemon sauce, beat butter, eggs and wine in the top section of a double boiler. Stir in lemon juice, cream and salt and heat mixture over boiling water until thickened, stirring constantly. Add lemon rind.
(4 servings)

VARIATIONS
☆ *Substitute artichoke hearts for the asparagus.*
☆ *Substitute ½ small onion for the chives.*

HINTS
☆ *While roasting, protect rib ends with foil.*
☆ *Remove cooked meat from bone and carve into thin slices.*

SUGGESTED SIDE DISHES
Cheesy potato slices
Buttered mixed vegetables

ROAST SADDLE OF LAMB WITH ALMOND TOPPING

1 boned saddle of lamb,
approximately 2 kg (4 lb)
1½ tsp salt
freshly ground black pepper
to taste
90 g (3 oz) finely chopped almonds
90 g (3 oz) rolled oats
3 tbsp chopped chives
3 tbsp melted butter
2 tsp chutney
1 egg white

PEACH PURÉE
410 g (13 oz) canned peaches,
drained and 2 tbsp syrup reserved
3 tbsp lemon juice

Season meat with salt and pepper. Shape meat into a roll and tie with string. Place meat on the rack of a roasting tin and roast at 160 °C (325 °F/gas 3) for 20 to 25 minutes per 500 g (1 lb) plus 20 minutes (medium) or 25 to 30 minutes per 500 g (1 lb) plus 25 minutes (well-done). Mix together almonds, oats, chives, butter and chutney. Beat egg white until stiff and fold into oat mixture. Spread over fat side of meat 30 minutes before end of cooking time. Allow meat to rest in warming drawer for 10 minutes before carving into thin slices and serving with peach purée.

To prepare the purée, purée peaches, syrup and lemon juice in a food processor or blender.
(10 servings)

HINT
☆ *Use the leftover egg yolk to make scrambled egg or home-made mayonnaise.*

SUGGESTED SIDE DISHES
Rice pilaff
Green bean bundles with dill

ROLLED FLANK OF LAMB WITH ORANGE STUFFING

1.5 kg (3 lb) whole flank and breast of lamb
1 tbsp cooking oil
1 tsp salt
freshly ground black pepper to taste
125 ml (4 fl oz) orange juice
125 ml (4 fl oz) meat stock (page 133)
1 tsp chopped fresh ginger root
1 tsp grated orange rind
1 tbsp plain flour

STUFFING
2 oranges
1 onion, chopped
15 g ($\frac{1}{2}$ oz) butter
90 g (3 oz) cooked rice
2 tsp dried or 2 tbsp chopped fresh parsley
$\frac{1}{2}$ tsp salt
freshly ground black pepper to taste

First prepare the stuffing. Cut away the rind, pith and skin of each orange. Carefully cut away the segments, leaving the membrane behind. Sauté onion in heated butter until translucent. Add orange segments and remaining stuffing ingredients and mix well.

To prepare the meat, bone the meat and remove all visible connective tissue. Spoon stuffing onto the meat, leaving 2 cm ($\frac{3}{4}$ inch) clear around the edges, then roll up and tie with string. Brown meat in heated cooking oil and season with salt and pepper. Heat remaining ingredients and add to meat. Cover with lid, reduce heat and simmer for 1$\frac{1}{2}$ to 2 hours or until meat is tender. Thicken sauce with a flour and water paste if necessary. Remove string and carve meat.

(8 servings)

VARIATION
Dried fruit stuffing: *Mix together 125 g (4 oz) mixed dried fruit, coarsely chopped, 3 tbsp lemon juice and 1 tsp grated lemon rind.*

HINTS
☆ *If flank of lamb is unavailable, use a boned shoulder.*
☆ *Substitute mint for the parsley.*

SUGGESTED SIDE DISHES
Fried potatoes
Brussels sprouts with almonds
Glazed carrots

ROLLED SHOULDER OF LAMB WITH LEEKS

1 shoulder of lamb roll, approximately 1.5 kg (3 lb)
15 g ($\frac{1}{2}$ g) butter
2 tsp cooking oil
1 tsp salt
freshly ground black pepper to taste
125 ml (4 fl oz) meat stock (page 133)
200 ml (6$\frac{1}{2}$ fl oz) dry white wine
3 large leeks, cut into 10 cm (4 inch) lengths

SAUCE
30 g (1 oz) butter
15 g ($\frac{1}{2}$ oz) flour
250 ml (8 fl oz) single cream
1 tbsp Pommery mustard
$\frac{1}{2}$ tsp salt
freshly gound black pepper to taste
4 slices pastrami (approximately 90 g/3oz), coarsely chopped

Brown meat in heated butter and cooking oil in a heavy-based saucepan. Season with salt and pepper and add heated stock and wine. Place meat in a casserole and bake at 160 °C (325 °F/gas 3) for 45 minutes per 500 g (1 lb) plus 40 minutes. Add leeks 30 minutes before end of cooking time. Remove meat and leeks from casserole and keep warm.

To prepare the sauce, make a paste from the butter and flour (beurre manié – page 153) and stir into liquid remaining in casserole. When thick and smooth, stir in cream, seasoning and pastrami and heat through. Carve the meat into thin slices and serve with the sauce and leeks.

(6 servings)

VARIATIONS
☆ *Substitute leg of lamb for the shoulder.*
☆ *Substitute flank or breast of lamb, boned and rolled, for the shoulder of lamb and brown without butter or cooking oil.*
☆ *Low-fat variation: Substitute 250 ml (8 fl oz) plain low-fat yoghurt for the 250 ml (8 fl oz) cream.*
☆ *Substitute bacon or smoked beef for the pastrami.*

HINT
☆ *Use the bones from the shoulder of lamb to prepare the meat stock (page 133).*

SUGGESTED SIDE DISHES
Parsley shell noodles
Vegetable casserole

ROLLED RIB OF LAMB WITH BACON STUFFING

1 rib of lamb (10 ribs), boned
1 tsp salt
freshly ground black pepper to taste

STUFFING
125 g (4 oz) rindless shoulder bacon, coarsely chopped
1 onion, chopped
1 clove garlic, crushed
90 g (3 oz) spinach, blanched and coarsely chopped
$\frac{1}{2}$ tsp salt
freshly ground black pepper to taste
grated nutmeg to taste

First prepare the stuffing. Fry bacon in a heavy-based saucepan until crisp. Add onion and garlic and sauté until onion is translucent. Add spinach and season with salt, pepper and nutmeg.

To prepare the meat, spoon stuffing over inside of meat, leaving 2 cm ($\frac{3}{4}$ inch) clear around the edges. Roll up meat and tie with string. Season with salt and pepper and place on the rack of a roasting tin. Roast at 160 °C (325 °F/gas 3) for 20 to 25 minutes per 500 g (1 lb) plus 20 minutes (medium) or 25 to 30 minutes per 500 g (1 lb) plus 25 minutes (well-done). Remove string and carve.

(8 servings)

VARIATION
☆ *Substitute smoked beef for bacon.*

SUGGESTED SIDE DISHES
Lemon rice
Ratatouille

Crispy roast leg of lamb

CRISPY ROAST LEG OF LAMB

1 leg or lamb, approximately
1.5 kg (3 lb)
1½ tsp salt
freshly ground black pepper to taste
2 tbsp lemon juice

GLAZE
2 tbsp soft brown sugar
2 tsp brandy
2 tsp lemon juice
1 tsp grated lemon rind

First prepare the glaze by mixing all the ingredients together well.

Season meat with salt, pepper and lemon juice. Place meat on the rack of a roasting tin and roast at 160 °C (325 °F/gas 3) for 20 to 25 minutes per 500 g (1 lb) plus 20 minutes (medium) or 25 to 30 minutes per 500 g (1 lb) plus 25 minutes (well-done). Baste meat frequently with glaze mixture during last 30 minutes of cooking time. Allow meat to rest in warming drawer for 10 minutes to facilitate carving.

(8 servings)

VARIATION

☆ *Substitute 1 tbsp apricot jam for the brown sugar.*

HINT

☆ *To extract the maximum amount of juice from a lemon, place the whole lemon in the pre-heated oven for 2 to 3 minutes or in the microwave oven for 15 seconds.*

SUGGESTED SIDE DISHES
Bacon and broccoli-stuffed potatoes
Chicory (endive) nut salad

PORK

Nowadays pork is low in fat and low in calories as it contains a low percentage of intramuscular fat, making it an ideal choice for everyone, including slilmmers. Rich in minerals and vitamin B1 (thiamine), a 90 g (3 oz) portion of pork without bone provides an adult with 45% of his daily protein needs.

Before roasting pork, remember to score the rind with a sharp knife or scorer at 2.5 cm (1 inch) intervals and rub in a mixture of salt and dry mustard. This will ensure a crisp rind.

Contrary to expectation, a pig's head contains a considerable amount of meat. The cheeks can be removed, cut into 2.5 cm (1 inch) cubes and used to make tasty stews. Connoissuers consider pigs' ears a delicacy. When roasting a pig's head, remember to cover the ears as well as the snout with foil as they are very thin and tend to burn easily.

QUALITY CHARACTERISTICS OF PORK

Colour

The meat of a young animal is greyish pink. Generally, the older the animal the darker the meat.

Texture

The meat and fat should feel firm to the touch and not leave an impression when pressed with a finger.

Bones

The surface of sawn bones should be red and porous. The ribs should have red flecks. The bones of an older animal are greyish white and chalky with no red flecks on the ribs.

Cartilage

The cartilage between the vertebrae is soft and jelly-like. In an older animal the cartilage is hard.

Fat

The fat is mostly white to creamy white. An oily appearance is indicative of an older animal.

Rind (skin)

The rind must be removed from cuts cooked using the moist-heat cooking method but the rind can be cooked separately as follows: Make diamond-shaped incisions in the rind, rub with cooking oil and salt and roast at 160 °C (325 °F/gas 3) for 25 minutes per 500 g (1 lb). For a crisp crackling increase the temperature to 200 °C (400 °F/gas 6) during the last 30 minutes.

HEAD

The head contains a large proportion of fat as well as edible parts such as the cheeks, tongue and ears.

USES
☆ Whole, soaked and cleaned: ....Roast
☆ Brawn: ....Simmer
☆ Trimmings:...................................Mince
☆ Tongue and cheeks: ....Pâté
☆ Cheeks:..Liver sausage

SHANK AND TROTTER OR HAND

The shank contains a large proportion of bone and little meat, but the meat contains a large proportion of white connective tissue (collagen) which makes this a less tender but tasty cut.

USES
☆ Trotters: ....Brawn
☆ Slices:...Braised dishes
☆ Whole shank, cured (pickled).........Simmer

Opposite Clockwise from top: Pork kebabs with garlic sauce (page 56); Pork fillet in filo pastry (page 54); and Kasseler rib with mango cream (page 57)

BLADE, SPARE RIB OR FOREQUARTER

The neck of the pig carcase is too short to remove separately and is removed with the blade and sparerib. This cut consists of the shoulder blade, backbone with dorsal vertebrae and five to seven ribs.

USES
☆ Whole, boned and stuffed: .... Roast (cushion)
☆ Thick rib chops: .... Grill (forequarter)
☆ Cubes: .... Stews
☆ Strips: .... Stir-fry

BREAST

The breast contains the breastbone, rib ends and a portion of the marrowbone.

USES
☆ Whole, boned and rolled: .... Pot-roast
☆ Cured: .... Green bacon (unsmoked bacon)
☆ Strips: .... Concertina kebabs, grill
☆ Portions: .... Spareribs, marinate and grill
☆ Cubes: .... Stews
☆ Trimmings: .... Mince

BELLY OR SPRING

The belly section is boneless with a thin muscle layer and a high percentage of white connective tissue.

USES
☆ Whole, rolled: .... Pot-roast or cook in cooking bag or foil
☆ Boned, cured and smoked: .... Streaky bacon
☆ Strips: .... Concertina kebabs, grill
☆ Trimmings: .... Mince

RIB OR RIB LOIN

A characteristic feature of the rib is the large eye muscle. This cut consists of seven to nine ribs, backbone and an even fat layer with rind.

USES
☆ Whole: .... Roast (chine)
☆ Rack: .... Roast (french and chine)
☆ Boned and rolled: .... Roast
☆ Cured and smoked: .... Kasseler rib
☆ Chops: .... Grill

FILLET

The fillet is a lean tender cut situated on the inside of the backbone.

USES
☆ Whole: .... Roast (preferably barded or basted)
☆ Slices: .... Grill, pan-grill

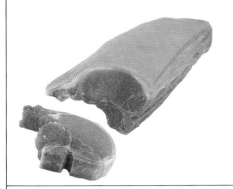

LOIN OR MIDLOIN

The loin contains the backbone, a T-shaped bone, a large eye muscle and a smaller fillet. The loin contains no ribs. If the loin is removed before the carcase is halved, it is referred to as the saddle.

USES

☆ Whole saddle:...........................Roast
☆ Whole loin:..............................Roast
☆ Boned and rolled:.....................Roast
☆ Loin and saddle chops: ....Grill
☆ Butterfly and medallion steaks: .. Grill, pan-grill

CHUMP

The chump contains the pelvic bone and several muscle layers.

USES

☆ Whole: ....Roast
☆ Boned: ....Roast
☆ Cured and/or smoked: ....Ham (could be left on leg)
☆ Chops: ....Grill
☆ Rump steaks ....Grill, pan-grill

LEG

The leg consists of marrowbone and several muscle layers. Larger carcases can be divided into three separate cuts, which are known as the silverside, topside and thick flank.

USES

☆ Whole: ....Roast
☆ Boned: ....Roast
☆ Cured and/or smoked: ....Ham
☆ Slices:.....................................Schnitzels, shallow-fry
    Pork olives, stew
☆ Strips:.....................................Stir-fry
☆ Cubes: ....Stews
    Kebabs, grill

PORK PIE

FILLING

750 g (1½ lb) lean leg of pork, cut into 2.5 cm (1 inch) cubes
250 g (8 oz) rindless back or shoulder bacon, chopped
1 small onion, grated
½ tsp dried or 2 tsp chopped fresh sage
freshly ground black pepper to taste
2 hard-boiled eggs

CREAM CHEESE PASTRY

250 g (8 oz) plain flour
½ tsp salt
60 g (2 oz) butter
1 egg, lightly beaten
155 to 200 g (5 to 6½ oz) cream cheese
egg for glazing

JELLY

2½ tsp powdered gelatine
250 ml (8 fl oz) white meat stock (page 133)
freshly ground black pepper to taste

First prepare the pastry. Sift flour and salt and rub in butter. Slowly mix in beaten egg, then the cream cheese to form a stiff dough. Wrap in cling film and refrigerate for 1 hour.

To prepare the filling, fry bacon until crisp and remove from saucepan. Brown meat in rendered bacon fat, drain and mix with bacon, onion, sage and pepper. Cool completely.

To assemble the pie, roll out pastry to fit a greased loaf tin. Spoon in half the filling, arrange boiled eggs lengthwise on top and spoon in remaining filling. Roll out rest of pastry to make a lid and position on top of filling. Pinch edges to seal well, then cut two small crosses in the lid. Decorate edges of pie and crosses with pastry. Brush with egg. Roll foil into small funnels and insert into each hole to keep it open during baking. Bake at 200 °C (400 °F/gas 6) for 25 minutes. Cover pastry with foil, shiny side out, reduce temperature to 180 °C (350 °F/gas 4) and bake for another 1½ to 2 hours. Leave pie to cool in tin, then turn out. Soak gelatine in cold meat stock until spongy. Heat gently in double boiler or microwave oven until gelatine is dissolved. Season and allow to cool. Remove foil funnels and pour jelly through holes. Chill for at least 4 hours.
(6 to 8 servings)

SUGGESTED SIDE DISH
Sweet and sour baby beetroot

German-style smoked pork

STUFFED THICK RIB

1.5 kg (3 lb) boned thick rib of pork, rind removed (cushion)

STUFFING

125 g (4 oz) stoned prunes, coarsely chopped
1 apple, peeled, cored and grated
good pinch salt
freshly ground black pepper
to taste

BASTING MIXTURE

3 tbsp cooking oil
juice of 1 large lemon
1 tsp dried or 1 tbsp chopped
fresh sage
1 tsp salt
freshly ground black pepper to taste

First prepare the stuffing by mixing all the ingredients together.

Prepare the basting mixture by mixing all the ingredients together.

To prepare the meat, trim excess fat according to own preference. Spoon stuffing into cavity and secure with string at 2.5 cm (1 inch) intervals. Place meat fat side uppermost on the rack of a roasting tin and roast at 160 °C (325 °F/gas 3) for 20 to 25 minutes per 500 g (1 lb) plus 20 minutes (medium) or 25 to 30 minutes per 500 g (1 lb) plus 25 minutes (well-done). Baste meat with basting mixture during last 30 minutes of cooking time. Allow meat to rest for approximately 10 minutes before carving.
(6 servings)

VARIATIONS

☆ Substitute any other dried fruit, such as apricots, for the prunes.
☆ Substitute apple juice for the lemon juice and add 1 tsp grated lemon rind.

SUGGESTED SIDE DISHES

Roast potatoes
Creamed spinach

GERMAN-STYLE SMOKED PORK

2 cured and smoked shanks of pork
1 onion, sliced
1 carrot, cut into chunks
1 bouquet garni (page 17)
enough water to cover

Place shanks in a large saucepan. Add onion, carrot and bouquet garni and cover with water. Bring to the boil, then reduce heat and simmer for 1 to $1\frac{1}{2}$ hours until meat is tender. Remove shanks from liquid, score rind and place under a pre-heated grill until crisp.
(4 servings)

VARIATION

☆ Substitute beer for half the water. Flat beer may also be used.

SUGGESTED SIDE DISHES

Boiled potatoes
Sauerkraut

PORK RIB ROLL WITH NUT AND APPLE STUFFING

1.5 kg (3 lb) rib of pork (8 ribs),
boned and rind removed
1 tsp salt
freshly ground black pepper to taste

STUFFING
1 onion, chopped
15 g ($\frac{1}{2}$ oz) butter
1 celery stalk, chopped
90 g (3 oz) walnuts, chopped
3 tbsp fresh breadcrumbs
1 cooking apple, peeled, cored and
grated
$\frac{1}{2}$ tsp dried or 1 tsp chopped fresh
rosemary
$\frac{1}{2}$ tsp salt
freshly ground black pepper to taste

First prepare the stuffing. Sauté onion in heated butter until translucent. Add celery, walnuts, breadcrumbs and apple and heat for a few minutes longer. Season with rosemary, salt and pepper.

To prepare the meat, trim excess fat according to preference. Spoon stuffing onto meat, leaving 2 cm ($\frac{3}{4}$ inch) clear around the edges, then roll and tie meat with string at 2.5 cm (1 inch) intervals. Season with salt and pepper. Place meat on the rack of a roasting tin, and roast at 160 °C (325 °F/gas 3) for 20 to 25 minutes per 500 g (1 lb) plus 20 minutes (medium) or 25 to 30 minutes per 500 g (1 lb) plus 25 minutes (well-done). Remove from oven and allow to rest for 10 minutes before carving.

(6 servings)

VARIATIONS
☆ Substitute toasted almonds for the walnuts.
☆ Substitute pork loin for the rib of pork.
☆ Substitute 1 pear, cored and cubed, for the cooking apple.

HINTS
☆ Roll meat from the thicker end towards the thinner end.
☆ To toast almonds: Spread a single layer on a baking tray and bake at 180 °C (350 °F/gas 4), turning them frequently until golden brown.

SUGGESTED DISH
Sweetcorn kernels

TOMATO AND MUSHROOM STEW

1.5 kg (3 lb) breast of pork, sawn into
6 portions
1 onion, quartered
2 cloves garlic, crushed
410 g (13 oz) canned whole
tomatoes
250 g (8 oz) button mushrooms,
wiped
125 ml (4 fl oz) meat stock (page 133)
150 ml ($\frac{1}{4}$ pint) dry white wine
1 tsp dried or 1 tbsp chopped fresh
thyme
1$\frac{1}{2}$ tsp salt
freshly ground black pepper to taste
1 tbsp plain flour
2 tsp dried or 2 tbsp chopped fresh
parsley

Brown meat in a heated heavy-based saucepan. Add onion and garlic and sauté until onion is translucent. Add tomatoes, mushrooms, heated meat stock, wine and remaining ingredients, except parsley. Cover with lid, reduce heat and simmer for 1 to 1$\frac{1}{2}$ hours or until meat is tender. Thicken sauce with a flour and water paste if necessary. Sprinkle with parsley.

(6 servings)

VARIATION
☆ Substitute shank for breast of pork.

SUGGESTED SIDE DISHES
Fettucine
Vegetables in season

PORK AND BEAN DISH

500 g (1 lb) shank of pork, sawn into
thick slices
500 g (1 lb) breast of pork, sawn into
6 portions
1 tbsp cooking oil
3 onions, sliced
3 cloves garlic, crushed
410 g (13 oz) canned whole
tomatoes, coarsely chopped
375 ml (12 fl oz) meat stock
(page 133)
5 tsp Worcestershire sauce
2 tsp salt
1 tsp freshly ground black pepper
500 g (1 lb) smoked boiling sausage,
sliced
200 g (6$\frac{1}{2}$ oz) haricot beans, soaked
and cooked
200 g (6$\frac{1}{2}$ oz) kidney beans, soaked
and cooked

Brown meat in heated cooking oil in a heavy-based saucepan. Add onion and garlic and sauté until onion is translucent. Heat tomato, meat stock and Worcestershire sauce and add to meat. Season with salt and pepper. Cover with lid, reduce heat and simmer for 1$\frac{1}{2}$ to 2 hours or until meat is tender. Add smoked sausages and beans and simmer until heated through.

(6 servings)

SUGGESTED SIDE DISH
Green salad

STUFFED PORK LOIN CHOPS

4 pork loin chops, 2.5 cm (1 inch)
thick

STUFFING
1 onion, chopped
15 g ($\frac{1}{2}$ oz) butter
90 g (3 oz) cooked brown rice
60 g (2 oz) dried apricots, finely
chopped
good pinch salt
freshly ground black pepper to taste

BASTING MIXTURE
1 tbsp cooking oil
4 tsp lemon juice
2 tsp dried or 2 tbsp chopped
fresh sage

First prepare the stuffing. Sauté onion in heated butter in a heavy-based saucepan until translucent. Add remaining ingredients and leave to cool.

Prepare the basting mixture by mixing all the ingredients together.

To prepare the meat, trim off excess fat according to preference. Cut a pocket in each chop, fill with a little stuffing and secure with a cocktail stick. Cook chops 10 cm (4 inches) under a pre-heated grill for 5 to 7 minutes in total (medium) or 7 to 10 minutes in total (well-done), basting frequently with basting mixture. Season with salt and pepper and serve.

(4 servings)

VARIATION
☆ Substitute Italian arborio rice for the cooked brown rice.

SUGGESTED SIDE DISHES
Deep-fried potato slices and
Cucumber salad

GINGER PORK CHOPS

6 pork chump chops
salt and freshly ground black pepper
to taste

MARINADE
1 clove garlic, crushed
2 tbsp chopped fresh ginger root
1 tbsp soft brown sugar
1 tbsp cooking oil
1 tbsp soy sauce
5 tbsp dry white wine

First prepare the marinade by mixing all the ingredients together.

Place meat in marinade and marinate for 3 to 4 hours. Remove from marinade and pat dry with paper towels. Cook meat 10 cm (4 inches) under a pre-heated grill for 5 to 7 minutes in total (medium) or 7 to 10 minutes in total (well-done), basting frequently with marinade. Season meat with salt and pepper and serve.

(6 servings)

SUGGESTED SIDE DISHES
Sauté potatoes
Glazed carrots
Buttered beans

PORK SHANK WITH YOGHURT

1.5 kg (3 lb) shank of pork, sliced
1 tbsp cooking oil
15 g ($\frac{1}{2}$ oz) butter
15 fresh pickling onions
2 cloves garlic, crushed
250 ml (8 fl oz) meat stock
(page 133)
1 tsp salt
freshly ground black pepper
to taste
1$\frac{1}{2}$ tsp paprika
2 tsp plain flour
150 ml ($\frac{1}{4}$ pint) plain yoghurt

Brown meat in heated cooking oil and butter in a heavy-based saucepan. Add onions and garlic and sauté until onions are translucent. Add heated meat stock and seasoning. Cover with lid, reduce heat and simmer for 1$\frac{1}{2}$ to 2 hours. Thicken the liquid with a flour and water paste. Remove from heat, stir in yoghurt and serve.

(6 servings)

VARIATION
☆ Substitute soured cream or cream for the yoghurt.

SUGGESTED SIDE DISH
Dried fruit salad

LEG OF PORK WITH CRACKLING AND BAKED APPLES

1 boned leg of pork, approximately
2 kg (4 lb)
1$\frac{1}{2}$ tsp salt
$\frac{1}{2}$ tsp dry mustard
freshly ground black pepper to taste

BAKED APPLES
8 cooking apples, cored
125 g (4 oz) mixed dried fruit
3 tbsp brandy
3 tbsp melted butter

MUSTARD SAUCE
3 eggs
125 ml (4 fl oz) white vinegar
185 g (6 oz) sugar
2 tsp dry mustard
410 g (13 oz) canned evaporated
milk
4 tbsp crushed green peppercorns
freshly ground black pepper to taste

To prepare meat, score rind and rub with a mixture of salt, mustard and pepper. Place meat on the rack of a roasting tin and roast at 160 °C (325 °F/gas 3) for 20 to 25 minutes per 500 g (1 lb) plus 20 minutes (medium) or 25 to 30 minutes per 500 g (1 lb) plus 25 minutes (well-done). Increase oven temperature to 200 °C (400 °F/gas 6) during last 30 minutes of cooking time.

To prepare the apples, make a horizontal incision around the middle of each apple and peel top half. Soak fruit in the brandy until plump. Mix with melted butter and stuff apples. Bake with leg of pork during last 40 minutes of cooking time or until apples are tender.

To prepare the mustard sauce, beat together the eggs, vinegar, sugar and dry mustard in top half of a double boiler. Stir the mixture over boiling water until thickened. Remove from heat and stir in evaporated milk, green peppercorns and black pepper. Serve pork with sauce and baked apples.

(8 to 10 servings)

VARIATIONS
☆ Substitute 3 tbsp horseradish sauce or 3 tbsp chopped fresh herbs or $\frac{1}{2}$ tsp each grated lemon and orange rind for the green peppercorns.
☆ Substitute quinces for the apples.

HINT
☆ Score the rind with a sharp knife to facilitate carving.

SUGGESTED SIDE DISHES
Savoury rice
Glazed mixed vegetables

PORK FILLET FLAMBE

625 g (1$\frac{1}{4}$ lb) fillet of pork steaks,
2.5 cm (1 inch) thick
30 g (1 oz) butter
2 tbsp brandy
410 g (13 oz) canned apricot halves
5 tbsp soured cream
1 tsp salt
freshly ground black pepper
to taste
1 tbsp lemon juice

Brown meat in heated butter in a heavy-based saucepan. Heat brandy, pour over meat and ignite. Shake the pan to and fro until flames are extinguished. Add heated apricots and juice and simmer for a few minutes. Add soured cream, seasoning and lemon juice.

(4 servings)

HINT
☆ Substitute peaches, figs or kiwi fruit for the apricots.
☆ Substitute rum or sherry for the brandy.

SUGGESTED SIDE DISHES
Courgettes cut into julienne
Herb potato croquettes

PORK FILLET IN FILO PASTRY

375 g (12 oz) whole fillet of pork
30 g (1 oz) butter
$\frac{1}{2}$ tsp salt
freshly ground black pepper
to taste
$\frac{1}{2}$ tsp dried or 1 tsp chopped
fresh mint
4 sheets filo pastry
2 tbsp melted butter

Brown meat in heated butter in a heavy-based saucepan. Seaon with salt, pepper and mint. Brush each sheet of filo pastry lightly with melted butter, pile the sheets on top of each other and place fillet diagonally across pastry. Roll the meat in the pastry, then brush with melted butter. Place meat in a greased roasting tin and bake at 160 °C (325 °F/gas 3) for 20 minutes and at 200 °C (400 °F/gas 6) for another 20 minutes.
(4 servings)

VARIATIONS
☆ *Brush browned fillet with melted butter and roll in breadcrumbs instead of filo pastry.*
☆ *Cut fillet into slices and prepare individual filo parcels.*
☆ *Substitute cream cheese pastry (page 41) for filo pastry.*

SUGGESTED SIDE DISH
Vegetable terrine

SCHNITZELS WITH A DIFFERENCE

6 thin slices of pork, cut from the leg
1 tsp salt
freshly ground black pepper to taste
60 g (2 oz) plain flour
2 eggs, beaten
60 g (2 oz) dried breadcrumbs
cooking oil

Place meat between two sheets of cling film and flatten slightly with the palm of the hand. Mix together salt, pepper and flour. Coat meat with flour, followed by beaten egg and breadcrumbs. Refrigerate for 30 minutes to allow breadcrumbs to set. Fry meat in heated cooking oil in a heavy-based frying pan until golden brown on both sides. Drain schnitzels on paper towels.
(6 servings)

VARIATIONS
Apricot cream schnitzels: *Mix 125 ml (4 fl oz) apricot yoghurt or apricot purée with 1 tsp lemon juice. Dip schnitzels in yoghurt or purée, then in flour, followed by beaten egg and finally in whole biscuit crumbs. Proceed as above.*
Kiwi-flavoured schnitzels: *Purée 1 fresh kiwi fruit. Dip schnitzels in fruit purée, then in the flour, followed by beaten egg and finally in breadcrumbs. Proceed as above.*
Schnitzels with a ginger crust: *Substitute 60 g (2 oz) ginger biscuit crumbs for the dried breadcrumbs. Proceed as above.*
Sesame seed schnitzels: *Substitute sesame seeds for half the dried breadcrumbs. Proceed as above.*

SUGGESTED SIDE DISHES
Boiled potatoes
Crisp salad

Leg of pork with crackling and baked apples (page 54)

PORK KEBABS WITH GARLIC SAUCE

500 g (1 lb) leg of pork, cut into
2.5 cm (1 inch) cubes
1 onion, quartered and loosened
1 red-skinned apple, cored and cut
into 2.5 cm (1 inch) cubes
lemon juice to prevent
discolouring of apple

GARLIC SAUCE
3 tbsp cooking oil
200 ml (6½ fl oz) soured cream
3 cloves garlic, crushed
2 tsp dried or 2 tbsp chopped
fresh parsley

First prepare the sauce by mixing all the ingredients together.

To prepare the meat, thread meat alternately with onion and apple onto bamboo skewers. Cook 10 cm (4 inches) under a pre-heated grill for approximately 10 minutes or until cooked, turning and basting meat frequently with the sauce. Serve immediately with remaining garlic sauce.

(4 to 6 servings)

VARIATION
☆ *Use 2 cm (¾ inch) strips of pork belly and thread them concertinawise and alternately with onion and apple, onto bamboo skewers.*

SUGGESTED SIDE DISHES
Chinese rice
Minty peas

PORK SCHNITZEL WITH BANANA

12 thin slices of pork, cut from
the leg
prepared mustard to taste
6 slices ham
6 slices Gruyère cheese
2 bananas, sliced
2 tsp lemon juice
freshly ground black pepper
to taste
2 tbsp plain flour
½ tsp salt
2 eggs, beaten
125 g (4 oz) dried breadcrumbs
cooking oil for frying

Front: Pork schnitzel with banana. Back: Pineapple-flavoured spareribs (page 57)

Flatten each slice of meat slightly with the palm of the hand, then spread each slice with mustard. Place ham, cheese and banana onto six slices of meat. Sprinkle lemon juice over and season with pepper. Place second slice of meat on top and secure with cocktail sticks. Season flour with salt and pepper. Coat meat with flour, then with beaten egg and finally with breadcrumbs. Place in refrigerator for at least 20 to 30 minutes to allow crumbs to set. Fry in heated cooking oil until golden brown and done on both sides. Drain on paper towels and serve immediately.

(6 servings)

VARIATIONS

☆ *Mix 4 tsp Parmesan cheese with the breadcrumbs.*
☆ *Substitute pears for the bananas.*

HINT

☆ *Cooking oil must be moderately hot, not smoking hot, otherwise the crumbs will burn.*

SUGGESTED SIDE DISHES
Potatoes with bacon
Buttered broccoli

PINEAPPLE-FLAVOURED SPARERIBS

1 kg (2 lb) pork spareribs

MARINADE
250 ml (8 fl oz) pineapple juice
125 ml (4 fl oz) dry white wine
1 tbsp soy sauce
1 tbsp clear honey
1 green pepper, seeded and chopped
1 clove garlic, crushed
2 tsp chopped fresh ginger root
1 tsp grated orange rind
5 tsp cornflour

Mix marinade ingredients, except cornflour, and marinate meat for 3 to 4 hours or in the refrigerator overnight. Remove from marinade and pat dry with paper towels. Cook 10 cm (4 inches) under a pre-heated grill for 12 to 15 minutes or until golden brown, basting frequently with marinade. Thicken remaining marinade with a cornflour and water paste. Cut between ribs into portions and serve with the sauce.

(6 servings)

VARIATIONS

☆ *Substitute mango or apricot juice for the pineapple juice.*
☆ *Substitute grated tangerine rind for the orange rind.*

HINT

☆ *To ensure that you have a supply of fresh ginger, chop large quantities of ginger root, moisten with cooking oil and store in an airtight container in the refrigerator.*

SUGGESTED SIDE DISHES
Baked sweet potatoes and
Chinese coleslaw or
Herb rice and
Courgettes

KASSELER RIB WITH MANGO CREAM

1 Kasseler rib, approximately
1.5 kg (3 lb)

MANGO CREAM
410 g (13 oz) canned mangoes, drained and juice reserved
200 ml ($6\frac{1}{2}$ fl oz) crème fraîche (page 154)
5 chives, chopped

Place meat on the rack of a roasting tin and brush with mango juice. Roast at 160 °C (325 °F/gas 3) for 10 minutes per 500 g (1 lb) or until meat is cooked. To prepare the mango cream, purée mangoes and remaining mango juice, add crème fraîche and chives and stir thoroughly.

Carve meat into chops and serve with mango cream.

(8 servings)

VARIATIONS

☆ *Substitute green of spring onion for the garlic.*
☆ *Substitute soured cream for the crème fraîche.*
☆ *Substitute canned gooseberries for the mangoes.*

HINTS

☆ *Bone the kasseler rib before cooking to facilitate carving (page 15).*
☆ *Grill kasseler rib chops over coals and serve with mango cram.*

SUGGESTED SIDE DISHES
Boiled potatoes
Brussels sprouts

SPINACH ROULADE WITH BACON

FILLING
250 g (8 oz) rindless streaky bacon, chopped
1 clove garlic, crushed
1 onion, chopped
250 g (8 oz) cream cheese
$\frac{1}{2}$ tsp dried or 2 tsp chopped fresh basil

ROULADE
60 g (2 oz) butter
60 g (2 oz) plain flour
250 ml (8 fl oz) milk
$\frac{1}{2}$ tsp salt
freshly ground black pepper to taste
good pinch grated nutmeg
4 eggs, separated
3 tbsp grated Parmesan cheese
625 g ($1\frac{1}{4}$ lb) spinach, cooked and chopped

First prepare the roulade. Make a white sauce (page 146) using the butter, flour and milk. Season with salt, pepper and nutmeg, then add beaten egg yolks, Parmesan cheese and spinach. Beat egg whites until soft peaks form and fold in. Line a Swiss roll tin with greaseproof paper and spoon in roulade mixture, smoothing the surface with the back of a metal spoon. Bake at 180 °C (350 °F/gas 4) for 20 minutes until golden brown and puffed. Turn out onto a moist cloth, allow to cool, then roll up like a Swiss roll.

To prepare the filling, fry bacon until crisp, then remove and allow to cool. Sauté garlic and onion in rendered fat until onion is translucent. Add bacon, garlic and onion to cream cheese and season with basil. Unroll roulade, remove greaseproof paper and spread on filling. Roll up and refrigerate for a few minutes before slicing. Roll up and refrigerate for a few minutes before slicing. Serve with herb mayonnaise (page 147).

(8 servings)

VARIATION

☆ *Substitute a crumbled blue cheese such as Stilton for the Parmesan cheese.*
☆ *Substitute 250 g (8 oz) packet frozen spinach, thawed and drained, instead of fresh.*

SUGGESTED SIDE DISHES
Wholemeal rolls
Tomato salad

HAM

Ham is prepared from a leg or shoulder of pork which has been cured and smoked.

Ham is mainly available in three different forms:
1. *Uncooked* This type of ham has to be cooked before use (the term 'gammon' is also regularly used in association with uncooked ham)
2. *Cooked* This type of ham is ready for eating.
3. *Uncooked* Certain types of ham are intended to be eaten raw. These hams are sold in paper-thin slices and are served cold. The label usually identifies the type of ham.

Select either of the following cooking methods to ensure a tender and succulent ham.

BOILING A HAM

1 ham, approximately 5 kg (11 lb)
1 to 2 carrots
1 large onion, pierced with 4 whole cloves
1 bay leaf
5 black peppercorns
1 tsp dry mustard
1 bunch fresh parsley
1 tbsp soft brown sugar

Cover ham with cold water and add remaining ingredients. Bring liquid to the boil, cover with lid, reduce heat and simmer for 30 minutes per 500 g (1 lb) until a thread of meat comes away easily. Allow to cool slightly, then remove rind. Return ham to cooking liquid and allow to cool before glazing (this will ensure a juicier ham).

VARIATIONS
☆ *Add any one of the following to the cooking liquid:*
- *pineapple rind or pineapple juice*
- *beer*
- *apple juice*
- *ginger ale*

BAKING A HAM IN FOIL

Preheat oven to 160 °C (325 °F/gas 3). Cover meat completely with a large sheet of foil, shiny side inside, and bake for 15 to 20 minutes per 500 g (1 lb). Remove ham from foil and remove the rind.

GLAZING A HAM

BASIC GLAZE
125 ml (4 fl oz) apple juice
2 tbsp honey
2 tsp dry mustard

Either boil the ham or bake in foil, cool slightly and remove rind. Score fat in a diamond pattern, then place ham on the rack of a roasting tin, fat side uppermost. Brush on glaze then bake at 160 °C (325 °F/gas 3) for 15 to 20 minutes. Brush on remaining glaze at regular intervals while baking the ham.

VARIATIONS
Green fig glaze: *Combine 375 g (12 oz) chopped green fig preserve, 3 tbsp medium cream sherry or port and 2 tbsp cooking oil.*

Cherry glaze: *Drain, then liquidize 410 g (13 oz) canned black cherries and combine with 1 tbsp cornflour, 2 tbsp cherry liqueur and 4 tsp grated orange rind.*

Fruit glaze: *Drain, then liquidize 410 g (13 oz) canned peach halves and combine with 2 tsp grated orange or lemon rind, 2 tbsp chopped ginger preserve, 1 tbsp soft brown sugar, 2 tbsp cooking oil and 3 tbsp port.*

Gooseberry glaze: *Drain, then liquidize 410 g (13 oz) canned gooseberries and combine with 1 tsp lemon juice and 15 ml grated lemon rind.*

ACCOMPANIMENTS

Serve the ham hot or cold with any of the following accompaniments:

Jellies

Quince or apple jelly.

Fruit

Brandied fruit: Place 90 g (3 oz) granulated sugar and 250 ml (8 fl oz) water in a heavy-based saucepan. Heat slowly, stirring continuously until sugar is dissolved. Add a sliver of lemon rind, 4 whole cloves, 1 cinnamon stick and 1 kg (2 lb) fresh fruit (cherries, figs, peaches, apricots) and simmer for 20 minutes or until the fruit is cooked but firm. Add 150 ml ($\frac{1}{4}$ pint) brandy or port while syrup is still boiling hot. Chill fruit before serving. (8 to 10 servings)

Pawpaw purée: In a blender, place 1 small pawpaw, seeded and peeled, 1 tsp grated orange rind, 3 tbsp orange juice, 1 tbsp chopped fresh mint and salt and white pepper to taste and blend until smooth. Chill and serve with glazed ham. (Makes 750 ml/1$\frac{1}{4}$ pints)

Fruit on a skewer: Thread 200 g (6$\frac{1}{2}$ oz) strawberries, 1 small pineapple, peeled and cubed, 1 bunch black grapes, 1 melon, seeded, peeled and cubed (or any fresh fruit in season) alternately onto bamboo skewers. Chill and serve with glazed ham. (10 to 15 kebabs)

Sugared pears: Prick 6 small pears with a fork and brush with melted butter. Roll in soft brown sugar, then place on baking sheet and bake at 180 °C (350 °F/gas 4) for 15 to 20 minutes or until slightly tender. (6 servings)
Variation: Add 1 tsp ground ginger to the brown sugar.

Sauces

Horseradish, mustard or fruit sauce.

SPECIAL HINTS

☆ *To calculate the required amount of ham per person, allow 155 g (5 oz) boneless, uncooked ham and 160 to 250 g (8 oz) uncooked ham on the bone.*

☆ *If ham is too salty, soak overnight in cold water, discard water, then bake or boil as described opposite.*

☆ *Cut raw ham into thick slices and bake in oven, or cook under pre-heated grill or in pan for 5 minutes per side. Alternatively, dip ham slices in flour, beaten egg and dried breadcrumbs and fry in heated cooking oil until golden brown.*

VEAL

Veal is the meat of calves under the age of six months. Generally it has very little exterior fat and no marbling. The fine velvety texture and the neutral flavour of veal are two characteristics which lend themselves superbly to the imagination of a creative cook. Sauces, herbs and spices, when used with flair (and care) in the preparation of veal, can result in a variety of truly delicious dishes, some of which are amazingly simple to prepare.

QUALITY CHARACTERISTICS OF VEAL

Colour
The colour of the meat should range from off-white to greyish-pink depending on the feeding of the animal.

Texture
The meat has a fine texture and should appear moist.

Fat
The outer layer of fat should be firm and creamy white.

Bones
Sawn bone surfaces should be very red and porous. The ribs on the inside of the carcase should be flecked with red.

Cartilage
The cartilage between the vertebrae should be white and jelly-like.

Opposite Top: Veal cordon bleu. Bottom: Osso bucco

VEAL TERRINE

250 g (8 oz) rindless streaky bacon

MEAT LAYER
750 g (1½ lb) shin of veal, thickly sliced
15 g (½ g) butter
1 tbsp cooking oil
125 ml (4 fl oz) meat stock (page 133)
125 g (4 oz) rindless bacon, chopped
2 onions, chopped
1 clove garlic, chopped
250 g (8 oz) lamb's liver, membrane removed

VEGETABLE LAYER
250 g (8 oz) courgettes, grated
1 clove garlic, crushed
good pinch salt
freshly ground black pepper to taste
4 tbsp soured cream
2 eggs, beaten
60 g (2 oz) walnuts, chopped (optional)

To prepare the meat layer, brown shin in heated butter and cooking oil in a heavy-based saucepan. Add heated meat stock, cover with lid, reduce heat and simmer for 1½ to 2 hours or until tender. Remove bones from meat. Fry bacon until crisp, add onion and garlic and sauté until onion is translucent. Add liver and fry lightly. Process all ingredients in a food processor. Moisten with a little stock if necessary.

Prepare the vegetable layer by mixing all ingredients together.

To assemble the terrine, line a terrine with bacon, then spoon in a meat layer followed by a vegetable layer. Fold bacon over vegetable layer, cover terrine with foil and bake in a *bain-marie* (page 153) at 180 °C (350 °F/gas 4) for 1 hour. Leave in turned-off oven to cool, then place a weight on top and refrigerate overnight. Turn out and slice.
(6 to 8 servings)

VARIATIONS
☆ Substitute 125 g (4 oz) ham for the bacon, adding 2 tsp butter to sauté the onion.
☆ Substitute toasted flaked almonds for the walnuts.

HINT
☆ Serve as a starter with lemon mayonnaise (page 147).

VEAL IN A CREAMY GARLIC SAUCE

1 kg (2 lb) boned thick rib of veal, cut into long, thin strips
15 g (½ oz) butter
1 tbsp cooking oil
3 spring onions, chopped
3 cloves garlic, crushed
125 ml (4 fl oz) meat stock (page 133)
2 tbsp medium cream sherry
1½ tsp salt
freshly ground black pepper to taste
125 ml (4 fl oz) single cream
2 tsp cornflour

Brown meat in heated butter and cooking oil in a heavy-based saucepan. Add onion and garlic and sauté until onion is translucent. Combine stock, sherry, salt and pepper and heat. Add to meat, cover pan with lid, reduce heat and simmer for 1 hour or until meat is tender. Mix cream and cornflour to a paste and stir into meat. Simmer for approximately 3 to 5 minutes, then serve.
(6 servings)

HINT
☆ To facilitate the peeling of garlic, pour boiling water over the cloves and leave for a few minutes.

SUGGESTED SIDE DISH
Buttered mixed vegetables

Front: Veal terrine. Back: Veal in a creamy garlic sauce

OSSO BUCCO

1.5 kg (3 lb) shank of veal, thickly sliced
1 tbsp cooking oil
15 g ($\frac{1}{2}$ oz) butter
$\frac{1}{2}$ tsp each dried or 1 tsp each chopped fresh sage and rosemary
1 large onion, chopped
1 clove garlic, crushed
1 carrot, sliced
1 celery stalk, chopped
1 tsp salt
freshly ground black pepper to taste
250 ml (8 fl oz) dry white wine
4 tbsp meat stock (page 133)
3 tbsp tomato paste

GREMOLATA
2 cloves garlic, chopped
2 tsp dried or 2 tbsp chopped fresh parsley
1 tsp grated lemon rind

Brown meat in heated cooking oil and butter in a heavy-based saucepan. Add sage, rosemary, onion, garlic, carrot and celery and fry until onion is translucent. Add seasoning. Cover with lid, reduce heat and fry for 3 minutes. Heat remaining ingredients and add to meat. Cover and simmer for 1$\frac{1}{2}$ to 2 hours or until meat is tender. Mix gremolata ingredients together and sprinkle over meat. Serve immediately.
(6 servings)

SUGGESTED SIDE DISH
Risotto

VEAL CORDON BLEU

12 slices of veal, 3 to 5 mm ($\frac{1}{8}$ to $\frac{1}{4}$ inch) thick, cut from the topside
4 tsp Dijon mustard
1 tbsp lemon juice
60 g (2 oz) Gruyère or mozzarella cheese, grated
6 slices ham
$\frac{1}{2}$ tsp salt
freshly ground black pepper to taste
60 g (2 oz) plain flour
2 eggs, beaten
125 g (4 oz) dried breadcrumbs
2 tbsp cooking oil
30 g (1 oz) butter

Place meat between two layers of cling film and flatten slightly with the palm of the hand. Spread meat slices with mustard and sprinkle with lemon juice. Sandwich grated cheese and a slice of ham between two slices of veal and secure with cocktail sticks. Add salt and pepper to flour and mix thoroughly. Dip meat in flour, then in beaten egg and finally in dried breadcrumbs. Refrigerate for 20 to 30 minutes to allow crumbs to set. Fry in heated cooking oil and butter until golden brown, then drain on paper towels. Remove cocktail sticks and garnish with lemon slices.
(6 servings)

VARIATIONS
☆ *Substitute fresh breadcrumbs, orange juice and crushed ginger root for the mustard, lemon juice, cheese and ham.*
☆ *Low-fat variation: Instead of shallow-frying, cook meat under a pre-heated grill for approximately 3 minutes per side.*

SUGGESTED SIDE DISHES
Boiled potatoes
Crisp salad

SUMMER VEAL STEW

1.5 kg (3 lb) boned neck of veal, cut
into cubes
15 g ($\frac{1}{2}$ oz) butter
1 tbsp cooking oil
1 large onion, chopped
3 tbsp plain flour
125 ml (4 fl oz) dry white wine
150 ml ($\frac{1}{4}$ pint) white meat stock
(page 133)
1 tsp salt
freshly ground black pepper to taste
500 g (1 lb) green beans
315 g (10 oz) fresh pickling onions,
peeled
and blanched for 10 minutes
3 carrots, cut into chunks
2 tsp dried or 2 tbsp chopped fresh
parsley

Brown meat in heated butter and oil in a heavy-based saucepan. Add onion and sauté until translucent. Add flour and fry for 1 minute. Heat wine and meat stock and add to meat with seasoning. Cover pan, reduce heat and simmer for 1 to 1$\frac{1}{2}$ hours or until meat is almost tender. Add green beans, onions and carrots 20 minutes before end of cooking time and simmer until cooked but still firm. Sprinkle with parsley.

(6 servings)

VARIATION
☆ *Substitute courgettes for the green beans.*

SUGGESTED SIDE DISH
Brown rice

VEAL ROLLS

8 slices of veal, 3 to 5 mm ($\frac{1}{8}$ to $\frac{1}{4}$ inch)
thick, cut from the topside
4 tsp cooking oil
10 fresh pickling onions
125 ml (4 fl oz) meat stock (page 133)
125 ml (4 fl oz) red wine
2 tomatoes, skinned and chopped
1 tsp dried or 1 tbsp chopped fresh
oregano
1 tsp salt
freshly ground black pepper to taste
1 tbsp plain flour

STUFFING
90 g (3 oz) cooked rice
4 spring onions, chopped
$\frac{1}{2}$ green pepper, seeded and
chopped
1 tbsp tomato purée
$\frac{1}{2}$ tsp salt
freshly ground black pepper
to taste
3 tbsp meat stock (page 133)

First prepare the stuffing by mixing all the ingredients together.

To prepare the meat, spoon a little stuffing onto each slice of meat, then roll up and secure with string or cocktail stick. Brown meat in heated cooking oil in a casserole, add onion and sauté until translucent. Add heated stock, wine, tomato, oregano, salt and pepper. Cover with lid and bake at 160 °C (325 °F/gas 3) for 1 hour or until meat is tender. Thicken sauce with a flour and water paste if necessary.

(4 servings)

VARIATIONS
☆ *Substitute slices of pork for the veal.*
☆ *Substitute a combination of breadcrumbs and nuts for the rice.*

SUGGESTED SIDE DISH
Parsley noodles

Veal rolls

KID AND GOAT

While kid and goat meats are favoured in the cuisines of the Mediterranean, West Indies, Middle East and Asia, they have yet to make any significant inroads into most Western cookery traditions. From a health point of view, the value of kid and goat meats should not be underestimated. As they contain little fat, they are ideal for those on low-fat diets.

Where climatic conditions favour goat husbandry for fibre or dairy production, kid meat (also marketed as capretto) and goat meat are by-products, particularly as far as the fibre breeds of Angora and Cashmere are concerned. Feral goats (crossbreeds from various species) are also used for goat meat, the majority being processed for export.

In Australia and New Zealand, plans for the introduction of the Boer goat of South Africa are well under way. This animal is specifically a meat breed, fast-growing and well-muscled, which should improve the quality of kid and goat meat available.

QUALITY CHARACTERISTICS OF KID AND GOAT MEAT

These are similar to the characteristics of suckling lamb (for kid) and mutton (for goat).

Kid is more likely to be available, with dressed carcase size in the 10-12 kg (22-26 lb) range. Its meat is light pink in colour with a covering of thin, creamy white fat. Kid has a high proportion of bone to meat, and this must be taken into consideration when calculating the amount required.

Goat meat should be bright pink in colour, signifying the goat is about 1-year-old and acceptable for most cooking methods as applied to quality mutton. A dark pink, almost plum colour, signifies meat is from an older animal, and should only be used for moist-heat cooking methods requiring long, slow cooking.

If either meat is not available in your area, lamb may be used as a substitute in recipes. Reduce the cooking time if the original recipe calls for goat meat.

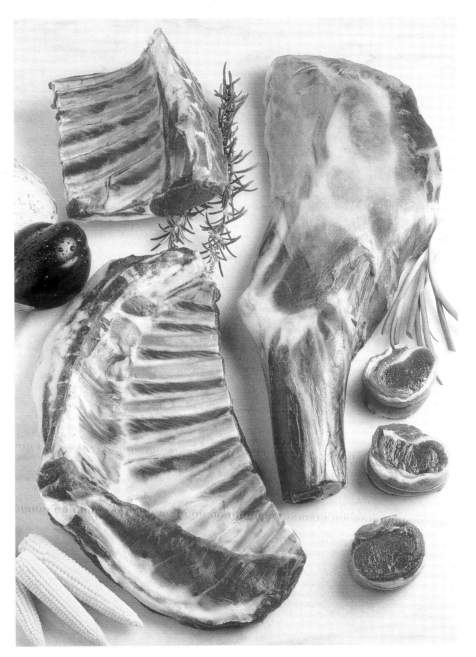

Opposite clockwise from top: Braised goat with leeks and mushrooms (page 68); Fruity casserole (page 71); and Chops with barbecue sauce (page 71)

NECK

The neck consists of the neck vertebrae and coarse-textured meat containing a large amount of white connective tissue (collagen). Long, slow cooking will convert this connective tissue into gelatine and make the meat tender. The yellow connective tissue (elastin) is not affected by heat and should therefore be removed prior to cooking.

USES
☆ Slices:......................................Braised dishes, casseroles
☆ Boned and minced: ....Minced dishes such as pies and meat balls

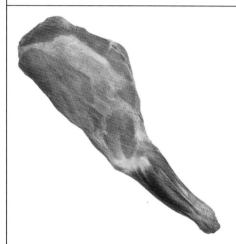

SHOULDER

The shoulder blade, marrowbone and shank bone are situated in the shoulder, which is covered with an even layer of fat. Attached to the shoulder blade is the softer cartilage section. If the shoulder is removed round, the upper portion of the thick rib is included.

USES
☆ Removed round with bone:.......Roast (kid); pot-roast, cook in cooking bag or foil (goat)
☆ Boned and rolled:.....................Roast (kid); pot-roast, casseroles, cook in cooking bag or foil (goat)
☆ Cubes: ....Kebabs, grill (kid); stews, casseroles (goat)

BREAST AND BELLY

The breast is sawn off with the belly for convenience. The cut contains the breastbone and ribs in a triangular shape where the belly joins the breast. A large proportion of white connective tissue occurs in the belly and the meat has a coarse texture. Breast and belly from kid has very little meat and cannot be used as indicated below.

USES
☆ Boned and rolled:.....................Pot-roast, casserole, cook in
....cooking bag or foil (goat)
☆ Cubes: ....Stews and casseroles (goat)
☆ Portions:.................................Stews, braised dishes, casseroles (goat)

THICK RIB (FOREQUARTER)

The thick rib consists of a few vertebrae, 5 to 6 ribs, part of the shoulder blade and an even layer of fat. If the shoulder is removed round, the upper muscle layer and fat layer of the thick rib are removed with the shoulder blade.

USES
☆ Boned and stuffed if shoulder has not been removed round (cushion):...................................Roast (kid); pot-roast (goat)
☆ Chops: ....Grill (kid); braised dishes, stews, casseroles (goat)
☆ Cubes: ....Stews and curries

RIB

The rib consists of vertebrae, ribs, a single eye muscle and an uneven fat layer. The meat has a fine texture.

USES

☆ Boned and rolled:.....................Roast (kid); pot-roast,
                                 casseroles, cook in cooking bag
                                 or foil (goat)

☆ Chops: ....Grill (kid); braised dishes, stews,
                                 casseroles (goat)

LOIN

A feature of the loin is the T-shaped vertebrae flanked by the very tender fillet on the one side and the eye muscle on the other. If removed before the carcase is halved, this cut is known as a saddle.

USES

☆ Whole loin:.............................Roast (kid); pot-roast (goat)
☆ Saddle:...................................Roast (kid); pot-roast (goat)
☆ Boned and rolled:.....................Roast (kid); pot-roast (goat)
☆ Chops: ....Grill (kid); braise, stew (goat)
☆ Saddle chops: ....Grill (kid); braise, stew (goat)

CHUMP

The chump contains the pelvic bone and a large proportion of meat. The chump can be left on the leg for a longer leg.

USES

☆ Whole: ....Roast (kid); pot-roast (goat)
☆ Boned: ....Roast (kid); pot-roast (goat)
☆ Chops: ....Grill (kid); braise, stew (goat)

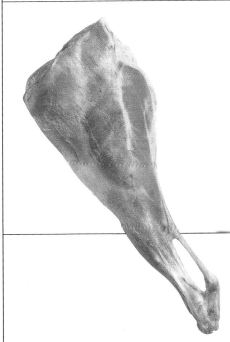

LEG

The leg contains the pelvic bone, marrowbone and shank bone and is possibly the most popular cut. A leg of kid or goat is long and thin and covered with a thin layer of fat.

USES

☆ Boned and rolled:.....................Roast (kid); pot-roast,
                                 casseroles, cook in cooking bag or
                                 foil (goat)

☆ With bone: ....Roast (kid); pot-roast, casseroles,
                                 cook in cooking bag or foil (goat)

☆ Cubes: ....Kebabs, grill (kid); stews, curries
                                 (goat)

SHANK

The shank contains the shank bone, meat with a coarse texture and a high percentage of white connective tissue.

USES

☆ Slices:....................................Stews, casseroles (goat)
☆ Meat stock

SPICY PEACH STEW

500 g (1 lb) shoulder of kid, boned
and cut into cubes
185 g (6 oz) rice
2 tbsp cooking oil
1 onion, chopped
1 tsp salt
freshly ground black pepper
to taste
$\frac{1}{2}$ tsp ground cinnamon
90 g (3 oz) dried peaches
250 ml (8 fl oz) meat stock (page 133)
2 tsp dried or 2 tbsp chopped fresh
parsley

Boil rice according to instructions on packet. Brown meat in heated cooking oil in a heavy-based saucepan. Add onion or sauté until translucent. Add seasoning. Add fruit and heated meat stock, cover with lid, reduce heat and simmer for 1 to 1½ hours or until meat is tender. Stir in rice and parsley.

(4 servings)

HINT

☆ If rice is cooked for too long and becomes mushy, spread it out in a large, flat roasting tin and place in oven at 160 °C (325 °F/gas 3) for 10 minutes.

SUGGESTED SIDE DISH
Orange-flavoured carrots

STUFFED LEG WITH A MUSTARD GLAZE

1 boned leg of kid, approximately
1 kg (2 lb)
1 tsp salt
freshly ground black pepper to taste

STUFFING
60 g (2 oz) fresh breadcrumbs
4 tbsp meat stock (page 133)
30 g (1 oz) walnuts, chopped
30 g (1 oz) mushrooms,
chopped
$\frac{1}{2}$ tsp grated orange rind
$\frac{1}{4}$ tsp salt
freshly ground black pepper to taste

MUSTARD GLAZE
4 tbsp meat stock (page 133)
1 tsp grated orange rind
juice of $\frac{1}{2}$ orange
1 tbsp brandy
1 tbsp French mustard

First prepare the stuffing by mixing all the ingredients together.

To prepare the meat, season inside of meat with half the salt and pepper. Stuff leg with stuffing, secure meat with string and season with remaining salt and pepper. Place meat fat side uppermost on the rack of a roasting tin and roast at 160 °C (325 °F/gas 3) for 20 minutes per 500 g (1 lb) plus 20 minutes (medium) or 25 minutes per 500 g (1 lb) plus 25 minutes (well-done).

Meanwhile prepare the glaze by mixing the ingredients together. Baste meat from time to time during the last 30 minutes of cooking time.

(4 servings)

HINT

☆ Mushrooms should not be washed or soaked as they tend to absorb a lot of water. They need only be wiped with a damp cloth.

SUGGESTED SIDE DISHES
Potato bake
Broccoli with cheese sauce

BRAISED GOAT WITH LEEKS AND MUSHROOMS

1.5 kg (3 lb) loin of goat, boned
1 tsp salt
freshly ground black pepper
to taste
2 leeks, sliced
125 g (4 oz) mushrooms, sliced
250 ml (8 fl oz) dry white wine
piece of lemon rind
1 tbsp plain flour
2 tbsp soured cream

Season inside of meat with half the salt and pepper. Shape meat into a roll and secure with string. Brown meat in a heated heavy-based saucepan, then add leeks and mushrooms and fry for a few minutes. Add remaining salt and pepper, heated wine and lemon rind. Cover with lid, reduce heat and simmer for 1½ to 2 hours or until meat is tender. Remove lemon rind and then thicken sauce with a flour and water paste. Stir in soured cream just before serving.

(6 servings)

SUGGESTED SIDE DISHES
Spinach and tomato bake
Jacket potatoes

MIDDLE EASTERN STYLE STEW

1 kg (2 lb) goat or kid chops
2 tsp dried or 2 tbsp chopped fresh
mint
2 tbsp cooking oil
2 onions, sliced
2 cloves garlic, crushed
3 tsp ground coriander
1 tbsp chopped ginger root
1 tsp salt
freshly ground black pepper to taste
250 ml (8 fl oz) meat stock (page 133)
good pinch saffron
2 tbsp lemon juice
2 tbsp flaked almonds
60 g (2 oz) raisins
1 tbsp cooking oil
250 ml (8 fl oz) plain yoghurt

Sprinkle mint over meat and leave to stand for 1 to 2 hours. Brown meat in heated cooking oil in a heavy-based saucepan. Add onion and garlic and sauté until onion is translucent. Add coriander and ginger and fry for a few minutes. Season with salt and pepper and add heated meat stock. Cover with lid*, reduce heat and simmer for 1½ to 2 hours or until meat is tender.

Meanwhile soak the saffron in lemon juice. Fry almonds and raisins in heated cooking oil, drain on paper towels and add to meat together with saffron and lemon juice. Stir in yoghurt just before serving.

(6 servings)

VARIATION

☆ Substitute 1 tsp turmeric for the saffron and add together with coriander and ginger.

HINT

☆ To casserole, prepare up to *, then place casserole in a pre-heated oven at 160 °C (325 °F/gas 3) for 2 to 2½ hours or until meat is tender, then proceed as above.

SUGGESTED SIDE DISH
Buttered noodles

Stuffed leg with a mustard glaze

CURRY MEAL-IN-ONE

1 kg (2 lb) breast of goat, sawn into
5 x 10 cm (2 x 4 inch) portions
1 tbsp cooking oil
2 onions, sliced
2 cloves garlic, crushed
4 tsp mild curry powder
1 tsp turmeric
1 tsp salt
freshly ground black pepper to taste
250 ml (8 fl oz) meat stock (page 133)
410 g (13 oz) canned whole
tomatoes, coarsely chopped
2 potatoes, quartered
6 carrots, quartered lengthwise
60 g (2 oz) seedless raisins
1 tbsp plain flour
185 ml (6 fl oz) plain yoghurt

Brown meat in heated cooking oil in a heavy-based saucepan. Add onion and garlic and sauté until onion is translucent. Add curry powder and turmeric and fry for 1 minute. Season with salt and pepper, then add heated meat stock and tomato. Cover with lid, reduce heat and simmer for $1\frac{1}{2}$ to 2 hours or until meat is almost tender. Add vegetables and raisins 30 minutes before end of cooking time and simmer until meat is tender and vegetables are cooked but still firm. Thicken liquid with a flour and water paste if necessary. Stir in yoghurt.
(6 servings)

HINT
☆ *If you don't possess a garlic press, place the garlic on a wooden board and sprinkle with salt. Using the flat edge of the knife blade, work the garlic and salt to a pulp.*

SUGGESTED SIDE DISH
Banana and coconut salad

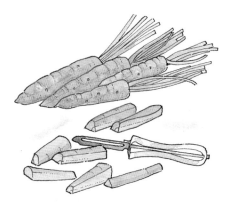

Curry meal-in-one

Chops with barbecue sauce

FRUITY CASSEROLE

1 kg (2 lb) shank of goat slices, 2 cm ($\frac{3}{4}$ inch) thick
15 g ($\frac{1}{2}$ oz) butter
1 tbsp cooking oil
1 large onion, chopped
1 clove garlic, crushed
1 cinnamon stick
1 bay leaf
1 tsp salt
$\frac{1}{2}$ tsp grated nutmeg
2 whole cloves
1 tbsp lemon juice
125 ml (4 fl oz) red wine
125 ml (4 fl oz) meat stock (page 133)
125 g (4 oz) dried apricots
125 g (4 oz) stoned prunes

Slash fat edges to prevent curling during cooking. Brown meat in heated butter and cooking oil in a heavy-based saucepan, add onion and garlic and sauté until translucent. Add seasoning. Heat lemon juice, wine and meat stock and add to meat. Add fruit, cover pan and simmer for 2 to 2$\frac{1}{2}$ hours or until meat is tender. Remove cinnamon and bay leaf.

(6 servings)

HINT

☆ *Wrap the cinnamon stick, bay leaf and cloves in a piece of muslin and secure with a long piece of string. Tie the bag to the handle of the saucepan for easy removal of the spices.*

SUGGESTED SIDE DISHES
Glazed sweet potatoes
Brown rice

CHOPS WITH BARBECUE SAUCE

12 to 16 kid rib chops, 2 cm ($\frac{3}{4}$ inch)

BARBECUE SAUCE
2 onions, chopped
1 clove garlic, crushed
1 green pepper, seeded and chopped
1 tbsp cooking oil
125 ml (4 fl oz) brown vinegar
410 g (13 oz) canned whole tomatoes, chopped
3 tsp Worcestershire sauce
$\frac{1}{4}$ tsp Tabasco
5 tsp soft brown sugar
1 tsp salt
2 tbsp fruit chutney

First prepare the sauce. Fry onion, garlic and green pepper in heated cooking oil in a heavy-based saucepan until onion is translucent. Add heated liquid and remaining ingredients and simmer for 30 minutes. Allow to cool.

To prepare the meat, marinate the meat in the sauce for 4 hours. Remove from marinade, pat dry with paper towels and cook 10 cm (4 inches) under a pre-heated grill for 7 to 10 minutes in total (medium) or 10 to 12 minutes in total (well-done), basting frequently with remaining sauce.

(4 to 6 servings)

HINT

☆ *Substitute 4 ripe skinned tomatoes for canned tomatoes.*

SUGGESTED SIDE DISHES
Wholegrain bread
Green salad

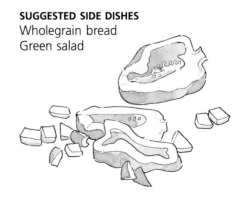

VARIETY MEATS

In times gone by, country folk would slaughter a sheep or goat for the pot regularly. In those days, variety meats (or offal, as they are often called) used to be much in demand, but today they are far less popular, particularly with the younger generation. This is unfortunate because not only is offal gourmet food but it also has a high nutritional value.

Perhaps it could do with some of the prestige and respect it receives in many European and Eastern countries, where offal and offal products are widely sold at speciality shops and remain part of the natural cookery traditions.

Everything removed during the dressing (slaughtering) of a carcase is regarded as offal. This includes the brains, lungs, tongue, trotters, tripe, kidneys, liver, sweetbreads and heart as well as the head, feet, tail, skin and horns.

STORAGE

Offal is a highly perishable product with a relatively short storage life. Offal should be removed from its packaging soon after purchase and stored (lightly covered with waxed paper or cling film) in the refrigerator. Fresh offal should be used within 24 hours or, if cooked, within 3 to 4 days.

Offal may also be frozen successfully at -18 °C (-2 °F) for a maximum of 3 months. To thaw, remove the offal from the freezer 24 hours prior to cooking and leave it to thaw, wrapped or in its container, in the refrigerator. Slow thawing is considered the best method as it reduces the drip loss and reduces the risk of spoilage.

Opposite Clockwise from top: Pork brawn (page 78); Braised oxtail with vegetables (page 79); and Port and caper pâté (page 76)

LIVER

Liver is a good source of complete proteins and is rich in vitamin A and the B-complex vitamins as well as mineral salts such as iron, calcium, phosphorus, copper and iodine. Calf's liver, with its fine texture and delicate flavour, is the most tender of all the liver types. Lamb's liver is also tender but is slightly stronger in flavour and darker in colour than calf's liver and is delicious grilled. Pig's liver has a strong flavour and can be grilled, stewed or casseroled. It is also ideal for pâtés. With its coarse texture and strong flavour ox liver is best stewed or braised.

HINTS
☆ To mince liver easily, first brown it in heated cooking oil.
☆ Use moist-heat cooking methods such as braising and stewing to cook ox liver.
☆ Calf and lamb's liver are excellent fried or grilled.
☆ Pig's liver is ideal for pâtés and terrines or in stews or caseroles.
☆ Pig's liver can be used in sausage meat and meat loaves.

To prepare liver
Rinse liver under a cold tap and remove the outer membrane, if any. If the liver is fresh, the membrane will slip off easily, otherwise soak the liver in lukewarm water for a few minutes. Remove any of the large tubes, as well. To tone down the strong flavour of ox or pig's liver, it may be soaked for one hour in milk or a weak solution of water and salt.

KIDNEYS
Ox kidneys weigh approximately 750 g (1½ lb), are coarse in texture and have a strong flavour, while calf's kidneys are smaller and more tender. Ox, calf and lamb's kidneys are usually surrounded by a layer of white fat known as kidney fat. Pig's kidneys have no fat and are

less tender than lamb and calf's kidneys. Pig's or ox kidneys may be braised or stewed while calf and lamb's kidneys may be grilled, braised or sautéed.

To prepare kidneys
If the kidneys are encased in fat, remove it and then peel off the outer membrane. If the kidneys are fresh, the membrane will slip off easily, otherwise soak them in lukewarm salted water or milk. Remove the inner cores and cut kidneys into cubes or strips before cooking. Because lamb and pig's kidneys are so small, they are usually only cut in half.

HEART
Because the heart is a hard-working organ it is tough and is therefore best cooked by braising or stewing. The heart is surrounded by a layer of fat which should be removed but the heart itself has very little intra-muscular fat and tends to be dry.

To prepare heart
Remove the fat surrounding the heart and wash thoroughly in lukewarm salted water. Remove the arteries and sinews. Leave the heart whole or cut it in half and stuff it or cut it into cubes or strips.

TONGUE
Ox tongue is the most popular because of its fine texture and excellent taste. Pig's tongue and lamb's tongue are also used but the latter is not readily available. Lamb's tongue and pig's tongue are usually served whole while ox tongue is served sliced. Tongue may be served fresh or pickled.

To prepare tongue
Place tongue in a large saucepan and cover with cold water. For extra flavour, add bouquet garni and vegetables such as carrots, onions or shallots and celery stalks. Bring to the boil, cover with lid, reduce heat and simmer for 3 to 4 hours

or until tender. Dip the tongue into cold water immediately and remove skin and tubes. The tongue will be juicier and tastier if allowed to cool in the cooking liquid before serving it cold and sliced.

SWEETBREADS

Sweetbreads are the thymus gland of a young animal, with calf's sweetbreads being the best. Fresh sweetbreads are soft and white or pink in colour.

To prepare sweetbreads

Rinse thoroughly under cold water, then soak for 1 to 2 hours in a weak solution of water and salt. Blanch the sweetbreads by placing them in cold water, bringing to the boil and simmering for about 1 minute. Remove the skin and outer membrane before cooking using any of the following cooking methods:

Poaching: After blanching and removing the skin and outer membrane, cover the sweetbreads with cold water. Add 1 tsp salt, 1 tsp vinegar or lemon juice or any seasoning of your choice such as bay leaf, peppercorns or sprig of parsley. Bring to the boil, cover with a lid, reduce the heat and simmer for approximately 15 minutes.

Stewing: After blanching and removing the skin and outer membrane, cut the sweetbreads into bite-sized portions. Roll them in plain flour seasoned with salt and pepper or breadcrumbs and brown in heated cooking oil or a mixture of cooking oil and butter. Add a little heated liquid. Cover with a lid, reduce the heat and simmer for approximately 15 minutes.

BRAINS

The delicate flavour and soft texture of brains make them the gourmet's favourite. Fresh brains are glossy and a greyish-pink.

To prepare brains

Soak them in cold salted water for 30 minutes. Remove the membrane and soak the brains again in lukewarm salted water to remove all traces of blood. If brains have been frozen, it is very difficult to remove the membrane; retain if necesary.

CAUL FAT

Caul fat is the lacy fat that lines an animal's stomach. Pig's caul is commonly used to line terrines or to wrap around sausages and patties. If the caul fat is too stiff to handle, soak it in lukewarm water until it is pliable. Caul fat can also be rendered and used to baste roast meat.

To prepare caul fat

It is only necessary to rinse it thoroughly in lukewarm salted water.

TRIPE

This is the stomach tissue of cud-chewing animals. Tripe has a very coarse texture and is fairly tough and, therefore, requires long, slow cooking. Tripe is usually sold prepared for use in recipes. It may be either smooth or honeycombed. The following instructions apply only to tripe taken straight from the animal.

To prepare tripe

Rinse it thoroughly in cold water, then soak it in warm water containing 2 tsp vinegar per litre (1¾ pints) of water. Rinse it again thoroughly in cold water, then scrape it clean with a blunt knife until it is white. Rinse again in cold water and cut as preferred.

To cook, cover tripe with cold water containing 1 tsp salt and 1 tbsp vinegar per litre (1¾ pints) of water. Bring to the boil, cover with lid, reduce heat and simmer for 2 to 3 hours or until tender.

OXTAIL

Long, slow cooking is required to make tasty stews and soup with oxtail. One oxtail will usually provide two to three servings.

To prepare oxtail

Remove all visible fat. Cut tail into pieces between the joints. Rinse thoroughly under running water.

TROTTERS

Usually pig's trotters are used for preparing brawn.

To prepare trotters

Immerse trotters in hot water (containing 2 tsp vinegar per litre/1¾ pints of water), then remove casings from trotters and scrape the rest clean. Rinse in clean cold water. Make an incision between the trotters right against the one side up to the first joint. Remove the trotter gland in one piece. Cut the trotters open at the first joint, chop or saw the shin bones in half and rinse thoroughly.

FAT

Take clean fat (for example, beef suet or pork fat) and cut it into cubes or mince it coarsely. Fry slowly until brown. Pour off the rendered fat and serve the crackling with polenta. The rendered fat may be substituted for cooking oil when sautéing onions and is excellent for seasoning a new cast-iron ridged pan.

HEAD

The head contains a large proportion of fat as well as edible parts such as the cheeks, tongue and ears.

To prepare the head

Rinse head in clean cold water. Cut the lower jaw loose from the upper jaw and remove the lower jawbone. Make an incision through the skin from the base to the point of the nose and cut the skin away from the bone of the nose. Use either of the following methods to remove the upper jaw and nose bones:
a) Saw an inverted V shape above the cheekbones with the apex high between the eyes. The brains can be left in the skull and may be spooned out after cooking,
b) Saw through the skull right between the eyes and obliquely downwards below the eyes in order to remove the bones. The brains may now be removed and used as preferred.
Remove all glands (below the ears, centre and lower jaw and tongue), giving special attention to the tongue, throat, ears and eyes where undesirable accretions may occur. Rinse head again.

SAVOURY LIVER STIR-FRY

1 kg (2 lb) lamb's liver, membrane removed
250 g (8 oz) rindless streaky bacon, coarsely chopped
315 g (10 oz) smoked sausage, thinly sliced
3 onions, thinly sliced
3 cloves garlic, crushed
1 green pepper, seeded and cut into julienne strips (optional)
1 tsp dried or 1 tbsp chopped fresh rosemary
1 tsp freshly ground black pepper
1 tsp salt
250 ml (8 fl oz) dry white wine
3 tbsp Worcestershire sauce
250 ml (8 fl oz) double cream

Cut liver into long, narrow strips. Stir-fry bacon, sausage and onion in a heavy-based saucepan until onion is translucent. Add oil if necessary. Add liver, garlic and green pepper if using and stir-fry until liver is done. Season with rosemary, pepper and salt. Add wine and Worcestershire sauce and bring to the boil, then boil rapidly for a few minutes to reduce and thicken the liquid. Stir in cream and heat through.

(8 servings)

HINT
☆ This dish can also be prepared in a wok or on a solid metal plate over hot coals for a barbecue party.

SUGGESTED SIDE DISH
Hot garlic bread or
Baked potatoes

LIVER AND SPAGHETTI CASSEROLE

500 g (1 lb) ox liver, membrane removed and cut into 2 cm ($\frac{3}{4}$ inch) slices
2 rashers rindless bacon, cut into smaller pieces
1 tbsp cooking oil
2 onions, sliced
4 tsp plain flour
meat stock (page 133)
410 g (13 oz) canned whole tomatoes, chopped and liquid reserved
1 tsp salt
freshly ground black pepper to taste
125 g (4 oz) spaghetti
60 g (2 oz) Cheddar cheese, grated

Front: Liver and spaghetti casserole. Back: Savoury liver stir-fry

Fry bacon until crisp and remove. Add cooking oil and fry liver. Add onion and sauté until translucent. Remove liver and onion with a slotted spoon and set aside. Add flour and fry for 2 to 3 minutes. Add sufficient meat stock to the reserved tomato juice to make up 250 ml (8 fl oz) and bring to the boil. Add heated liquid, liver and onion mixture, bacon, seasoning and tomatoes, cover with lid, reduce heat and simmer for 20 to 30 minutes.

Cook spaghetti according to directions on packet and drain. Spoon spaghetti into a flat oven dish and top with liver mixture. Sprinkle cheese over and bake at 160 °C (325 °F/gas 3) for 20 minutes or until heated through.

(4 to 6 servings)

VARIATIONS
☆ Substitute macaroni for the spaghetti.
☆ Substitute dry white wine for the meat stock.

SUGGESTED SIDE DISH
Carrot salad

Left: Liver and bacon en croûte. Right: Tongue salad (page 77).

PORT AND CAPER PATE

500 g (1 lb) sheep's liver, membrane
removed and sliced
60 g (2 oz) butter
6 rashers rindless streaky bacon,
coarsely chopped
1 medium onion, grated
1 clove garlic, crushed
125 ml (4 fl oz) port
$\frac{1}{2}$ tsp salt
1 tsp freshly ground black pepper
90 ml (3 fl oz) single cream
1 tsp lemon juice
3 tbsp mayonnaise
1 tbsp finely chopped capers
30 g (1 oz) clarified butter
(page 154)
2 tsp dried or 2 tbsp chopped fresh
parsley

Fry liver in heated butter in a heavy-based saucepan. Add bacon and fry until crisp. Add onion and garlic and sauté until onion is translucent. Add port, salt, pepper and cream and simmer for 3 minutes. Add lemon juice and mayonnaise and liquidize, then stir in capers and mix well. Place in individual ramekin dishes and seal with clarified butter mixed with parsley.
(8 servings)

SUGGESTED SIDE DISH
Melba toast

LIVER AND BACON EN CROUTE

375 g (12 oz) lamb's liver, membrane
removed and coarsely chopped
30 g (1 oz) butter
2 tsp fresh breadcrumbs
2 hard-boiled eggs
1 small onion, coarsely chopped
2 tsp dried or 2 tbsp chopped
fresh parsley
1 tsp lemon juice
$\frac{1}{2}$ tsp salt
freshly ground black pepper to taste
10 rashers rindless streaky bacon
10 croûtes (page 154)

Fry liver in heated butter until cooked. Place liver and remaining ingredients except bacon and croûtes in a food processor or blender and chop coarsely. Roll bacon rashers firmly and secure with cocktail sticks, then cook under a pre-heated grill until crisp. Spoon liver mixture onto croûtes and garnish with bacon rolls. Serve immediately.

(10 servings)

VARIATIONS

☆ *Fry the bacon until crisp, then chop and sprinkle over liver.*

☆ *Serve liver mixture on a bed of creamy mashed potatoes instead of on a croûte.*

SUGGESTED SIDE DISH
Green salad with avocado

KIDNEY KEBABS

4 lamb's kidneys, membrane and
core removed, cut into cubes
8 cocktail sausages
90 g (3 oz) button mushrooms

BASTING MIXTURE
4 tbsp lemon juice
2 tbsp cooking oil
1 onion, finely chopped
1 clove garlic, crushed
1 tsp grated lemon rind
1 tsp salt
pinch cayenne pepper

Mix basting ingredients together. Thread kidney cubes, sausages and mushrooms alternately onto skewers. Place on the rack of a grill pan and brush with basting mixture. Cook 10 cm (4 inches) under a pre-heated grill for approximately 5 minutes per side, basting frequently with the basting mixture.

(4 servings)

VARIATIONS

☆ *Wrap kidneys in bacon before threading onto skewers.*

Fruit kebabs: *Substitute ham or bacon for the cocktail sausages; pineapple cubes for the mushrooms; and pineapple juice for the lemon juice.*

SUGGESTED SIDE DISHES
Garlic bread and a crisp mixed salad

KIDNEYS IN SOUR SAUCE

10 sheep's kidneys, membrane and
core removed, cut into dice
4 tbsp plain flour
1 tsp salt
freshly ground black pepper to taste
1 large onion, sliced
2 tsp cooking oil
2 tsp butter
200 ml (6½ fl oz) meat stock (page
133)
2 tbsp vinegar
1 tsp sugar

Combine flour, salt and pepper and roll kidneys in mixture. Sauté onion in heated cooking oil and butter in a heavy-based saucepan until onion is translucent. Add kidneys and brown. Heat meat stock, vinegar and sugar and add to meat. Cover with lid, reduce heat and simmer for 10 to 15 minutes or until tender. Do not allow to boil or kidneys would toughen.

(6 servings)

VARIATION

☆ *Substitute 200 g (6½ oz) sheep's liver for half the sheep's kidneys.*

SUGGESTED SIDE DISHES
Sautéed tomatoes
Scrambled egg with parsley
Creamy mashed potatoes

OX TONGUE WITH SWEET AND SOUR SAUCE

1 pickled ox tongue
1 onion, quartered
1 celery stalk, cut into chunks
2 carrots, cut into chunks
2 bay leaves
5 black peppercorns

SWEET AND SOUR SAUCE
250 ml (8 fl oz) apple cider
200 g (6½ oz) brown sugar
6 ginger nuts, crumbed
1 bay leaf
2 tbsp lemon juice
90 g (3 oz) raisins
½ tsp ground cinnamon
8 whole cloves
60 g (2 oz) flaked almonds, toasted
(optional)
1 small onion, thinly sliced
1 tsp salt
freshly ground black pepper to taste

Cover tongue with cold water and add onion, celery, carrots, bay leaves and peppercorns. Bring to the boil, cover with lid, reduce heat and simmer for 3 to 4 hours until tender. Dip into cold water immediately and remove skin. Return to liquid and leave to cool.

To prepare the sauce, mix all the ingredients together and simmer for approximately 10 minutes. Remove cloves and bay leaf. Serve the sauce separately with the sliced tongue.

(8 servings)

VARIATION

☆ *Cut the tongue into thin slices and place in a dish. Pour sweet and sour sauce over and bake at 160 °C (325 °F/ gas 3) for 20 minutes.*

SUGGESTED SIDE DISHES
Pearl wheat
Baby carrots

TONGUE SALAD

500 g (1 lb) cooked pickled tongue,
cut into long, narrow strips
(page 73)
90 g (3 oz) smoked beef,
thinly sliced
2 carrots, cut into julienne strips
1 celery stalk, cut into julienne strips
6 lettuce leaves

SALAD DRESSING
3 tbsp cooking oil
3 tbsp wine vinegar
2 tbsp meat stock (page 133)
1 tsp soft brown sugar
1 tsp prepared mustard
1 tbsp chopped mixed fresh herbs

Mix salad dressing ingredients and marinate tongue and smoked beef in half the salad dressing for 1 hour. Arrange meat, carrots and celery on lettuce leaves, sprinkle remaining salad dressing over and serve.

(6 servings)

HINTS

☆ *To prepare carrot curls, use a potato peeler to cut thin strips of carrot. Roll the strips, secure with cocktail sticks and place in iced water for 30 minutes.*

☆ *Serve the salad as a starter.*

SUGGESTED SIDE DISH
Wholemeal bread

CRUMBED BRAINS

250 g (8 oz) brains (page 74)
125 ml (4 fl oz) meat stock (page 133)
2 tbsp plain flour
1 tsp salt
fresh ground black pepper to taste
1 egg, beaten
90 g (3 oz) dried breadcrumbs
cooking oil
2 tsp dried or 2 tbsp chopped fresh
parsley

Soak brains in lukewarm salted water for 30 minutes, then drain well. Bring meat stock almost to boiling point and poach brains for 20 minutes. Remove from meat stock, drain well and cut into slices. Mix flour, salt and pepper. Roll slices in flour mixture, then in beaten egg and finally in dried breadcrumbs. Refrigerate for 20 to 30 minutes to allow crumbs to set, then brown brains quickly in heated cooking oil. Drain on paper towels and sprinkle parsley over.

(2 servings)

HINT

☆ *Serve as a starter with Hollandaise sauce.*

EASTERN OX TRIPE

1.5 kg (3 lb) cleaned ox tripe
(page 74)
1 onion, chopped
3 cloves garlic, crushed
1 tbsp cooking oil
15 g ($\frac{1}{2}$ oz) butter
2 tsp mild curry powder
$\frac{1}{2}$ tsp each aniseed and ground
coriander
18 fresh pickling onions
6 carrots, peeled and cut into chunks
3 potatoes, peeled and quartered
150 ml ($\frac{1}{4}$ pint) meat stock (page 154)
2 tsp salt
freshly ground black pepper to taste
5 tsp lemon juice
4 to 6 ginger nuts, crumbed

Cover tripe with cold water and simmer for approximately 3 hours or until tender. Drain and cut into strips. Sauté onion and garlic in heated cooking oil and butter in a heavy-based saucepan until onion is translucent. Add curry powder, aniseed and coriander and fry

for another minute. Add remaining ingredients except lemon juice and biscuit crumbs. Cover with lid, reduce heat and simmer until vegetables are tender but still firm. Add lemon juice and thicken sauce with biscuit crumbs.

(6 servings)

VARIATION

☆ *For a stronger flavour, add chopped chilli.*

SUGGESTED SIDE DISHES
Lentils
Tomato and onion salad

SPICED OX HEART

1 kg (2 lb) ox heart, hard parts and
sinews removed,
cut into cubes
1 tbsp cooking oil
15 g ($\frac{1}{2}$ oz) butter
2 large onions, chopped
1 clove garlic, crushed
2 tsp salt
freshly ground black pepper
to taste
375 ml (12 fl oz) meat stock
(page 133)
2 bay leaves or lemon leaves
3 whole cloves
$\frac{1}{2}$ tsp each mixed spice and
grated nutmeg
2 tbsp lemon juice
4 tbsp plain flour

Brown meat in heated cooking oil and butter in a heavy-based saucepan. Add onion and garlic and sauté until onion is translucent. Season with salt and pepper. Heat meat stock and add to meat together with remaining ingredients except lemon juice and flour. Cover with lid, reduce heat and simmer for $2\frac{1}{2}$ to 3 hours or until meat is tender. Remove bay leaves or lemon leaves and stir in lemon juice. Thicken sauce with a flour and water paste.

(6 servings)

HINT

☆ *For easy removal, tie the whole cloves and bay leaves in a piece of muslin.*

SUGGESTED SIDE DISHES
Buttered carrots
Marinated broccoli

PORK BRAWN

4 shanks of pork
500 g (1 lb) lean pork
1 bay leaf
5 black peppercorns
5 whole cloves
2 onions, grated
1 tbsp cooking oil
1 tbsp mild curry powder
1 tsp turmeric
2 tsp salt
1 tsp grated lemon rind
3 tbsp apricot jam
3 tsp lemon juice
90 ml (3 fl oz) vinegar

Cover meat with cold water. Tie bay leaf, peppercorns and cloves in a piece of muslin and add. Bring to the boil, cover with lid, reduce heat and simmer until meat is tender. Remove meat from bones and cube. Reserve cooking liquid. Sauté onion in heated cooking oil in a heavy-based saucepan, add curry powder and turmeric and fry for 1 minute. Add salt, lemon rind, jam, lemon juice, vinegar and 300 ml ($\frac{1}{2}$ pint) cooking liquid and bring to the boil. Cover with lid, reduce heat and simmer for 5 minutes. Add curry mixture to meat and simmer for 30 minutes. Spoon into moulds, refrigerate and allow to set.

(8 servings)

SUGGESTED SIDE DISHES
Wholemeal bread
Crisp salad
Fruit kebabs

OXTAIL WITH BANANA AND APPLE

2 oxtails, cut into joints
2 tbsp cooking oil
2 onions, chopped
1 tbsp mild curry powder
2 tsp salt
freshly ground black pepper
to taste
1 tbsp smooth apricot jam
1 tbsp fruit chutney
1 tbsp lemon juice
200 ml ($6\frac{1}{2}$ fl oz) meat stock
(page 133)
2 potatoes, grated
2 cooking apples, cored and thinly
sliced
2 bananas, thinly sliced

Remove excess fat from oxtail and brown meat in heated cooking oil in a heavy-based saucepan. Add onion and sauté until translucent. Add curry powder and fry for another minute. Add salt, pepper, jam, chutney, lemon juice and heated meat stock. Cover with lid, reduce heat and simmer for 3 to $3\frac{1}{2}$ hours or until meat is almost tender. Add potatoes and simmer for another 20 minutes. Add fruit 5 minutes before the end of the cooking time.

(6 servings)

SUGGESTED SIDE DISHES
Brown rice
Cucumber and dill salad

BRAISED OXTAIL WITH VEGETABLES

1 oxtail, cut into joints
1 tbsp cooking oil
1 onion, chopped
2 tsp salt
freshly ground black pepper to taste
2 bay leaves
2 whole cloves
500 ml (16 fl oz) meat stock
(page 133)
410 g (13 oz) canned whole
tomatoes, quartered
8 fresh pickling onions
2 celery stalks, sliced
2 large carrots, peeled and cut into
chunks
8 new potatoes
90 g (3 oz) mushrooms, wiped and
sliced
4 tbsp medium cream sherry
4 tsp dried or 3 tbsp chopped fresh
parsley

Remove excess fat from oxtail and brown meat in heated cooking oil in a heavy-based saucepan. Add onion and sauté until translucent. Add seasoning, heated meat stock and tomato, cover with lid, reduce heat and simmer for 3 hours or until meat is tender. Add vegetables and sherry and simmer for another 30 minutes. Remove bay leaves, then sprinkle with parsley.

(2 to 3 servings)

HINT
☆ *Reduce the amount of liquid called for and use a slow-cooker.*

SUGGESTED SIDE DISH
Savoury rice

Front: Crumbed brains (page 78). Back: Oxtail with banana and apple (pages 78 to 79)

UNUSUAL DISHES

The recipes in this chapter come from all over the world and are authentic in their ingredients and origins. They will certainly appeal to those cooks who like to seek out unusual recipes and/or ingredients and who don't mind spending time in the kitchen preparing what can sometimes be time-consuming recipes.

GREEK-STYLE BAKED LAMB WITH PASTA

This is without doubt one of the favourite celebration dishes among Greeks, whether on the mainland or the islands.

1.6 kg (3$\frac{1}{4}$ lb) boned leg of lamb, sliced thickly
4 cloves garlic, peeled and halved
6 tbsp olive oil
500 g (1 lb) very ripe fresh tomatoes, peeled and finely chopped
2 tbsp tomato purée
salt and freshly ground black pepper to taste
1 tbsp Greek *rigani* or oregano
400 g (14 oz) *orzo* (rice-shaped pasta)

Put the meat in a roasting dish with the garlic and 150ml/$\frac{1}{4}$ pint boiling water. Add the olive oil, tomatoes, tomato purée and salt and pepper. Sprinkle with the *rigani*.

Bake at 220 °C (425 °F/gas 7) for 45 to 50 minutes, turning the meat and basting from time to time. Add 300 ml/$\frac{1}{2}$ pint more boiling water and add the pasta. Season again and reduce the heat to 200 °C (400 °F/gas 6) and bake for a further 40 minutes or until the pasta is cooked. You may need to add a little more water if the pasta starts to dry out.
(6 servings)

Opposite clockwise from top: Sosaties (page 86); Bobotie (page 84); and Lamb and spinach bredie (this page)

BARBECUED LAMB, PARSEE STYLE

Yoghurt and lemon juice are commonly used as meat tenderizers, in Indian dishes but in this recipe, fresh papaya (pawpaw) is used instead.

500 g (1 lb) boned leg of lamb
1 clove garlic, chopped
2.5 cm (1 inch) piece fresh ginger root, chopped
1$\frac{1}{2}$ tsp whole cumin
4 black peppercorns
2 tbsp whole coriander
1 tsp chilli powder
1 tsp sugar
1 tsp salt
60 g (2 oz) fresh papaya (pawpaw), peeled and chopped
2 tbsp vinegar
3 tbsp vegetable oil
2 limes or lemons, cut in wedges

Trim any fat from the meat. Cut into 2.5 cm (1 inch) cubes and set aside. Grind the garlic, ginger, cumin seeds, black peppercorns, coriander seeds, chilli powder, sugar, salt and papaya to a smooth paste. Add the vinegar and grind for a further minute. Add the oil and mix well together. Add the ground mixture to the meat and coat thoroughly. Cover and refrigerate to marinate for 10 hours. Stir occasionally.

Prepare the barbecue or heat the grill. Thread a few pieces of meat onto each skewer and cook, turning frequently, for about 15 minutes, until the lamb is tender and well browned. Serve hot.
(4 servings)

SUGGESTED SIDE DISHES
Poppadums
Cucumber raita
Rice and chutney

LAMB AND SPINACH BREDIE

Sorrel may be added for a touch of sourness but if it is not readily available, it may be replaced by an apple or lemon juice.

1.5 kg (3 lb) breast of lamb, cut into 6 portions
315 g (10 oz) spinach
1 tbsp plain flour
4 tsp cooking oil
2 onions, chopped
1 clove garlic, crushed
1 large cooking apple, cored and coarsely chopped
300 ml ($\frac{1}{2}$ pint) meat stock (page 133)
2 tsp salt
freshly ground black pepper to taste
2 potatoes, quartered

Rinse spinach thoroughly and remove any hard stems. Pat dry with paper towels. Roll meat in plain flour and brown in heated cooking oil in a heavy-based saucepan. Add onion and garlic and sauté until onion is translucent. Add apple, heated meat stock, salt and pepper and bring to the boil. Cover with lid, reduce heat and simmer for 1$\frac{1}{2}$ to 2 hours or until meat is tender, adding more meat stock if necessary. Add the potatoes 30 minutes before the end of the cooking time, and the spinach 10 minutes before serving.
(6 servings)

VARIATIONS
Broccoli bredie: *Substitute 315 g (10 oz) broccoli florets for the spinach and 1 tbsp lemon juice for the apple.*
Tomato bredie: *Substitute 1 kg (2 lb) ripe tomatoes for the spinach and add 1 tsp sugar. Omit apple and meat stock.*
Pumpkin bredie: *Substitute 500 g (1 lb) pumpkin for the spinach. Omit apple and add 1 cinnamon stick and a pinch of ground ginger.*

SPICED BEEF BUNDLES

750 g (1½ lb) minced beef
1 tbsp cooking oil
2 onions, finely chopped
2 cloves garlic, crushed
1 large potato, peeled and diced
1 tsp ground mixed spice
1½ tsp salt
freshly ground black pepper
to taste
125 ml (4 fl oz) meat stock
(page 133)
cooking oil for deep-frying

SODA WATER PASTRY
500 g (1 lb) plain flour
2 tsp baking powder
1 tsp salt
500 g (1 lb) butter
1 tbsp brandy
250 ml (8 fl oz) soda water
whole cloves

Fry meat in heated cooking oil until it turns colour. Add onion and garlic and sauté until onion is translucent. Add potato, mixed spice, salt, pepper and heated meat stock. Bring to the boil, cover with lid, reduce heat and simmer for about 30 minutes. Leave to cool.

To prepare the pastry, sift flour, baking powder and salt. Rub in butter until mixture resembles coarse breadcrumbs. Add brandy and enough soda water to form a fairly soft dough. Roll out pastry very thinly and cut into 7.5 cm (3 inch) squares. Place a little of the meat mixture in the centre of each square and draw up the corners, securing them with a clove. Deep-fry until golden brown. Drain on kitchen paper and serve hot or cold.

(approximately 20)

BAKED LIVER PATTIES

500 g (1lb) liver
1 onion, finely chopped
pinch grated nutmeg
½ tsp ground coriander
1½ tsp salt
freshly ground black pepper to taste
1 tbsp vinegar
1 egg, beaten
2 tbsp plain flour
½ tsp baking powder
1 caul fat

Place liver in boiling water for 1 minute and remove membrane. Shred liver with a fork. Add all ingredients except caul fat to liver and mix well. Spoon liver mixture onto caul fat, fold over and secure with cocktail sticks. Place in ovenproof dish and bake at 160 °C (325 °F/ gas 3) for 1 hour or until cooked.

(4 to 6 servings)

VARIATIONS

☆ Substitute green (page 153) or smoked bacon for the caul fat if the latter is not available.

☆ Cut caul fat into 15 cm (6 inch) squares. Place tablespoonfuls of prepared liver on caul fat, fold fat over and secure with cocktail sticks. Cook slowly over coals until cooked.

HINT

☆ If the caul fat is hard and difficult to handle, simply dip it in hot water.

SUGGESTED SIDE DISHES
Hot French bread
Curried green beans

MOCK VENISON

It is believed that this recipe may have originated in the Cape district of South Africa during the 1600s.

1 boned leg of mutton,
approximately 2 kg (4 lb)
250 g (8 oz) speck, cut into strips
345 ml (11 fl oz) red wine or wine vinegar
125 ml (4 fl oz) meat stock (page 133)
2 tbsp cooking oil
2 tsp salt
freshly ground black pepper to taste
1 tsp dried or 1 tbsp chopped fresh rosemary
2 tsp ground coriander
250 ml (8 fl oz) soured cream

Lard (page 11) meat with speck and marinate it in red wine or wine vinegar and meat stock for 48 hours, turning it regularly. Remove meat but reserve marinade. Dry meat thoroughly with kitchen paper and brown in heated cooking oil in a heavy-based saucepan. Heat reserved marinade and add to meat together with salt, pepper, rosemary and coriander. Bring to the boil, cover with lid, reduce heat and simmer for approximately 1½ hours or until meat is tender. Stir in soured cream and heat through.

(6 servings)

VARIATION

☆ Substitute crème fraîche (page 154) for the soured cream.

SUGGESTED SIDE DISHES
Stewed sweet potatoes
Green peas

Left to right: Mock venison; Baked liver patties (page 82); and Spiced beef bundles (page 82)

SHEEP'S OFFAL WITH APRICOTS

The preparation of traditional dishes such as brawn, cured meat and offal used to be a ritual whenever an animal was slaughtered on farms. It was common practice on these occasions to send such a dish to neighbours as a token of friendship. Dried apricots and spices are a contemporary addition to this recipe.

1 sheep's offal (head, tripe and trotters), cleaned
3 tbsp vinegar
5 whole cloves
5 black peppercorns
2 bay leaves or lemon leaves, crushed
2 onions, chopped
2 tbsp cooking oil
5 tsp mild curry powder
2 tsp turmeric
4 tsp apricot jam
2 tsp salt
125 g (4 oz) dried apricots, soaked in water until plump
4 potatoes, quartered

Cut offal into pieces, place them in a heavy-based saucepan and cover with cold water. Add vinegar. Tie cloves, peppercorns and bay leaves or lemon leaves in a piece of muslin and add. Bring to the boil, cover with lid, reduce heat and simmer for 3 hours or until tender. In the meantime, sauté onion in heated cooking oil until translucent. Add curry powder and turmeric and fry for 1 minute. Add apricot jam and salt and mix well. Remove spice bag from saucepan and add onion mixture together with apricots and potatoes. Simmer until tender. Remove meat from bones and serve.
(4 servings)

VARIATIONS
☆ *Tie sheep's brains in omasum (page 156) and cook with offal.*
☆ *Add 1 sheep's neck to offal.*

HINT
☆ *Mash some of the potatoes to thicken the sauce.*

SUGGESTED SIDE DISH
Rice or freshly baked bread

TRADITIONAL CAPE LAMB PIE

In 1659, the first free bakers in the Cape baked and sold meat pies with both an upper crust and a lower crust. Later single crust pies appeared on the scene and these soon assumed a special place on South African menus.

1.5 kg (3 lb) neck or shank of lamb, boned and cut into cubes
5 tsp cooking oil
2 onions, chopped
125 g (4 oz) rindless shoulder bacon, coarsely chopped
$\frac{1}{2}$ tsp mixed spice
2 tsp salt
freshly ground black pepper to taste
125 ml (4 fl oz) meat stock (page 133)
125 ml (4 fl oz) dry white wine
5 tsp lemon juice
2 hard-boiled eggs
milk and egg beaten together for glazing

PASTRY
125 g (4 oz) butter
125 ml (4 fl oz) soured cream
$\frac{1}{2}$ egg, beaten
185 g (6 oz) plain flour
pinch salt

First prepare the pastry. Grate butter and lightly stir in soured cream. Add egg and stir. Sift flour and salt, add to butter mixture and mix to a stiff dough. Place in refrigerator until well chilled, then roll out thinly into a rectangle. Fold top third of the dough down and bottom third up. Place in a plastic bag and refrigerate for 30 minutes. Repeat the process of rolling, folding and resting twice more.

To prepare the meat, brown it in heated cooking oil, add onion and bacon and fry until onion is translucent. Add seasoning, heated stock, wine and lemon juice. Cover with lid, reduce heat and simmer for 1$\frac{1}{2}$ hours or until meat is almost tender. Remove bones. Spoon into pie dish and allow to cool. Top with sliced hard-boiled egg. Roll out pastry and carefully place it on top of cooled meat. Trim edges, then brush pastry with egg and milk mixture to glaze. Bake at 200 °C (400 °F/gas 6) for 35 minutes or until golden brown.
(6 servings)

VARIATION
☆ *Substitute thick rib of lamb for the neck or shank of lamb and add 1 tbsp sago to thicken.*

HINT
☆ *A lightly beaten extra large egg will yield about 3 tbsp. Measure out 5 tsp for the puff pastry and use the rest to glaze the pastry.*

SUGGESTED SIDE DISHES
Green beans
Cinnamon pumpkin

BOBOTIE

Bobotie is increasingly popular as an unusual meat dish. The first reference to bobotie dates back to 1609 when it appeared in an old Dutch cookbook. The origin of the recipe is unknown.

1 kg (2 lb) minced lamb or beef
1 thick slice white bread
375 ml (12 fl oz) milk
2 onions, chopped
2 tbsp cooking oil
2 tbsp mild curry powder
2 tsp turmeric
1$\frac{1}{2}$ tsp salt
freshly ground black pepper to taste
2 tbsp lemon juice
60 g (2 oz) seedless raisins
5 tsp chopped almonds
2 eggs
4 bay leaves or orange or lemon leaves

Soak bread in 125 ml (4 fl oz) milk until soft, then mash with a fork. Sauté onion in heated cooking oil in a heavy-based saucepan until translucent. Add curry powder and turmeric and fry for 1 minute. Add mince and fry until it turns colour. Add bread, salt, pepper, lemon juice, raisins and almonds. Cover with lid, reduce heat and simmer for a few minutes. Spoon mixture into a greased pie dish. Beat eggs and remaining milk together and pour over mince. Arrange bay leaves or orange or lemon leaves on top and bake at 160 °C (325 °F/gas 3) for 30 minutes.
(6 servings)

SUGGESTED SIDE DISHES
Pilau rice
Stewed peaches

Traditional Cape lamb pie

SOSATIES

This traditional Malay dish is made from cubes of lamb threaded onto wooden skewers and marinated in a curry sauce. The word 'sosatie' is possibly derived from the Indonesian word 'satay', which describes a similar pork dish, or is a corruption of two Indonesian words, *saté* – meaning sauce – and *sesaté* meaning skewered meats.

1.5 kg (3 lb) boneless lamb (leg, thick rib or shoulder), cut into cubes
375 g (12 oz) speck, cut into cubes
1 onion, quartered and loosened
125 g (4 oz) dried apricots

MARINADE
250 ml (8 fl oz) buttermilk
4 bay leaves, crushed
2 cloves garlic, crushed
1 onion, chopped
freshly ground black pepper to taste

CURRY SAUCE
4 large onions, chopped
2 tbsp cooking oil
1 tbsp curry powder
1 tsp turmeric
5 tbsp apricot jam
4 bay leaves
375 ml (12 fl oz) vinegar
1 tsp salt
freshly ground black pepper to taste
1 tbsp plain flour

Mix marinade ingredients. Place meat in a suitable container, pour marinade over meat and marinate overnight in refrigerator. Drain well.

To prepare the curry suace, sauté onion in heated cooking oil until translucent. Add curry powder and turmeric and fry for 1 minute. Add remaining ingredients, except flour, and simmer for a few minutes. Allow to cool, then pour over meat and leave to marinate for 1 to 2 days in the refrigerator.

To assemble the sosaties, thread meat, speck, onion and apricots alternately onto wooden skewers. Grill over low coals for approximately 20 minutes or until cooked.

Remove and discard bay leaves from curry sauce, then thicken sauce with a flour and water paste. Serve sauce separately.
(6 servings)

HINTS
☆ *Thread meat loosely onto skewers to enable meat to cook evenly.*
☆ *Cover ends of wooden skewers with foil or soak them in water before threading on meat to prevent them from scorching.*

SUGGESTED SIDE DISH
Farmhouse bread and butter

SPICY HOMEMADE SAUSAGES

These unusual home-made sausages are deliciously spicy.

2 kg (4 lb) beef
1 kg (2 lb) pork
4 tsp salt
3 tbsp coriander seeds toasted and ground
$\frac{1}{2}$ tsp ground cloves
freshly ground black pepper to taste
315 g (10 oz)) speck, cut into 3 mm ($\frac{1}{8}$ inch) cubes
5 tbsp vinegar
1 tbsp brandy
100 g ($3\frac{1}{2}$ oz) sausage casings

Cut meat into 5 cm (2 inch) cubes and combine with seasoning and spices. Mince the meat, add speck and sprinkle vinegar and brandy over. Mix lightly but thoroughly, then stuff mixture loosely into casings.
(approximately 3.5 kg/7lb)

HINT
☆ *Handle meat as little as possible to ensure a loose texture.*

VARIATION
☆ *Add 5 tsp Worcestershire sauce with the vinegar and brandy.*

SUGGESTED SIDE DISH
Ratatouille

Spicy homemade sausages

☆ *Ask your butcher to saw through the breastbone to facilitate the cutting of the portions afterwards.*
☆ *Soak very salty and dry cured mutton in cold water overnight before cooking it.*
☆ *Once boiled and dried, wrap the cured mutton in muslin. It should keep for up to 1 week in a well-ventilated cool place.*
☆ *The meat will be pink inside due to the addition of saltpetre to the brine.*
☆ *Breast of lamb is so tender it does not need to be precooked.*

SUGGESTED SIDE DISH
Corn-on-the-cob

BEEF JERKY

Before refrigeration, housewives had to plan carefully to prevent food from perishing. The old-fashioned method of preserving meat is still used today to produce one of Australia's favourite snacks.

2 whole silversides, approximately
12 kg (25 lb)
315 g (10 oz) coarse salt
90 g (3 oz) soft brown sugar
$1\frac{1}{2}$ tsp saltpetre
1 tbsp bicarbonate of soda
1 tbsp freshly ground black pepper
60 g (2 oz) coriander seeds,
toasted and ground
300 ml ($\frac{1}{2}$ pint) vinegar

Remove all visible connective tissue from meat. Cut meat into long strips approximately 2.5 cm (1 inch) thick. Mix dry ingredients together. Place meat in layers in a suitable container and sprinkle salt mixture over each layer. Sprinkle with vinegar and leave overnight. Dip meat into hot vinegar and water mixture (375 ml/12 fl oz vinegar to 5 litres/9 pints boiling water), then hang in a cool draughty place to dry.
(approximately 6 kg/13 lb)

HINTS
☆ *About 50 to 60% of the meat mass is lost during the drying process.*
☆ *Do not store meat in plastic containers as it will become mouldy. Store it wrapped in muslin or freeze it tightly wrapped in cling film.*

Cured breast of mutton

CURED BREAST OF MUTTON

In the past curing and drying was the usual method of preserving meat.

1 breast of mutton,
approximately 1.5 kg (3 lb)
1 tbsp soft brown sugar
225 g (7 oz) coarse salt
$\frac{1}{2}$ tsp saltpetre
3 tbsp coriander seeds, toasted
and ground

Mix brown sugar, salt, saltpetre and coriander and rub into meat. Place meat in a glass, earthenware or plastic container and refrigerate for 2 to 3 days. Hang meat in a cool, well-ventilated place to dry. Place meat in a saucepan, cover with cold water and bring to the boil. Cover with lid, reduce heat and simmer for 1 hour or until meat is almost tender. Remove from liquid and allow to cool. Hang meat in a cool place to dry the surface, then cook meat over moderate coals until brown and crisp. Cut into portions and serve.
(6 servings)

MINCE

Whether used for hamburgers, meat loaf, pies or a pasta dish, mince is always a hit! Mince is quick and easy to prepare and with a little imagination it can be transformed into a variety of delicious dishes for breakfast, lunch, dinner, party and picnic.

STORING MINCE

In the refrigerator: Mince goes off easily and can only be kept in the refrigerator for two to three days. Unwrap the mince and cover it lightly with waxed paper to prevent it from drying out.

In the freezer: Freeze mince in family-sized portions in airtight containers. To ensure rapid freezing as well as thawing and to save freezer space, use flat square containers.

FREEZING TIMES FOR MINCE
Raw minced beef (lean): 6 months
Raw minced pork: 2 months
Raw minced lamb: 2 to 3 months

Freeze raw mince without any additions as certain ingredients such as garlic, breadcrumbs and herbs may undergo unpleasant flavour changes during the freezing process.

HINTS
☆ *Good quality mince has a cherry-red colour with a crumbly texture and should be free of any bits of connective tissue and excess fat.*
☆ *Minced beef tends to be dry. Combine two-thirds minced beef with one-third minced pork, lamb or veal for added flavour and to improve the texture and juiciness of the mince.*

Opposite clockwise from top: Stuffed aubergines (page 92); Pasta with mince (page 95); and Pork and broccoli terrine (page 93)

CUTS SUITABLE FOR MINCE			
BEEF	**MUTTON/LAMB**	**PORK**	**VEAL**
Neck Chuck Blade Flank Topside Shin	Thick rib (Forequarter) Flank (remove outer connective tissue)	Blade and spare rib Flank Cheeks	Neck Thick rib (Shoulder) Silverside Topside Thick flank

☆ *Coarsely minced meat is suitable for rissoles and pasta dishes, whereas finely minced meat should be used for terrines, meat loaves and stuffings.*
☆ *Cold minced meat dishes require more seasoning than hot dishes.*
☆ *Do not discard juices that collect around rissoles or a baked meat loaf as this will dry them out. Leave the meat loaf or rissoles in the meat juices to cool so that the juices can be re-absorbed.*
☆ *Add the following to rissoles:*
- *Replace breadcrumbs with grated apple or carrot, chopped dried fruit or chopped nuts.*
- *Use fresh or dried herbs such as oregano and parsley.*
- *Replace vinegar with white wine.*
☆ *Apart from baking, rissoles may also be fried or simmered in liquid or cooked on a skewer over a barbecue or under a pre-heated grill.*
☆ *If rissoles are being fried, cover them with beaten egg and breadcrumbs. Do not fry rissoles in very hot oil or cook them for too long as the meat will dry out. Ten minutes for frying and 20 to 30 minutes for baking is usually sufficient.*

PORTION SIZES
90 g (3 oz): Mince combined with other food, such as lasagne or moussaka.
125 g (4 oz): Pure mince without any additions.

MINCE AND VEGETABLE ROLL

750 g (1½ lb) minced beef
1 tsp salt
freshly ground black pepper to taste
½ tsp dried or 1 tsp chopped fresh thyme
1 egg, beaten
1 onion, chopped
1 tbsp cooking oil
155 g (5 oz) courgettes, grated
1 large carrot, peeled and grated
125 g (4 oz) Cheddar cheese, grated
6 rashers rindless streaky bacon

Mix mince, salt, pepper, thyme and egg thoroughly. Place mixture on a piece of cling film or foil and shape into a rectangle measuring 45 × 30 cm (18 × 12 inches). Sauté onion in heated cooking oil until translucent. Add vegetables and fry lightly. Place vegetables on top of mince and sprinkle cheese over. Roll up meat like a Swiss roll, using the cling film or foil to assist you. Place on a greased baking sheet and arrange rashers of bacon on top. Bake at 160 °C (325 °F/gas 3) for 45 to 60 minutes or until meat is cooked.
(6 servings)

SUGGESTED SIDE DISHES
Potato croquettes
Tomato, onion and mozzarella salad

TOMATO MINCE PIES

500 g (1 lb) minced beef
2 onions, chopped
2 cloves garlic, crushed
2 tbsp cooking oil
1 tsp salt
freshly ground black pepper
to taste
$\frac{1}{2}$ tsp dried or 2 tsp chopped fresh
thyme
1 tsp dried or 1 tbsp chopped fresh
oregano
410 g (13 oz) canned whole
tomatoes, chopped

PASTRY
250 g (8 oz) plain flour
5 tsp baking powder
good pinch salt
60 g (2 oz) butter
90 ml (3 fl oz) tomato purée
4 tbsp water
1 egg, beaten

To prepare the meat, sauté onion and garlic in heated cooking oil until onion is translucent. Add mince and fry until it turns colour. Season mince with salt, pepper, thyme and oregano. Heat tomatoes and add to meat. Simmer until cooked and thickened. Allow to cool.

To prepare the pastry, sift flour, baking powder and salt together and rub in butter. Mix tomato purée with the water and add to flour mixture to make a stiff dough. Wrap pastry in cling film and refrigerate for 30 minutes before rolling out.

For individual pies, roll pastry out thinly and cut into circles with a biscuit cutter. Brush edges of pastry with beaten egg and cold water. Place a spoonful of the filling in the centre of each circle, keeping the edges clear. Cover with a second circle of pastry and press edges of pastry down with a fork. Prick top with a fork, brush with beaten egg and place on a greased baking sheet. Bake at 200 °C (400 °F/gas 6) for 20 minutes or until golden brown and cooked.
(6 servings)

VARIATION
☆ For a single pie, spoon meat mixture into a pie dish and top with a circle of pastry. Prick surface with a fork, brush with beaten egg to glaze and bake at 200 °C (400 °F/gas 6) for 30 minutes.

HINTS
☆ Handle pastry as little as possible and keep ingredients as cold as possible.
☆ To ensure a light crust and to prevent shrinkage, it is necessary to place the pastry in the refrigerator to rest before rolling it out.

SUGGESTED SIDE DISHES
Carrots with soured cream
Cabbage and nut salad

MEAT LOAF WITH BANANA

750 g (1$\frac{1}{2}$ lb) minced beef
250 g (8 oz) minced lean pork
2 slices white bread
90 ml (3 fl oz) milk
1 onion, grated
4 tsp prepared mustard
2 tsp salt
freshly ground black pepper
to taste
3 bananas, peeled and mashed
250 g (8 oz) rindless streaky bacon
3 hard-boiled eggs, shelled

Soak the bread in the milk, squeeze out and add to mince. Mix in remaining ingredients excpet bacon and eggs. Grease a loaf tin or terrine and line it with the bacon. Spoon in half the meat mixture and arrange hard-boiled eggs down the middle. Spoon remaining mince on top and bake at 160 °C (325 °F/gas 3) for 1 hour or until mince is cooked. Allow to stand for approximately 10 minutes before turning out onto a meat platter.
(6 servings)

VARIATIONS
☆ Prepare individual meat loaves in small loaf tins. Remember to reduce the cooking time accordingly.
☆ Substitute banana-flavoured drinking yoghurt for the milk.

HINTS
☆ To prevent bananas from turning brown, dip unpeeled bananas in boiling water or sprinkle peeled and sliced bananas with lemon juice.
☆ To ensure a loose texture, mix the minced meat lightly with a fork.

SUGGESTED SIDE DISH
Fried potato slices

AUBERGINE FRITTERS WITH MINCE

500 g (1 lb) minced beef
90 g (3 oz) rindless streaky bacon,
coarsely chopped
2 onions, chopped
2 tbsp plain flour
3 tbsp tomato purée
2 tsp sugar
1 tsp dried or 1 tbsp chopped mixed
fresh herbs
1 tsp salt
freshly ground black pepper
to taste
125 ml (4 fl oz) meat stock (page 133)
125 ml (4 fl oz) dry white wine

AUBERGINE FRITTERS
1 onion, chopped
30 g (1 oz) butter
1 aubergine, grated
2 eggs, beaten
125 g (4 oz) plain flour
60 g (2 oz) Cheddar cheese, grated
2 tsp baking powder
1 tsp salt
cooking oil for deep frying

To prepare the meat, fry bacon until crisp, add onion and sauté until tarnslucent. Add mince and fry until it turns colour. Add flour and remaining ingredients and simmer for 20 minutes.

To prepare the aubergine fritters, sauté onion in melted butter until translucent. Add remaining ingredients and mix well. Fry spoonfuls of the batter in hot cooking oil until golden brown. Drain on paper towels, then fill with meat mixture.
(6 servings)

VARIATIONS
☆ Prepare 10 small fritters. Spoon minced meat mixture into a serving dish and arrange fritters on top.
☆ Use 250 ml (8 fl oz) meat stock instead of 125 ml (4 fl oz) dry white wine and 125 ml (4 fl oz) meat stock.

HINT
☆ To prevent aubergine from absorbing too much liquid and becoming bitter, cut in half lengthwise, sprinkle with salt and drain in a colander for 30 minutes. Rinse, then dry thoroughly with paper towels.

SUGGESTED SIDE DISH
Mixed salad

CURRIED MINCE

1 kg (2 lb) minced beef
2 onions, chopped
1 clove garlic, crushed
1 tbsp cooking oil
4 tsp mild curry powder
1 tsp turmeric
90 ml (3 fl oz) orange juice
200 ml (6½ fl oz) coconut milk (page 154)
1 tbsp chopped ginger root or ½ tsp ground ginger
1 bay leaf
3 tbsp seedless raisins
2 tbsp fruit chutney
2 cooking apples, cored and grated
2 tbsp vinegar
1 carrot, grated
1 cinnamon stick
freshly ground black pepper to taste
1½ tsp salt

Sauté onion and garlic in cooking oil until translucent. Add mince and fry until it turns colour. Add curry powder and turmeric and fry for 1 minute. Heat orange juice and coconut milk and add to mince with remaining ingredients. Cover, reduce heat and simmer for 30 minutes. Remove bay leaf and cinnamon.
(6 servings)

VARIATIONS
☆ Substitute meat stock for the coconut milk.
☆ Slice cooking apples thinly and add 15 minutes before the end of the cooking time.
☆ Substitute apricot or mango juice for the orange juice.

HINT
☆ To prevent curry from staining tablecloths and clothing, omit the turmeric.

SUGGESTED SIDE DISHES
Fruit rice
Sambals

Curried mince

Rissoles with hazelnut sauce

STUFFED AUBERGINES

315 g (10 oz) minced beef
6 small aubergines
1 onion, chopped
2 tsp cooking oil
$\frac{1}{2}$ tsp salt
freshly ground black pepper
to taste
1 tsp Dijon mustard
125 g (4 oz) Cheddar cheese,
grated
pinch grated nutmeg
90 ml (3 fl oz) single cream
315 g (10 oz) spinach, blanched
and chopped
5 tsp grated Parmesan cheese
$\frac{1}{2}$ tsp dried or 2 tsp chopped fresh
parsley

First prepare the aubergines by halving them lengthwise. To form hollows for the mince mixture, remove some of the flesh from the centre and reserve.

To prepare the mince, sauté onion in heated cooking oil until translucent. Add mince and chopped reserved aubergine and fry until mince turns colour. Add salt, pepper and remaining ingredients except Parmesan and parsley. Spoon some of the mixture into each hollowed-out aubergine. Sprinkle Parmesan and parsley over and bake at 160 °C (325 °F/gas 3) for 30 minutes.
(6 servings)

HINT

☆ *Use any leftover mince mixture as a sandwich filling.*

SUGGESTED SIDE DISHES
Mixed salad
Garlic bread

RISSOLES WITH HAZELNUT SAUCE

500 g (1 lb) minced beef
1 tsp salt
freshly ground black pepper
to taste
125 ml (4 fl oz) plain low-fat yoghurt
1 slice wholemeal bread, crumbed
1 apple, cored and grated
5 tbsp seedless raisins
1 small onion, chopped
chopped fresh dill

HAZELNUT SAUCE
250 ml (8 fl oz) meat stock
(page 133)
1 tsp dried or 1 tbsp chopped
fresh dill
2 tsp plain flour
30 g (1 oz) butter
$\frac{1}{2}$ tsp salt
freshly ground black pepper to taste
125 ml (4 fl oz) single cream
3 tbsp chopped toasted hazelnuts

To prepare the rissoles, mix all ingredients, except dill, together lightly with two forks and shape into rissoles. Place in an ovenproof dish and bake at 160 °C (325 °F/gas 3) for 30 minutes.

To prepare the sauce, heat meat stock and dill and reduce to 125 ml (4 fl oz) over high heat. Make a paste of flour and soft butter and stir in. Remove from heat and stir in salt, pepper, cream and nuts. Stir until thickened and then pour over rissoles. Sprinkle with chopped fresh dill and serve.
(4 servings)

SUGGESTED SIDE DISHES
Vegetables in season

SCONE DOUGH MEAT ROLL

500 g (1 lb) minced beef
125 g (4 oz) ham, chopped
1 onion, chopped
125 g (4 oz) button mushrooms, cut into quarters
1 green pepper, seeded and chopped
1 clove garlic, crushed
2 tsp butter
2 tsp cooking oil
2 tsp plain flour
good pinch salt
freshly ground black pepper to taste
2 tsp Worcestershire sauce
200 ml (6$\frac{1}{2}$ fl oz) meat stock (page 133)

DOUGH
250 g (8 oz) plain flour
2 tsp baking powder
$\frac{1}{2}$ tsp salt
185 ml (6 fl oz) milk
3 tbsp cooking oil

To prepare the filling, fry onion, mushrooms, green pepper and garlic in heated butter and cooking oil until onion is translucent. Add mince and fry until it turns colour. Add ham. Mix flour, salt, pepper and Worcestershire sauce and add to mince. Add heated meat stock, cover with lid, reduce heat and simmer for 15 to 20 minutes until cooked, then leave to cool slightly.

To prepare the scone dough, sift dry ingredients together. Mix milk and oil, add to dry ingredients and mix to the consistency of scone dough. Place dough on waxed paper and roll out to approximately 2 cm ($\frac{3}{4}$ inch) thick. Spread filling over dough, then roll up like a Swiss roll, using the paper to assist you. Place on a greased baking sheet, brush with milk and bake at 200 °C (400 °F/gas 6) for 30 minutes or until golden brown and cooked.
(6 servings)

VARIATION
☆ Add 2 tsp dried or 2 tbsp chopped fresh parsley or other herb to dry ingredients when making the dough.

HINT
☆ To make it easier to transfer the meat roll to a serving dish, place the meat roll on an upside down baking sheet before baking.

PORK AND BROCCOLI TERRINE

500 g (1 lb) minced pork
250 g (8 oz) broccoli
good pinch salt
pinch grated nutmeg
freshly ground black pepper to taste
4 tbsp double cream
4 eggs, beaten
1 onion, chopped
2 cloves garlic, crushed
1$\frac{1}{2}$ tsp salt
1 tsp dried or 1 tbsp chopped fresh rosemary
1 tbsp brandy
200 g (6$\frac{1}{2}$ oz) rindless streaky bacon

Blanch broccoli in boiling water. Drain and place in a food processor. Add salt, nutmeg, pepper and 2 tbsp cream and purée. Add 2 beaten eggs and set mixture aside.

Add remaining ingredients except bacon to mince and mix well. Line a greased terrine with bacon, reserving some rashers for the top. Spoon in half the mince, followed by the broccoli mixture. Spoon in remaining meat and top with a layer of bacon. Bake in a *bain-marie* (page 153) at 180 °C (350 °F/gas 4) for 1 hour or until mince mixture is set. Allow terrine to cool before unmoulding it.
(6 servings)

VARIATION
☆ For a special occasion, line and also cover the terrine with unsweetened shortcrust pastry (page 121) or cream cheese pastry (page 51). Bake at 220 °C (425 °F/gas 7) for 10 minutes, then reduce heat to 180 °C (350 °F/gas 4) and bake for another hour.

HINTS
☆ When cooked, place terrine in refrigerator one to three days before serving to allow flavours to develop.
☆ Chilling dulls the flavour so bring the terrine to room temperature before serving.

SUGGESTED SIDE DISHES
Melba toast
Marinated mushrooms

Scone dough meat roll

HAMBURGERS WITH BANANA CURRY SAUCE

345 g (11 oz) minced lean beef
155 g (5 oz) minced pork or veal
1 onion, chopped
1 thick slice bread
125 ml (4 fl oz) meat stock
(page 133)
1 tsp salt
freshly ground black pepper to taste
2 tsp dried or 2 tbsp chopped
fresh parsley
1 tbsp lemon juice
6 hamburger buns

BANANA CURRY SAUCE
3 onions, chopped
2 tbsp cooking oil
1 tsp mild curry powder
5 tsp plain flour
2 tbsp wine vinegar
3 tbsp meat stock (page 133)
good pinch salt
5 tsp apricot jam
1 tbsp brown sugar
4 bananas, sliced

To prepare the hamburgers, use a fork to mix together all the ingredients, except buns, lightly. Shape into patties and cook over barbecue or under a pre-heated grill for approximately 7 to 10 minutes per side or until cooked.

To prepare the sauce, sauté onion in heated oil in a heavy-based saucepan until translucent. Add curry powder and flour and fry for 1 minute. Heat vinegar and meat stock and add to onion together with remaining ingredients except bananas. Simmer for 3 minutes, then add bananas and heat through.

To serve, place a lettuce leaf and a slice each of tomato and onion on each buttered bun and top with a hamburger. Serve the sauce separately.
(6 servings)

VARIATIONS
☆ Add 1 tbsp crushed green peppercorns to the mince and serve with a mushroom sauce.
☆ Substitute fruit chutney for the apricot jam.

Cheeseburger: Omit sauce, place a slice of Gruyère or Cheddar cheese on each cooked hamburger and place under a pre-heated grill until the cheese has melted.

HINTS
☆ Hamburgers may be frozen in layers separated by a sheet of foil.
☆ The ideal thickness of an uncooked hamburger is about 2.5 cm (1 inch).

SUGGESTED SIDE DISH
Mixed salad

CIRCLE MINCE PIE

1 kg (2 lb) minced lean pork
4 tsp dried or 3 tbsp chopped fresh
parsley
2 onions, finely chopped
1 apple, cored and grated
1 tsp each dried or 1 tbsp each
chopped fresh sage and mixed
herbs
$1\frac{1}{2}$ tsp salt
freshly ground black pepper
to taste
155 g (5 oz) Cheddar cheese, grated
410 g (13 oz) frozen puff pastry,
thawed
1 egg, beaten

Mix all ingredients, except cheese, pastry and egg, together lightly with a fork. Roll pastry out on a floured surface into a rectangle measuring 50 x 30 cm (20 x 12 inches). Spread three-quarters of the mince over the centre of the pastry. Sprinkle cheese down the middle of the mince and spoon remaining meat on top. Moisten edges of pastry and bring together on top of mince. Press edges together in a zig-zag pattern and shape into a circle. Place in a greased pie dish and brush with beaten egg. Bake at 220 °C (425 °F/gas 7) for 10 minutes, then at 180 °C (350 °F/gas 4) for 50 minutes. Transfer to a serving platter with the aid of two egg slices.
(6 servings)

HINTS
☆ For best results, ensure that the pastry is chilled, work in a cool area and roll out the pastry on a marble slab or other cool surface.
☆ Do not use self-raising flour to dust the surface when rolling out puff pastry as it will make the pastry spongy instead of crisp.

SUGGESTED SIDE DISHES
Brussels sprouts and celery
Buttered tomatoes

STUFFED FRENCH LOAF

250 g (8 oz) minced beef
250 g (8 oz) minced pork of veal
1 onion, chopped
1 clove garlic, crushed
2 celery stalks, chopped
2 tbsp cooking oil
2 tsp mild curry powder
2 tsp plain flour
125 g (4 oz) mushrooms, sliced
2 tbsp tomato purée
125 ml (4 fl oz) meat stock
(page 133)
1 tsp salt
freshly ground black pepper
to taste
1 large French loaf, 1-day-old
2 bananas, sliced
200 ml ($6\frac{1}{2}$ fl oz) soured cream
pinch salt and white pepper
2 eggs
3 tbsp plain flour

Fry onion, garlic and celery in heated cooking oil until onion is translucent. Add mince and fry until it turns colour. Add curry powder and flour and fry for 1 minute. Add mushrooms, tomato purée, heated meat stock, salt and pepper and simmer for 10 minutes.

Remove top crust from French loaf and hollow out the centre. Place bread on a large piece of foil. Spoon mince into cavity and top with banana slices. Beat soured cream, salt, pepper, eggs and flour with a fork and pour over banana. Fold foil around sides of loaf but do not cover topping. Bake at 180 °C (350 °F/gas 4) for 20 minutes, then remove foil and bake another 10 minutes or until topping is set and bread is slightly crisp.
(6 servings)

VARIATIONS
☆ Substitute crème fraîche (page 154) for the soured cream.

Savoury banana mince pie: Spoon mince into a dish and arrange banana slices on top. Pour soured cream and egg mixture over and bake at 160 °C (325 °F/gas 3) for 20 minutes.

HINT
☆ Make crumbs from leftover bread.

SUGGESTED SIDE DISH
Cucumber and green pepper salad

Circle mince pie (page 94)

PASTA WITH MINCE

500 g (1 lb) minced beef
1 onion, chopped
2 cloves garlic, crushed
2 tsp cooking oil
4 tomatoes, skinned and chopped
155 ml ($\frac{1}{4}$ pint) meat stock
(page 133)
90 ml (3 fl oz) red wine
2 tsp Worcestershire sauce
2 tsp soy sauce
1 tsp salt
freshly ground black pepper
to taste
2 tbsp chopped fresh parsley
2 tsp plain flour
500 g (1 lb) macaroni

Sauté onion and garlic in heated cooking oil in a heavy-based saucepan until onion is translucent. Add mince and fry until it turns colour. Heat remaining ingredients, except macaroni, and add to mince mixture. Cover with lid, reduce heat and simmer for 15 minutes. Thicken with a paste of flour and water. Cook macaroni according to instructions on packet, then drain. Serve macaroni piping hot with meat sauce poured over.

(4 to 6 sevings)

VARIATION
☆ Serve savoury mince on brown or white rice, mashed potatoes or any other pasta.

HINTS
☆ This mince mixture freezes well for up to two months. Cool thoroughly and pack in an airtight container.
☆ Allow about 90 g (3 oz) uncooked pasta per person.

SUGGESTED SIDE DISH
Carrot salad

STEAKS

Beef steaks remain a great favourite. In order to ensure that the steak is tender, it is necessary to purchase good quality meat that has been well-hung or aged. Steaks should also be correctly packed, sealed, refrigerated, frozen and thawed in order to retain the succulence of the meat.

COOKING HINTS FOR STEAKS

☆ *Keep steaks at room temperature for 20 minutes before cooking. Steaks cooked in a cold or frozen state will be dry due to the loss of meat juices.*
☆ *Steaks should have a minimum thickness of 2 cm ($\frac{3}{4}$ inch) since thinner steaks tend to be dry when cooked.*
☆ *Slash fat edges at 2.5 cm (1 inch) intervals to prevent the meat from curling during cooking. When the steak curls up, liquid collects in the hollows with the result that the steak is cooked in moist heat instead of dry heat and becomes tough.*
☆ *Do not add salt to uncooked steaks. Salt draws out the meat juices, producing dry meat.*
☆ *To turn meat, use tongs rather than a fork which pierces the meat and causes loss of meat juices.*
☆ *Don't use a meat mallet to tenderize steaks as it damages the meat fibres causing the meat juices to escape. Well-hung or aged meat does not need to be tenderized.*
☆ *Commercial meat tenderizers give steaks a floury texture.*
☆ *Steaks may be grilled in three ways: in a ridged pan, under a pre-heated grill or over a barbecue. They may also be fried.*

☆ *Preheat the grill or ridged pan before adding the meat. Low temperatures require a longer cooking time, resulting in the loss of more meat juices.*
☆ *Steak should preferably be grilled until rare or medium to ensure maximum tenderness and juiciness. Well-done meat tends to be dry.*
☆ *For best results grilled steak should be served immediately.*
☆ *Cooked, leftover steaks can be cut into thin slices and used in a salad.*

GRILLING TIMES
Rare: 5 to 7 minutes in total
Medium: 7 to 10 minutes in total

Opposite clockwise from top: Mock pesto sauce and Oven-roasted porterhouse (page 101); and Flambé fillet steaks with vegetables (page 100)

STEAKS			
FOREQUARTER	**MEAT CUT**	**THICKNESS**	
Rib-eye steak	Prime rib	2.5 cm (1 inch)	Boneless
Prime rib steak	Prime rib	2.5 cm (1 inch)	Contains bone
HINDQUARTER			
Thin flank steak	Thin flank		Boneless
Wing rib steak	Wing rib	2.5 cm (1 inch)	Contains bone
Scotch fillet	Wing rib	2.5 cm (1 inch)	Boneless
Entrecôte steak	Sirloin	2.5 cm (1 inch)	Boneless
T-bone steak	Sirloin	2.5 cm (1 inch)	Contains bone
Porterhouse steak			
British	Sirloin	2.5 cm (1 inch)	Boneless
American	Sirloin	5 cm (2 inches)	Contains bone
Minute steak	Thick flank	(3 to 4 servings)	
	(round muscle)	5 mm ($\frac{1}{4}$ inch)	Boneless
Rump steak	Rump	2.5 cm (1 inch)	Boneless
Point rump steak	Rump	2.5 cm (1 inch)	Boneless
Topside steak	Topside	2.5 cm (1 inch)	Boneless
Fillet steaks		5 mm ($\frac{1}{4}$ inch)	Boneless
Filet minute	Fillet	5 mm ($\frac{1}{4}$ inch)	Boneless
Filet mignon	Fillet	5 mm ($\frac{1}{4}$ inch)	Boneless
Piccata	Fillet	5 mm ($\frac{1}{4}$ inch)	Boneless
Tournedos	Fillet	2.5 cm (1 inch)	Boneless
Fillet steak	Fillet	2.5 cm (1 inch)	Boneless
Châteaubriand	Fillet	Whole	Boneless
		(500 to 750 g/	
		1 to 1$\frac{1}{2}$ lb)	

TYPES OF STEAK

Prime rib steak is cut from the prime rib in the forequarter. It is characterized by the rib, backbone, dorsal vertebrae, large eye muscle and an edging of fat opposite the rib.

Wing rib steak is cut from the wing in the hindquarter. This steak resembles the prime rib steak but is smaller.

Scotch fillet is cut from the boned sirloin and wing rib. It is a boneless steak characterized by the large eye muscle and an edging of fat. This steak resembles the entrecôte steak.

T-Bone steak is cut from the sirloin from the section nearest the wing rib. It is easily identified by the T-shaped bone flanked by a large eye muscle on one side and a smaller fillet on the other.

Porterhouse steak is cut from the sirloin from the section nearest the rump.

The steak resembles the T-bone but the fillet is larger and the steak is usually 5 cm (2 inches) thick. Only one Porterhouse steak can be cut from a hindquarter but because of its thickness the steak is usually enough to serve two persons. (See also glossary page 156.)

Fillet steak The fillet is situated under the lower backbone and runs from the sirloin to the rump. The meat has a fine texture and is boneless and very lean. The fillet in the sirloin section is usually removed separately and cut into fillet steaks. The fillet in the rump section is known as Châteaubriand. It weighs approximately 500 g (1 lb) and is normally sufficient to serve two persons.

Thin flank steak can be found between two layers of connective tissue in the flank nearest the leg, on the inside of the hindquarter. The steak is round without bone or fat. Score meat in a diamond pattern before cooking.

Rib-eye steak The large eye muscle can be removed from the prime rib along the natural seams and sliced into rib-eye steaks. These steaks consist of a large eye muscle without bone and without an edging of fat. The texture is slightly coarser than that of the fillet.

Minute steak When the connective tissue in the inner layer of muscle of the thick flank is removed, the whole muscle is then referred to as the mock fillet. The steaks cut from this are known as minute steaks and are about 5 mm ($\frac{1}{4}$ inch) thick, boneless and without fat.

Rump steak is cut from the boned rump and features a large muscle layer edged with fat.

Point rump steak is cut from the triangular muscle layer in the rump and is boneless with an edging of fat.

Entrecôte steak is also known as sirloin steak and is similar to Scotch fillet. The boneless steaks, cut from the boned sirloin, consist of a large eye muscle and an edging of fat.

Topside steak is cut from the triangular muscle layer in the topside more generally used for roasting. The upper surface is scored into a diamond pattern and the steak fried in butter on both sides. For optimum tenderness it should be served rare.

Tenderized steak These steaks are cut about 2 cm ($\frac{3}{4}$ inch) thick from the large muscle layers of the topside, silverside and thick flank. The steaks are then passed through a tenderizing machine which pierces the meat fibres. The steaks can be marinated and grilled or used for a stew as they tend to be dry because of meat juices escaping from the broken meat fibres.

1 Prime rib steak
2 Wing rib steak
3 Scotch fillet (boneless sirloin)
4 T-bone steak
5 Fillet steak
6 Rump steak
7 Entrecôte steak
8 Rib-eye steak
9 Point rump steak
10 Porterhouse steak
11 Minute steak
12 Thin flank (skirt) steak
13 Topside steak
14 Tenderized steak

GRILLED T-BONE STEAKS WITH CHEESE AND STUFFED MUSHROOMS

4 T-bone steaks
1 onion, finely chopped
4 reserved mushroom stems
(see stuffed mushrooms below), chopped
15 g ($\frac{1}{2}$ oz) butter
1 tsp coarse-grained mustard
125 g (4 oz) Gruyère cheese, grated

STUFFED MUSHROOMS
4 large black mushrooms, wiped
1 tbsp melted butter
2 slices ham, chopped
3 chives, snipped
30 g (1 oz) fresh breadcrumbs
freshly ground black pepper
to taste

First prepare the stuffed mushrooms. Remove stems and set aside for steaks. Place mushrooms, round side uppermost, on a baking sheet and brush with melted butter. Cook for 3 minutes under a pre-heated grill. Mix remaining stuffing ingredients and spoon stuffing onto each mushroom.

To prepare the meat, slash fat edges of meat at 2.5 cm (1 inch) intervals to prevent curling during cooking. Heat a ridged pan until smoking hot and cook meat for 5 to 7 minutes in total (rare) or 7 to 10 minutes in total (medium). Cook the mushrooms together with the steaks for 3 minutes.

Meanwhile sauté onion and reserved mushroom stems in heated butter until onion is translucent. Remove from heat and add mustard and cheese. When meat is cooked, remove immediately from ridged pan, spread topping over each steak and place together with mushrooms under a pre-heated grill until cheese has melted.

(4 servings)

VARIATION
☆ Add 60 g (2 oz) grated Cheddar cheese to stuffing for mushrooms.

HINT
☆ To keep mushrooms fresh, remove cling film from mushrooms and refrigerate between layers of paper towels in an airtight container.

SUGGESTED SIDE DISH
Wholemeal rolls

Grilled T-bone steaks with cheese and stuffed mushrooms

GRILLED FILLET STEAK WITH HERBS

4 fillet steaks
1 tbsp cooking oil
1 tbsp lemon juice
4 tsp dried or 3 tbsp chopped fresh parsley
2 cloves garlic, crushed
1 tsp dried or chopped fresh basil
freshly ground black pepper
to taste
1 tsp salt

Mix oil, lemon juice, parsley, garlic, basil and pepper. Roll steak in mixture and leave in refrigerator for 1 hour. Place meat on the rack of a grill pan and cook 10 cm (4 inches) under a pre-heated grill for 5 to 7 minutes in total (rare) or 7 to 10 minutes in total (medium), basting meat with remaining oil mixture. Season with salt and serve immediately.

(4 servings)

SUGGESTED SIDE DISH
Potato fritters

FILLET WITH CHICKEN LIVER TOPPING

6 fillet steaks
15 g ($\frac{1}{2}$ oz) butter
1 tbsp cooking oil
$\frac{1}{2}$ tsp salt
freshly ground black pepper
to taste
6 croûtes (page 154)

CHICKEN LIVER TOPPING
125 g (4 oz) rindless streaky bacon,
chopped
1 onion, chopped
1 clove garlic, crushed
250 g (8 oz) chicken livers, chopped
$\frac{1}{2}$ tsp salt
freshly ground black pepper to taste
1 cooking apple, peeled, cored and
grated
2 tbsp medium cream sherry
2 tsp dried or 2 tbsp chopped fresh
parsley
125 ml (4 fl oz) crème fraîche
(page 154)
snipped chives to garnish

First prepare the topping. Fry bacon lightly, add onion, garlic and chicken livers and fry until onion is translucent. Season with salt and pepper, then add apple. Cover with lid, reduce heat and simmer for 15 minutes or until liver is cooked. Spoon into food processor and chop coarsely. Stir in sherry, parsley and crème fraîche.

Fry meat on both sides in heated butter and cooking oil in a heavy-based saucepan for approximately 7 to 10 minutes in total. Season with salt and pepper. Place meat on croûtes, spoon chicken liver mixture over and garnish with chives. Serve immediately.

(6 servings)

VARIATIONS
☆ *Substitute brandy for the sherry.*
☆ *Add 125 g (4 oz) chopped mushrooms to the topping.*

HINTS
☆ *Chicken liver may be mashed with a fork if a food processor is not available.*
☆ *Croûtes can be prepared beforehand and stored in an airtight container.*

SUGGESTED SIDE DISHES
Thin green beans and onions
Crisp salad

Fillet with chicken liver topping

FLAMBE FILLET STEAKS WITH VEGETABLES

6 fillet steaks
30 g (1 oz) butter
3 tbsp brandy
salt and freshly ground black pepper
to taste
chopped fresh herbs to garnish

VEGETABLES
2 tbsp cooking oil
1 green pepper, seeded and cut into
julienne strips
1 red pepper, seeded and cut into
julienne strips
250 g (8 oz) mushrooms, sliced
1 clove garlic, chopped
$\frac{1}{2}$ tsp dried or 2 tsp chopped fresh
basil

Fry meat in heated butter in a heavy-based frying pan for approximately 7 minutes in total.

To prepare the vegetables, heat a heavy-based saucepan with cooking oil and sauté the green and red peppers, mushrooms and garlic until cooked but still crisp. Add basil, then spoon vegetables onto a serving plate and place fillet steaks on top. Heat brandy, pour over steaks and ignite. When flames have burnt out, season dish with salt and pepper, garnish with fresh herbs and serve imemdiately.

(3 servings)

VARIATION
☆ *Substitute carrots for the green and red peppers.*

SUGGESTED SIDE DISH
Buttered shell noodles

MARINATED RIB-EYE STEAKS

6 rib-eye steaks
salt and freshly ground black pepper
to taste

MARINADE
2 onions, chopped
2 cloves garlic, crushed
125 ml (4 fl oz) vinegar
3 tbsp soft brown sugar
5 tsp coarse-grained mustard
410 g (13 oz) canned whole
tomatoes, chopped

Mix marinade ingredients and marinate meat for 4 hours or overnight. Remove meat from marinade and pat dry with paper towels. Place on the rack of a grill pan and cook 10 cm (4 inches) under a pre-heated grill for 5 to 7 minutes in total (rare) or 7 to 10 minutes in total (medium). Baste meat with remaining marinade during last 3 minutes of the cooking time. Season meat with salt and pepper to taste and serve immediately.

(6 servings)

SUGGESTED SIDE DISHES
Potato chips
Green salad

WING RIB STEAKS WITH CRUMB TOPPING

6 wing rib steaks

CRUMB TOPPING
3 tbsp grated Parmesan cheese
5 tsp dried breadcrumbs
good pinch cayenne pepper
1 tsp dry mustard

First prepare the crumb topping by mixing all the ingredients together.

Place meat on the rack of a grill pan and cook 10 cm (4 inches) under a pre-heated grill for 5 to 7 minutes in total (rare) or 7 to 10 minutes in total (medium). Season steaks with salt and pepper to taste and sprinkle topping over 1 to 2 minutes before the end of the cooking time and grill until golden brown. Serve immediately.

(6 servings)

VARIATION
☆ Substitute seasoned dried breadcrumbs for the plain breadcrumbs.

SUGGESTED SIDE DISH
Ratatouille

OVEN-ROASTED PORTERHOUSE WITH MOCK PESTO SAUCE

1 Porterhouse steak

MOCK PESTO SAUCE
30 g (1 oz) chopped fresh parsley
3 cloves garlic, crushed
5 tbsp chopped walnuts
3 tbsp chopped fresh basil
2 tbsp cooking oil
2 tbsp grated Parmesan cheese
freshly ground black pepper to taste
250 ml (8 fl oz) crème fraîche
(page 154)

First prepare the sauce by mixing all the ingredients together.

Place meat on a rack in a roasting tin and roast at 160 °C (325 °F/gas 3) for 15 to 20 minutes per 500 g (1 lb) plus 15 minutes (rare) or 20 to 25 minutes per 500 g (1 lb) plus 20 minutes (medium). Allow meat to rest for 10 minutes, then carve into thin slices and serve with mock pesto sauce.

(3 to 4 servings)

HINTS
☆ Mock pesto sauce can be stored in a jar in the refrigerator for at least one month if the crème fraîche is not added to the remaining ingredients. Stir in the crème fraîche just before serving.
☆ Peel garlic, cover with oil and refrigerate in an airtight container for up to 3 months. Use garlic oil in pesto sauce and salad dressings.

SUGGESTED SIDE DISH
Carrots in orange liqueur

Wing rib steaks with crumb topping

RUMP STEAK WITH SWEET WINE SAUCE

2 rump steaks
½ tsp salt
freshly ground black pepper to taste

SWEET WINE SAUCE
3 tbsp port
125 ml (4 fl oz) white meat stock
(page 133)
½ tsp salt
freshly ground black pepper
to taste
2 spring onions, chopped
1 tsp prepared mustard
3 tsp plain flour

First prepare the sauce by mixing all ingredients together and bringing to the boil. Thicken sauce with a paste of flour and water and keep warm.

Slash the fat edges of the meat at 2.5 cm (1 inch) intervals to prevent curling during cooking. Preheat a ridged pan until smoking hot and grill the meat for 5 to 7 minutes in total (rare) or 7 to 10 minutes in total (medium). Season with salt and pepper and serve with the sweet wine sauce.

(2 servings)

VARIATION
☆ Substitute any sweet wine such as sherry or Madeira for the port.

SUGGESTED SIDE DISHES
Crisply fried onion rings
Tomato and lettuce salad

SMOKED CHATEAUBRIAND

500 g (1 lb) whole fillet
1 tbsp cooking oil
freshly ground black pepper
to taste
2 tbsp hardwood shavings

SAUCE
410 g (13 oz) canned peaches in
fruit juice
good pinch dried or 1 tsp chopped
fresh mint

Brush meat with oil and sprinkle black pepper over evenly, pressing it firmly onto meat. Sprinkle shavings along the sides of a heavy-based sacuepan. Place a rack in the saucepan and position the meat on top. Cover the saucepan tightly by placing a layer of foil over the top, followed by the lid. Place the saucepan on the cooker and turn heat to high for 40 minutes, then turn down to low for 10 minutes. Serve immediately with sauce.

To prepare the sauce, liquidize peaches and half of the juice. Add mint.

(4 servings)

VARIATIONS
☆ Substitute canned apricots for the canned peaches.
☆ Substitute porterhouse steak for the whole fillet.

HINT
☆ The wood shavings must be dry hardwood. Any resin in the wood tends to melt and to produce no smoke. Use apple or pear wood, or hickory chips if available.

SUGGESTED SIDE DISHES
Stir-fried courgettes
Rice timbales

SCOTCH FILLET WITH PRUNE STUFFING

4 Scotch fillets
salt and freshly ground black pepper
to taste

STUFFING
10 prunes, pitted and chopped
3 tbsp medium cream sherry
2 tsp grated lemon rind
1 tsp grated ginger root

First prepare the stuffing. Soak prunes in sherry for 15 minutes, then add remaining ingredients.

To prepare the meat, make an incision in each steak to form a pocket. Fill with stuffing and secure with cocktail sticks. Preheat a ridged pan until smoking hot and cook the meat for 5 to 7 minutes in total (rare) or 7 to 10 minutes in total (medium). Season the meat with salt and black pepper to taste and serve immediately.

(4 servings)

VARIATION
Mushroom stuffing: Mix together 90 g (3 oz) mushrooms, thinly sliced, 30 g (1 oz) fresh breadcrumbs, 5 tbsp double cream, 1 clove garlic, crushed, 1 tsp salt and freshly ground black pepper to taste.

HINTS
☆ Place meat in the freezer until firm before making the incision to form a pocket.
☆ If pitted prunes are unavailable, use a pair of kitchen scissors dipped in oil to remove the stones.

SUGGESTED SIDE DISHES
Parsley potatoes
Pumpkin slices with cinnamon

PRIME RIB STEAKS WITH VEGETABLE TOPPING

4 prime ribs steaks
½ tsp salt
freshly ground black pepper to taste

TOPPING
5 tsp sugar
5 tsp white vinegar
pinch cayenne pepper
1 small cucumber, thinly sliced
10 radishes, cut into julienne strips
2 spring onions, chopped

First prepare the topping. Mix sugar and vinegar until sugar has dissolved. Mix with remaining ingredients and allow to rest for 10 minutes. Drain and set aside.

To prepare the meat, slash fat edges 2.5 cm (1 inch) intervals to prevent meat from curling during cooking. Heat a ridged pan until smoking hot, then grill meat for 5 to 7 minutes in total (rare) or 7 to 10 minutes in total (medium). Season meat with salt and pepper and top with drained topping.

(4 servings)

HINT
☆ Steaks can also be grilled over a barbecue. The fire is ready when you are able to hold your hand 10 cm (4 inches) from the coals for 4 seconds. Cook for the same time as in a ridged pan.

SUGGESTED SIDE DISH
Hot herb or garlic bread

Front: Prime rib steak with vegetable topping   Back: Smoked Châteaubriand

GRILLED THIN FLANK STEAK

1 thin flank (skirt) steak, connective
tissue removed
freshly ground black pepper
to taste

MARINADE
3 tbsp Worcestershire sauce
3 tbsp soy sauce
2 tbsp chopped ginger root
2 tsp grated lemon rind
2 tsp dried or 2 tbsp chopped fresh
rosemary

First prepare the marinade by mixing all
the ingredients together. Pour marinade
over steak and marinate for at least 6 to
8 hours. Remove meat from marinade
and pat dry with paper towels. Cook 10
cm (4 inches) under a pre-heated grill for
5 to 7 minutes in total (rare) or 7 to 10
minutes in total (medium), basting meat
regularly with remaining marinade. Cut
the meat at a 45° angle into thin slices.
Season with pepper.
(2 servings)

SUGGESTED SIDE DISH
Creamy potato bake

BARBECUES

Just the thought of a sizzling summer barbecue is enough to make your mouth water. A few new ideas, hints and recipes for serving meat are always welcome for this quick, easy and informal way of entertaining.

AFFORDABLE BARBECUES

For many people, chops and sausages are synonymous with barbecues, which goes to prove how easily one ends up in a rut when it comes to preparing meat for outdoor cooking.

PURCHASING

Buy meat according to the number of guests. It is important to calculate portion sizes in advance as this will prevent overspending on meat.

When purchasing meat for a barbecue, always look for quality and make sure that the meat is reasonably well-hung or aged. It is vitally important to have meat that is tender and succulent.

ECONOMICAL MEAT CUTS
Kebabs
Meat can be cut into cubes, strips or slices.

HINTS
☆ *A variety of fruit and/or vegetables interspersed with meat can be threaded onto a skewer.*
☆ *Experiment with exotic marinades.*
☆ *Use cocktail sticks, bamboo sticks or metal skewers, which also enhance the appearance of the kebab.*
☆ *Serve kebabs with rice, pitta bread or any other bread or vegetable to suit your taste.*

Opposite top: Kasseler rib chops with rosemary mustard (page 109). Bottom: Lamb chops with barbecue sauce (page 107)

Ribs
Beef, lamb or pork ribs can make an entire meal.
Lamb: Serve chops or portions with a glaze or with a barbecue sauce.
Pork: Serve spareribs, strips of rib with a honey glaze or portions in a curry marinade.
Beef: Serve flat rib with barbecue sauce or crumbed ribs.

Whole cuts
Some whole cuts, such as a butterflied leg of lamb, beef fillet, Scotch fillet, fillet or pork loin, can be cooked successfully over the coals. The cooked cut is then carved and served to the guests. This is a very economical way to entertain as more people can be fed per kg (2 lb) of meat, thus reducing wastage.

Pot dishes
Prepare curry dishes in a three-legged pot over the coals, or rissoles or toad-in-the-hole in a flat-based pot.

Hamburgers
An economical way of entertaining is to let your guests create their own hamburgers. Prepare a number of hamburger patties plus a few sauces and place lettuce, tomato, onion, pineapple and slices of cheese in separate bowls.

HINT
☆ *Use the following to determine the temperature of the coals:*
Hot coals *are ash-grey in colour and allow you to keep your hand 10 cm (4 inches) above the coals for 2 to 3 seconds.*
Moderate coals *are totally grey in colour and allow you to keep your hand 10 cm (4 inches) above the coals for 3 to 4 seconds.*
Cool coals *are covered with a layer of grey ash and allow you to keep your hand 10 cm (4 inches) above the coals for 4 to 5 seconds.*

GLAZED LEG OF LAMB ON A SPIT

2 kg (4 lb) whole leg of lamb
2 tsp salt
freshly ground black pepper to taste

PEACH GLAZE AND SAUCE
1 kg (2 lb) canned yellow peaches, drained and puréed
90 ml (3 fl oz) brandy
3 tbsp chopped ginger root
3 tbsp soft brown sugar
$1\frac{1}{2}$ tsp cornflour

Remove the shank and pelvic bone, leaving the marrowbone in the middle. Thread the spit through the centre of the leg, parallel to the marrowbone, and tie string around the thicker part of the meat to make the shape of the joint as even as possible. Place a drip pan under the meat and arrange coals around it. Spit-roast about 15 cm (6 inches) above moderate coals for $1\frac{1}{2}$ hours, adding fresh coals from a second fire to ensure a constant temperature. Mix glaze ingredients, except cornflour, and baste meat frequently during the last 30 minutes. When meat is done, remove from spit and leave in a warm place for 15 minutes before carving into thin slices. Heat remaining glaze and thicken with a paste of cornflour and water. Serve with the meat.
(8 to 10 servings)

HINTS
☆ *A meat thermometer should register 70 °C (160 °F) when the leg of lamb is cooked.*
☆ *Cooking time may be shortened to 1 or $1\frac{1}{4}$ hours if the leg of lamb is grilled in a covered spit.*

SUGGESTED SIDE DISHES
Cracked wheat salad
Courgette salad

SMOKED RIB OF LAMB

Smoking may be done in a gas smoker which is simple to use. Unlike conventional barbecuing, smoker-cooking needs little, if any attention.

1 rib (rack) of lamb (8 ribs, 15 cm/6 inches long)
125 g (4 oz) Cheddar cheese, grated
315 g (10 oz) mushrooms, wiped and sliced
3 chives, snipped
2 tsp dried or 2 tbsp chopped fresh parsley
$\frac{1}{2}$ tsp salt
freshly ground black pepper to taste

Ask your butcher to remove the backbone to facilitate carving. Mix remaining ingredients together. Make an incision between the skin layer and the eye muscle and stuff cavity with cheese mixture. Secure with cocktail sticks if necessary. Place meat fat side uppermost on the rack of a smoker and set flame at its highest. Cook for approximately $1\frac{1}{2}$ hours (medium) or approximately 2 hours (well-done).
(4 servings)

HINT
☆ *This dish may also be prepared in a covered barbecue over moderate coals. Halve the cooking time.*

SUGGESTED SIDE DISH
Tomato and celery salad

LEG OF PORK WITH MANGO SAUCE

1 boned leg of pork, approximately 2 kg (4 lb), rind removed
410 g (13 oz) canned apple pie filling
410 g (13 oz) canned mango slices, drained and diced
2 tsp salt
freshly ground black pepper to taste
$\frac{1}{2}$ tsp dry mustard
250 ml (8 fl oz) unsweetened mango and pineapple juice
5 tsp cornflour

Combine apple pie filling and mango and use a third of the mixture to stuff the leg. Fold meat over and secure with string. Rub meat with seasoning, then place meat fat side uppermost on the grid of a pre-heated covered barbecue, positioning it over the drip pan. Insert a meat thermometer, cover with lid and cook to an internal temperature of 70 °C (160 °F).

Heat remaining fruit together with fruit juice and thicken with a paste of cornflour and water and serve with the leg of pork.
(8 servings)

VARIATION
☆ *Substitute canned lychees for the apple pie filling.*

SUGGESTED SIDE DISHES
German potato salad
Marinated broccoli

PORK NOISETTES WITH GINGER TOPPING

! boned loin of pork, approximately 1.5 kg (3 lb)
1 tsp salt
freshly ground black pepper to taste

GINGER TOPPING
2 onions, finely chopped
2 cloves garlic, crushed
3 tbsp chopped ginger root
15 g ($\frac{1}{2}$ oz) butter
2 tsp cooking oil
5 tsp soy sauce
5 tsp Worcestershire sauce
4 gingernuts, crumbed

First prepare the topping. Fry onion, garlic and ginger in heated butter and cooking oil until onion is translucent. Add soy and Worcestershire sauce and thicken with gingernut crumbs.

Sprinkle half the salt and pepper over inside of meat, then roll and tie meat with string at 2.5 cm (1 inch). Using a sharp knife, cut the meat between the strings into even slices. Grill noisettes over moderate coals for 7 to 10 minutes in total (medium) or 10 to 12 minutes in total (well-done). Season with salt and pepper and serve covered with ginger topping.
(6 servings)

HINT
☆ *Remove the rind before preparing a roll of pork – the rind tends to toughen when exposed to moist heat.*

SUGGESTED SIDE DISH
Green apple and lettuce salad

LAMB CHOPS WITH BARBECUE SAUCE

1.25 kg (2½ lb) boned loin of lamb
1½ tsp salt
freshly ground black pepper to taste

BARBECUE SAUCE
2 onions, chopped
3 cloves garlic, crushed
1 green pepper, seeded and finely chopped
1 tbsp cooking oil
410 g (13 oz) canned whole tomatoes, chopped
4 tbsp tomato paste
2 tbsp Worcestershire sauce
3 tbsp soft brown sugar
3 tbsp dry white wine or vinegar
1 tsp French mustard
freshly ground black pepper to taste
½ tsp salt

First prepare the barbecue sauce. Fry onion, garlic and green pepper in heated cooking oil until onion is translucent. Add remaining ingredients, cover, reduce heat and simmer for a few minutes.

Season inside of meat with half the salt and pepper. Shape into a roll and insert skewers through roll at 2.5 cm (1 inch) intervals. Using a knife, slice through meat between each skewer to form pinwheels. Cook meat over moderate coals or under a pre-heated grill for 7 to 10 minutes in total (medium) or 10 to 12 minutes in total (well-done). Season meat with remaining salt and pepper and serve with barbecue sauce.
(6 servings)

HINT
☆ *The barbecue sauce can be frozen successfully.*

SUGGESTED SIDE DISHES
Baked sweet potatoes
Salad platter

Left to right: Leg of pork with mango sauce; Pork noisettes with ginger topping; and Smoked rib of lamb

CURRIED LAMB STEW

1 kg (2 lb) of lamb, sliced
1 tbsp cooking oil
1 onion, sliced
3 cloves garlic, crushed
3 tbsp chopped ginger root
1 tbsp mild curry powder
1 tsp aniseed (optional)
1 dried chilli, crushed
$1\frac{1}{2}$ tsp salt
freshly ground black pepper
to taste
250 ml (8 fl oz) meat stock
(page 133)
125 ml (4 fl oz) unsweetened
apricot juice
1 tbsp lemon juice
12 fresh pickling onions
12 new potatoes
315 g (10 oz) carrots, cut into
chunks
500 g (1 lb) mixed dried apricots,
prunes, apples and sultanas

Brown meat in heated cooking oil in a heavy cooking pot. Add onion, garlic and ginger and fry until is translucent. Add curry powder, aniseed and chilli and fry for 1 minute. Season with salt and pepper. Add heated stock, apricot and lemon juice. Cover and simmer over moderate coals for $1\frac{1}{2}$ hours or until meat is tender. Add onion, potatoes and carrots and simmer for approximately 15 minutes. Add dried fruit and simmer until vegetables are cooked and dried fruit is tender.
(6 servings)

HINTS

☆ *If dried chilli is not available, increase curry powder to 4 tsp.*
☆ *Leave to simmer undisturbed, only checking occasionally that there is sufficient liquid. If necessary, add a little heated meat stock.*
☆ *Dumplings may be added – simply ensure there is sufficient liquid in the pot.*
☆ *Stews requires long, slow cooking over low heat. Add coals from a second fire from time to time to maintain a constant temperature under the pot.*
☆ *Add a few slices of potato to the meat to thicken the sauce.*

SUGGESTED SIDE DISHES
Brown rice
Banana salad with coconut

ROAST BEEF WITH SMOKED MUSSEL AND MUSHROOM SAUCE

Cooking in a covered barbecue is a new way of entertaining all year round in any climate, producing delicious meals for serving either indoors or out. Covered barbecues are available in a variety of sizes and brands.

1 well-hung or aged wing rib roll,
prime rib roll or rump,
approximately 1.5 to 2 kg (3 to 4 lb)
$1\frac{1}{2}$ tsp salt
freshly ground black pepper
to taste

SAUCE
30 g (1 oz) butter
125 g (4 oz) canned smoked mussels,
drained and oil reserved
1 large onion, chopped
250 g (8 oz) mushrooms, sliced
5 tsp plain flour
1 tsp salt
2 tbsp medium cream sherry
250 ml (8 fl oz) single cream

Insert a meat thermometer into the thickest part of the meat and place on grid above drip pan in a pre-heated covered barbecue. Cover with the lid and cook to an internal temperature of 60 °C (140 °F) (rare) or 65 °C (150 °F).
Meanwhile prepare the sauce. Combine butter and reserved oil, heat and sauté onion in mixture until translucent. Add mushrooms and fry lightly. Add flour and salt and stir until smooth. Add sherry, cream and smoked mussels and heat through.
(8 to 10 servings)

VARIATIONS

☆ *Substitute smoked oysters for the smoked mussels.*
☆ *Low-fat variation: Substitute plain yoghurt for the cream.*

HINT

☆ *When cooking meat in a covered barbecue, use a meat thermometer to determine when the meat is cooked. The weather can affect the cooking time – a longer cooking time should be allowed on cold or windy days and less in very hot weather.*

SUGGESTED SIDE DISH
Avocado and lychee salad

STUFFED CHUMP CHOPS

6 lamb chump chops
$\frac{1}{2}$ tsp salt
freshly ground black pepper
to taste

CHEESE AND HERB STUFFING
30 g (1 oz) fresh breadcrumbs
3 chives, snipped
$\frac{1}{2}$ tsp dried or 2 tsp chopped fresh
rosemary
60 g (2 oz) Gruyère cheese, grated
1 tsp lemon juice
2 tbsp toasted flaked almonds

First prepare the stuffing by combining the ingredients.
Make an incision in each chop to form a pocket, stuff chops and secure with cocktail sticks. Cook chops over moderate coals for 7 to 10 minutes in total (medium) or 10 to 12 minutes in total (well-done). Season, then serve.
(6 servings)

SUGGESTED SIDE DISH
Vegetable parcels

SPANISH-STYLE SAUSAGE

500 g (1 lb) pork sausages
2 tbsp cooking oil
2 large onions, chopped
2 cloves garlic, crushed
1 green pepper, seeded and cut into
julienne strips
500 g (1 lb) brown rice
$1\frac{1}{2}$ tsp salt
freshly ground black pepper
to taste
2 litres ($3\frac{1}{2}$ pints) white meat stock
(page 133)
500 g (1 lb) smoked sausage, sliced
500 g (1 lb) cocktail sausages
250 g (8 oz) button mushrooms
315 g (10 oz) frozen peas
410 g (13 oz) canned tomatoes,
coarsely chopped
2 tbsp tomato paste
2 tbsp medium cream sherry

Brown pork sausages in heated cooking oil in a shallow saucepan over moderate coals. Don't prick the sausages as this will cause a loss of meat juices. Move sausages to edge of pan and add onion, garlic and green pepper and fry until onion is translucent. Add rice, salt, pepper and meat stock and simmer for approximately 45 minutes, or until sausages and rice are cooked. Slice pork sausages and return to pan. Add remaining ingredients and simmer for another 10 minutes, adding more stock if necessary.

(10 servings)

HINTS

☆ *Use a shallow saucepan to prevent the rice from cooking to a pulp at the bottom of a deep saucepan.*

☆ *If a large shallow saucepan is not available, a paella pan will work just as effectively.*

KASSELER RIB CHOPS WITH ROSEMARY MUSTARD

8 Kasseler rib chops

ROSEMARY MUSTARD
2 tsp dried or 2 tbsp chopped fresh rosemary
2 tsp French mustard
2 tsp coarse-grained mustard
125 ml (4 fl oz) double cream
125 ml (4 fl oz) plain yoghurt

First prepare the sauce by mixing all ingredients together well.

Slash fat edges of meat at 2.5 cm (1 inch) intervals to prevent curling during grilling. Grill over moderate coals for approximately 5 minutes in total. Serve chops with rosemary mustard.

(8 servings)

HINT

☆ *Kasseler ribs are always pink even when cooked. This is due to the curing process.*

SUGGESTED SIDE DISH
Dried fruit salad

Front: Spanish-style sausage. Back: Curried lamb stew

MICROWAVE MEALS

For many years it was believed that red meat did not microwave well, that it always looked dull and unappetizing and tasted different. Those days are long gone. The discovery of variable power, the addition of herbs and spices to give colour and flavour, the use of basting mixtures and marinades have all contributed to the success of meat dishes cooked in the microwave oven. The introduction of the browning dish and the combination microwave oven has done much to popularize microwave meat cookery. Today meat cookery can be an unqualified success by combining favourite red meat recipes with modern technology.

Recipes for this book were tested in a 650/700-watt oven as this is the standard middle-of-the-range microwave oven available today.

☆ Do remember that power supply may differ from region to region and at certain times of the day, which affects the length of the cooking time. Use the cooking times given in the recipe as a guide only.
☆ A very important rule to remember is to undercook rather than overcook red meat.

Other factors which may influence the cooking time of meat are: the initial temperature, the shape and size of the meat, the fat distribution, the amount of power used during cooking, the meat cut used, and the amount of connective tissue and bone present in the cut.

Opposite top: Minute steak schnitzels (page 113). Bottom: Beef and pineapple stew (page 116)

HINTS
☆ Although it saves energy, red meat cooked in the microwave oven using moist-heat cooking methods takes almost as long as foods cooked conventionally. This is because long, slow cooking is required to convert the connective tissue into gelatine.
☆ To ensure an even heat distribution, cut vegetables and meat into similar sizes and shapes for stews and casseroles.
☆ Fat and sugar attract microwave energy which may lead to overcooking in some areas.
☆ Shield thinner parts of meat, sides of rolled meat and roasts with foil and remove halfway through the cooking time. Ensure that the foil is applied smoothly and that it does not touch the sides of the microwave oven.
☆ Large roasts or pieces of meat should be turned during the cooking time to ensure even heating.

SUITABLE CONTAINERS
☆ Round or oval containers in proportion to the prepared dish.
☆ Cooking bags secured with string or cellotape.
☆ Microwave pressure cookers, foil containers and browning dishes used according to the manufacturer's instructions.
☆ Paper towels or paper plates are useful to prevent splashing, to line certain dishes or absorb moisture.

UNSUITABLE CONTAINERS
☆ Cut glass, crystal, certain plastic, polystyrene, metal and china with metal rim.

TO IMPROVE THE APPEARANCE OF MEAT
☆ Top meat with dried or fresh breadcrumbs, grated cheese, paprika or fresh or dried herbs.
☆ Use the browning dish or brown under a pre-heated grill.
☆ Bard the meat with bacon.

POWER SETTINGS		
POWER	COMMON SETTING	USES
100%	high/full power	Browning meat Preheating browning skillet Cooking smaller cuts
70%	medium high/medium	Preparing tender roasts Cooking mince dishes Baking meat loaves Preparing dishes containing delicate ingredients such as eggs, cream and yoghurt
50%	medium/medium low	Cooking of pot-roasts, casseroles, stews Simmering/braising
30%	medium low/ low/defrost	Thawing both uncooked and cooked meat Simmering oxtail, tripe, tongue
10%	low/warm	Keeping foods at serving temperature

MICROWAVE ROASTING CHART

BEEF

Microwave	Time per 500 g (1 lb)	Internal temperature	Internal temperature after standing time
Rare	6 to 8 minutes	50 to 55 °C (120 to 130 °F)	55 to 60 °C (130 to 140 °F)
Medium	10 to 12 minutes	60 to 65 °C (140 to 150 °F)	65 to 70 °C (150 to 160 °F)

Combination	Time per 500 g (1 lb)	Combination setting	
Rare	10 to 12 minutes	30% microwave power 180 °C convection	
Rare	6 to 8 minutes	60% microwave power 200 °C convection	
Medium	15 to 20 minutes	30% microwave power 200 °C convection	
Medium	8 to 10 minutes	60% microwave power 299 °C convection	

LAMB AND MUTTON

Microwave	Time per 500 g (1 lb)	Internal temperature	Internal temperature after standing time
Medium	10 to 12 minutes	60 to 65 °C (140 to 150 °F)	65 to 70 °C (150 to 160 °F)
Well-done	12 to 14 minutes	65 to 70 °C (150 to 160 °F)	70 to 80 °C (160 to 170 °F)

Combination	Time per 500 g (1 lb)	Combination setting	
Medium	18 to 20 minutes	30% microwave power 180 °C convection	
Medium	9 to 11 minutes	60% microwave power 200 °C convection	
Well-done	20 to 22 minutes	30% microwave power 190 °C convection	
Well-don	12 to 15 minutes	60% microwave power 200 °C convection	

PORK

Microwave	Time per 500 g (1 lb)	Internal temperature	Internal temperature after standing time
Medium	10 to 12 minutes	60 to 65 °C (140 to 150 °F)	65 to 70 °C (150 to 160 °F)
Well-done	12 to 14 minutes	65 to 70 °C (150 to 160 °F)	70 to 80 °C (160 to 170 °F)

Combination	Time per 500 g (1 lb)	Combination setting	
Medium	18 to 20 minutes	30% microwave power 200 °C convection	
Medium	9 to 12 minutes	60% microwave power 220 °C convection	
Well-done	20 to 25 minutes	30% microwave power 200 °C convection	
Well-done	12 to 15 minutes	60% microwave power 220 °C convection	

ADVANTAGES OF THE MICROWAVE OVEN

☐ Microwave cooking saves considerable time by eliminating the need for preheating an oven or saucepan.

☐ Energy costs are minimized dramatically compared with an electric or gas cooker.

☐ Reheating cooked meat dishes is rapid and successful.

☐ The thawing and cooking of red meat is rapid and with no loss of meat juices or undue shrinkage.

☐ Vitamins and water-soluble mineral salts as well as flavour are retained because of reduced evaporation. Additional salt is therefore unnecessary but if used, it should be added at the end of the cooking time.

☐ No (or minimal) fat or cooking oil is needed for microwave cooking. This is a definite advantage in the quest for a healthier life-style.

☐ The microwave oven is easy to keep clean and reduces washing-up and is therefore labour-saving.

☐ It is compact and space-saving and easy to transport.

☐ The microwave oven keeps the kitchen cool and cooking odours are kept to a minimum.

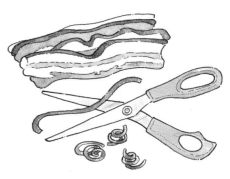

SHORT CUTS

☆ Uncooked bacon rind may be turned into an instant snack by placing the rind on an unwaxed paper plate, covering it with another paper plate and microwaving on 100% for 2 to 6 minutes (depending on the quantity of rind) until crisp.

☆ Heat brandy and other spirits for flambéing by microwaving on 100% for 30 seconds before igniting.

☆ Dry 60 g (2 oz) fresh breadcrumbs on 100% for 4 to 5 minutes. Stir every minute.

☆ Make crisp crumbs by tossing 185g (6 oz) dried breadcrumbs in 4 tbsp melted butter. Microwave on 100% for 4 to 6 minutes until crisp.

BREAST OF LAMB STEW

1 kg (2 lb) breast of lamb, sawn into
portions
1 onion, chopped
1 clove garlic, crushed
15 g ($\frac{1}{2}$ oz) butter
410 g (13 oz) canned whole
tomatoes,
chopped and liquid reserved
2 tbsp lemon juice
1 tsp sugar
$\frac{1}{2}$ tsp salt
freshly ground black pepper
to taste
2 tsp plain flour

Microwave onion, garlic and butter on
100% for 1 minute. Heat browning
dish according to the manufacturer's
instructions and brown meat for $2\frac{1}{2}$ to
3 minutes per side. Mix remaining
ingredients, except reserved tomato
liquid, and spoon over meat. Cover
with lid or cling film and microwave
on 100% for 5 minutes. Stir well, then
microwave on 50% for 20 minutes. Stir
and add heated tomato liquid to cover
meat. Microwave on 50% for another
20 to 25 minutes. Thicken sauce if
necessary with a flour and water paste
and microwave for 1 minute on 100%
or until sauce has thickened.
(6 servings)

VARIATIONS
☆ *Add 1 aubergine, cubed, to the
onion.*
☆ *Add 250 g (8 oz) courgettes, sliced,
10 minutes before end of cooking time.*
☆ *Make dumplings (page 134) and
add 10 to 15 minutes before end of
cooking time.*

SUGGESTED SIDE DISH
Buttered noodles

Breast of lamb stew

MINUTE STEAK SCHNITZELS

4 thin slices of beef, cut from
the thick flank (round) or topside
prepared mustard
30 g (1 oz) plain flour
1 tsp salt
freshly ground black pepper
to taste
1 egg, beaten
90 g (3 oz) dried breadcrumbs
4 tbsp cooking oil

Place meat between two layers of cling
film and flatten slightly with the palm
of the hand. Spread a little mustard on
one side of each steak. Season flour
with salt and pepper. Roll meat in flour,
then in egg and lastly in breadcrumbs.
Place meat in refrigerator for 20 to 30
minutes to allow breadcrumbs to set.
Preheat a browning dish according to
the manufacturer's instructions, add oil
and microwave on 100% for 1 minute.
Place steaks on browning dish and
microwave on 100% for $1\frac{1}{2}$ to 2 min-

utes. Turn and microwave for another
$1\frac{1}{2}$ to 2 minutes. Drain on paper towels
and serve immediately.
(4 servings)

VARIATION
☆ *Substitute thin slices of pork or
lamb for the beef.*

SUGGESTED SIDE DISHES
Creamed potatoes
Red and/or green cabbage with apple
and caraway seed

Ham and onion tart

HAM AND ONION TART

FILLING
155 g (5 oz) ham, chopped
4 large onions, chopped
30 g (1 oz) butter
2 tbsp plain flour
125 ml (4 fl oz) milk
125 ml (4 fl oz) single cream
3 eggs
$\frac{1}{2}$ tsp salt
freshly ground black pepper
to taste
1 tsp dried or 1 tbsp chopped
fresh marjoram
125 g (4 oz) Cheddar cheese, grated
1 tsp paprika

PASTRY
250 g (8 oz) plain flour
$\frac{1}{2}$ tsp salt
125 g (4 oz) cold butter, grated
approximately 4 tbsp iced water

First prepare the pastry. Sift dry ingredients together. Rub in butter, then add sufficient iced water to form a stiff dough. Roll out and line a 25 cm (10 inch) glass pie dish. Prick pastry with a fork, cover with a paper towel and fill with dried beans or rice. Microwave on 100% for 2 to 3 minutes, then remove paper towel and beans or rice and place pastry shell 10 cm (4 inches) under a pre-heated grill until golden brown and crisp.

To prepare the filling, microwave onion and butter on 100% for 4 minutes until softened. Stir in flour, microwave for 1 minute, then add ham. Beat milk, cream, eggs, salt, pepper and marjoram together. Add to onion mixture, mix well, then pour into pre-baked pastry shell. Sprinkle with cheese and then paprika. Microwave on 70% for 12 to 14 minutes until filling has set.

(4 to 6 servings)

VARIATION
☆ Substitute 1 onion and 200 g ($6\frac{1}{2}$ oz) mushrooms, wiped and sliced, for the 4 large onions.

HINT
☆ Combination oven: Temperature 200 °C, microwave on 30% for 25 to 30 minutes.

SUGGESTED SIDE DISH
Crisp green salad

PORK ROLL WITH SAVOURY PARSLEY STUFFING

1 kg (2 lb) boned belly of pork, rind removed
1½ tsp salt
freshly ground black pepper to taste
200 ml (6½ fl oz) peach juice
1 tbsp lemon juice
2 tsp apricot jam
1 tbsp plain flour

STUFFING
1 onion, chopped
4 tsp dried or 3 tbsp chopped fresh parsley
15 g (½ oz) butter
90 g (3 oz) cooked rice
½ tsp salt
freshly ground black pepper to taste

First prepare the stuffing by microwaving onion, parsley and butter on 100% for 1 minute. Add rice and seasoning and allow to cool.

To prepare the meat, sprinkle half the salt and pepper over inside of meat and spoon stuffing over. Roll up meat and secure with string. Heat browning dish according to the manufacturer's instructions. Place meat in browning dish and microwave on 100% for 5 minutes, turning every minute. Mix peach juice, lemon juice and apricot jam and heat in microwave oven. Add heated liquid to meat, cover and microwave on 50%, calculating the cooking time according to weight (see chart on page 112). Turn meat after half the cooking time has elapsed. If necessary, thicken the sauce with a flour and water paste and microwave on 100% for 1 minute or until thickened.

(4 to 6 servings)

VARIATIONS
☆ Add 2 celery stalks, chopped, to the stuffing.
☆ Add 60 g (2 oz) chopped almonds or pecan nuts to the stuffing.

HINT
☆ Combination ovens – see the chart on page 112.

SUGGESTED SIDE DISHES
Carrot and parsnip purée
Sweet potatoes

BRAISED BEEF WITH VEGETABLES

1 kg (2 lb) boned chuck or flat rib of beef
1 tsp salt
freshly ground black pepper to taste
1 clove garlic, crushed
2 tsp French mustard
1 tbsp paprika
1 tbsp plain flour
2 tsp dried or 2 tbsp chopped mixed fresh herbs
250 g (8 oz) potatoes, quartered
250 g (8 oz) frozen, sliced carrots
250 g (8 oz) frozen green peas or green beans
250 g (8 oz) rice, soaked in 625 ml (1 pint) water for 1 hour
1 tbsp plain flour

Mix salt, pepper, garlic and mustard and spread over inside of meat. Roll up meat and tie at intervals with string. Rub paprika, flour and half the herbs over outside of meat. Cover ends of roll with foil to ensure even cooking. Place meat in a cooking bag and secure with string. Pierce the top of the bag to allow steam to escape. Mix potatoes with remaining paprika and herbs, place in a cooking bag, secure with string and pierce. Place carrots, peas and rice, including the soaking water, in separate cooking bags, secure with string and pierce. Place all cooking bags in a suitable container, positioning the meat on top of the vegetable bags. Microwave on 100% for 45 minutes, then allow to stand for 15 minutes. Carefully remove meat from cooking bag and discard foil and string. Pour cooking liquid into a suitable container and thicken with a flour and water paste if necessary. Carve meat and serve with vegetables.

(6 servings)

VARIATIONS
☆ Substitute boned breast or shoulder of lamb for beef.

HINT
☆ If using fresh vegetables, add 5 to 6 tsp water to the vegetables in the cooking bags.

SUGGESTED SIDE DISH
Green salad

TASTY MINCE PIE

500 g (1 lb) minced beef
30 g (1 oz) butter
1 medium onion, chopped
1 clove garlic, crushed
1 tbsp plain flour
125 ml (4 fl oz) meat stock (page 133)
30 ml (2 tbsp) tomato purée
200 g (6½ oz) mushrooms, wiped and sliced
1 tsp salt
freshly ground black pepper to taste
good pinch dried or ½ tsp chopped fresh oregano

TOPPING
250 ml (8 fl oz) plain yoghurt
2 large eggs, beaten
3 tbsp self-raising flour
125 g (4 oz) Cheddar cheese, grated
good pinch salt
freshly ground black pepper to taste
1 tsp paprika

Microwave butter, onion and garlic in a casserole on 100% for 2 minutes. Add mince and mix well with a fork. Microwave on 100% for 5 minutes, stirring once. Add flour, heated meat stock and tomato purée. Mix well and microwave on 70% for 5 to 7 minutes or until thick. Add mushrooms and seasoning and transfer to an ovenproof dish.

To prepare the topping, beat all ingredients together except paprika. Pour over mince mixture, sprinkle top with paprika and microwave on 70% for 12 to 15 minutes or until topping has set.

(4 to 6 servings)

VARIATIONS
☆ Substitute 1 small aubergine, peeled and diced, for the mushrooms.
☆ Low-fat variation: Substitute low-fat mozzarella or quark for the Cheddar cheese.
☆ Substitute 200 g (6½ oz) minced pork for 200 g (6½ oz) of the minced beef.

HINT
☆ For combination oven: Temperature 180 °C, microwave on 30% for 20 to 30 minutes until topping has set.

SUGGESTED SIDE DISH
Cucumber and dill salad

SCOTCH FILLET WITH HORSERADISH AND BEETROOT CREAM SAUCE

1.5 kg (3 lb) whole Scotch fillet
2 tbsp cooking oil
2 tbsp brandy
2 cloves garlic, crushed
2 tbsp mustard seeds, crushed
freshly ground black pepper to taste
pinch allspice

SAUCE
2 beetroots, peeled and finely grated
2 tbsp fresh horseradish, peeled and grated
125 ml (4 fl oz) double cream
good pinch salt

First prepare the sauce by mixing all the ingredients together.

Preheat a browning dish according to the manufacturer's instructions. Tie meat with string to obtain an even shape. Place oil in dish and microwave for 30 seconds on 100%. Brown meat for 4 minutes on 100%, turning meat every minute. heat brandy, pour over meat and ignite. Mix garlic, mustard seeds, black pepper and allspice and sprinkle over meat. Place meat on a rack and, calculating the time by consulting the chart on page 112, microwave on 70%, turning meat once during the cooking time. Allow to rest before carving and serving with the sauce.

(6 servings)

VARIATION
☆ Substitute 4 Scotch fillet or rib-eye steaks for the whole cut. Microwave in a pre-heated browning dish on 100% for 2 minutes, turn and microwave for another 2 to 4 minutes.

SUGGESTED SIDE DISHES
Fried potatoes and onions
Vegetable medley

BEEF AND PINEAPPLE STEW

750 g (1½ lb) boned chuck steak, cut into cubes
1 onion, sliced
3 tbsp plain flour
410 g (13 oz) canned pineapple pieces,
drained and juice reserved
meat stock (page 133)
1 red pepper, seeded and cut into julienne strips
2 celery stalks, cut into chunks
3 carrots, cut into julienne strips
1 tbsp chopped ginger root
1 tbsp wine vinegar
1 bay leaf
1 tsp salt
freshly ground black pepper to taste
2 tbsp soy sauce

Preheat a browning dish according to the manufacturer's instructions. Brown meat and onion on 100% for 4 to 5 minutes. Stir in flour and microwave for another minute. Add sufficient meat stock to the reserved pineapple juice to make up 470 ml (¾ pint). Add to meat together with remaining ingredients, cover and microwave on 100% for 10 minutes. Reduce power to 50% and microwave for 1 to 1½ hours or until tender. Remove bay leaf.

(6 servings)

VARIATIONS
☆ Substitute topside or thick flank for the chuck steak.
☆ Substitute 1 tsp ground ginger for the fresh ginger.

HINT
☆ For combination oven: Temperature 180 °C, microwave on 30% for 1 to 1½ hours or until tender.

SUGGESTED SIDE DISHES
Brown rice
Glazed pumpkin

BOBOTIE

500 g (1 lb) minced beef
500 g (1 lb) minced pork
1 slice white bread
3 tbsp milk
2 onions, finely chopped
1 tbsp cooking oil
5 tsp mild curry powder
1 tsp turmeric
1 tbsp apricot jam
1 tbsp lemon juice
2 tbsp flaked almonds
1 tsp salt
freshly ground black pepper to taste
6 bay leaves or lemon leaves

TOPPING
3 eggs
375 ml (12 fl oz) milk
½ tsp salt
1 tsp paprika

Soak bread in milk and mash with a fork. Sauté onion in cooking oil in a bowl on 100% for 3 to 4 minutes. Add curry powder, turmeric and jam and microwave on 100% for 30 seconds. Add meat and remaining ingredients, except bay leaves or lemon leaves, and stir with a fork. Spoon meat mixture into a greased dish and arrange bay leaves on top. Microwave on 70% for 10 minutes. Combine topping ingredients, except paprika, beating thoroughly. Pour over meat, sprinkle with paprika and microwave on 70% for another 8 to 10 minutes until custard has set.

(6 to 8 servings)

VARIATION
☆ Add 60 g (2 oz) seedless raisins to the meat mixture.

SUGGESTED SIDE DISHES
Yellow raisin rice
Tomato salad

HAM WITH HONEY-NUT TOPPING

1.5 to 2 kg (3 to 4 lb) smoked ham
1 small onion
4 whole cloves
2 bay leaves
5 black peppercorns
470 ml (¾ pint) apricot juice
250 ml (8 fl oz) water

Ham with honey-nut topping

HONEY-NUT TOPPING
125 g (4 oz) chopped almonds
155 g (5 oz) thick creamy honey
1 tbsp each grated lemon and
orange rind

Place ham in a suitable microwave dish together with onion studded with cloves, bay leaves, peppercorns, apricot juice and water and cover with lid or cling film.

Calculate the cooking time at 10 minutes per 500 g (1 lb) and microwave on 70%, turning ham twice during the cooking time. Remove ham from liquid and cut away rind, leaving a thin fat layer over surface of meat. Score fat in a diamond pattern. Return ham to cooking liquid to cool completely.

Mix topping ingredients and spread over ham. Place ham in a shallow microwave dish and microwave for another 5 to 8 minutes per 500 g (1 lb), basting ham frequently with glaze. Allow to stand for 10 minutes before serving.
(10 to 12 servings)

VARIATIONS
☆ *Substitute any of the following for the apricot juice:*
- *pineapple skins and pineapple juice*
- *beer or cider*
- *grape juice*

☆ *See pages 58 and 59 for other glaze variations.*

SUGGESTED SIDE DISHES
Spiced peaches
Buttered cauliflower and broccoli

PRESERVED MEATS

Preserved meats are meats that have been prepared for instant use. Vienna sausages, frankfurters, smoked boiling sausages, ham, smoked beef and salami are only some of the large variety available. Preserved meats can be used to make anything, from quiches, savoury tarts, salads and spreads to fillings for pancakes and stuffings for potatoes and vegetables. Economical meals can be created using preserved meats with the addition of other ingredients.

BUYING PRESERVED MEATS
Make sure that the vacuum pack is free of air bubbles, which shorten the shelf life of the contents. If it is a good vacuum, the meat may be stored in the refrigerator for up to three weeks. Insist that cold meat be sliced fresh, while you wait.

To ensure that the meat is fresh, buy preserved meats at a delicatessen or supermarket with a large turnover.

STORING PRESERVED MEATS
Store preserved meats according to the instructions on the package.

Cut meat may be stored in an airtight container in the refrigerator for up to two days, while whole polonies or vacuum-packed preserved meats may be stored in the refrigerator for up to three weeks.

When an airtight package has been damaged or broken, transfer the contents to an airtight plastic container and use within two days.

FREEZING PRESERVED MEATS
Preserved products undergo changes in taste and texture when frozen. Only vacuum-packed meats may be frozen, and then for no longer than a month.

ADVANTAGES OF PRESERVED MEATS
☆ *They are an affordable red meat product which helps to balance the meat budget.*
☆ *They are tasty without requiring many additions.*
☆ *They are time-saving and convenient since they may be served as is.*
☆ *A large range of different products is available.*

COOKING PRESERVED SAUSAGES
Handle sausages carefully with meat tongs or an egg-slice. Forks damage the sausage casings, thus affecting the texture and taste.

Heating in water: Bring water to the boil in a saucepan. Add sausages and heat for 5 to 8 minutes without allowing the water to boil. Boiling may cause the casings to split.

Grilling: Brush sausages with a basting mixture or cooking oil and cook 10 cm (4 inches) from the coals or under a pre-heated grill for 5 minutes in total, turning regularly.

Frying: Heat a mixture of cooking oil and butter in a frying pan and stir-fry sausages until warmed through and golden brown.

Microwaving: Bring one medium-sized sausage to room temperature and microwave for 20 seconds on 100%. Add on an extra 10 seconds for each additional sausage.

Opposite clockwise from top: Hot potato salad with frankfurters (page 124); Savoury tart (page 121), and Ham-and-tongue croquettes (page 123)

TYPES OF PRESERVED MEATS

Liver sausage is prepared from sheep, ox or pig's liver. The meat is minced twice before being stuffed into casings. The mixture can also be stored in sterilized jars for later use.

Bratwurst is prepared from pork and beef. The meat is coarsely ground the first time, then seasoned and ground with a finer disc.

Bockwurst is a white sausage prepared from pork, beef and speck. More speck is added for a finer texture while leaner meat is used for a coarser sausage. After being ground, the sausage meat is processed into an emulsion which is blended with ice and seasoning. The sausage is boiled.

Bierwurst is prepared mainly from beef. Once it has been processed into an emulsion, mustard seeds are added. Depending on the type of casing used, this sausage may be smoked, cured, and then boiled before being offered for sale.

Smoked beef The round muscle of the silverside is particularly suitable for this purpose. The meat is cured for 16 to 18 hours, then smoked and hung for a week to dry before being sliced into paper-thin slices.

Smoked boiling sausages are prepared from a mixture of beef and pork. After the meat has been processed to an emulsion, additional coarsely ground beef and pork are added and the sausage meat is then stuffed into casings. The sausages are subsequently smoked and boiled.

Frankfurters and Vienna sausages are also prepared from beef and pork. Frankfurters are stuffed into thicker casings than Viennas.

Mettwurst and Teewurst are fine-textured, uncooked spreadable sausages which are prepared from beef and cured pork.

French polony is prepared from an emulsion of beef and pork, spices and salt and is stuffed into casings in a variety of sizes.

Mortadella is prepared from cured beef or pork. The German mortadella is seasoned with small cubes of speck and green almonds whereas the Italian mortadella is seasoned with peppercorns.

Cervelat is a German sausage prepared from minced beef and pork. It has a fine textrue and cuts easily into thin slices.

Salami is prepared from finely chopped beef or pork. It is seasoned wth herbs, spices and garlic, depending on its origin. It is sometimes lightly smoked. Salami is dried in controlled humidity rooms where special conditions apply.

Ham is prepared from cured or cured and smoked pork, which is always cooked before use.

Parma ham is prepared from pork and is never smoked or cooked. It is cured and left to mature under conditions similar to those applying to salami.

Meat rolls are generally an emulsion of beef and pork which is mixed with peppercorns, sliced hard-boiled eggs or olives, or flavoured as indicated.

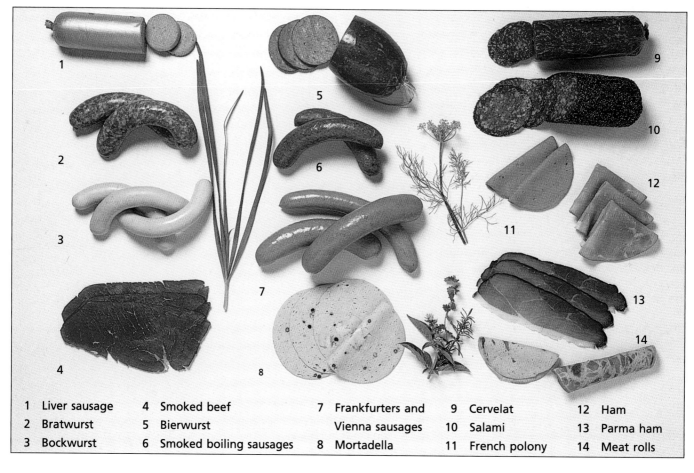

1	Liver sausage	4	Smoked beef	7	Frankfurters and	9	Cervelat	12	Ham
2	Bratwurst	5	Bierwurst		Vienna sausages	10	Salami	13	Parma ham
3	Bockwurst	6	Smoked boiling sausages	8	Mortadella	11	French polony	14	Meat rolls

SAVOURY TART

FILLING
250 g (8 oz) smoked boiling sausage, coarsely chopped
250 g (8 oz) rindless shoulder or back bacon, chopped and crisply fried
1 onion, chopped
2 tsp dried or 2 tbsp chopped fresh parsley
125 g (4 oz) Cheddar cheese, grated

SHORTCRUST PASTRY
185 g (6 oz) plain flour
pinch salt
90 g (3 oz) chilled butter, diced
3 tbsp iced water
2 tsp lemon juice

WHITE SAUCE
60 g (2 oz) butter
3 tbsp plain flour
$\frac{1}{2}$ tsp dry mustard
pinch cayenne pepper
$\frac{1}{2}$ tsp salt
freshly ground black pepper to taste
500 ml (16 fl oz) milk
3 eggs, beaten

First prepare the pastry. Sift together the flour and salt. Rub butter into flour until it resembles breadcrumbs. Mix water and lemon juice. Stir in and mix to a dough. Wrap in cling film and chill for 30 minutes. Place pastry on a lightly floured surface and roll out. Line a greased pie dish with pastry and prick base with a fork.

To prepare the white sauce, melt butter, add flour and seasoning and stir for 1 minute. Add heated milk and stir until thick and smooth. Cool slightly, then beat in eggs.

To prepare the filling, add sausages, bacon, onion, parsley and half the cheese to the white sauce and mix well. Pour filling into a pastry-lined pie dish, sprinkle with remaining cheese and bake at 180 °C (350 °F/gas 3) for 35 to 40 minutes.

(10 to 12 servings)

HINT
☆ *To colour and crisp the pastry shell before adding the filling, bake it blind (page 153).*

SUGGESTED SIDE DISH
Spinach salad

Savoury tart

SPINACH RAMEKINS

315 g (10 oz) pastrami, chopped
1 onion, chopped
1 tsp cooking oil
1 tsp butter
500 g (1 lb) fresh spinach, stalks removed and chopped
good pinch dried or $\frac{1}{2}$ tsp chopped fresh tarragon
2 tsp dried or 2 tbsp chopped fresh parsley
good pinch salt
freshly ground black pepper to taste
3 tbsp double cream
1 tsp grated lemon rind

Sauté onion in heated cooking oil and butter until translucent. Add spinach and stir-fry for 3 to 5 minutes. Add seasoning, cream and lemon rind. Spoon into liquidizer or food processor, add pastrami and liquidize to a purée. Spoon into greased ramekins and bake at 180 °C (350 °F/gas 4) for 10 to 15 minutes until heated through.

(6 servings)

HINT
☆ *Substitute small serving dishes for the ramekins.*

SUGGESTED SIDE DISH
Wholemeal bread

MEAT ROLL AND PASTA BAKE

155 g (5 oz) meat roll, cubed
250 g (8 oz) shell pasta
410 g (13 oz) canned chopped
tomatoes
1 onion, finely chopped
2 tsp Worcestershire sauce
1 tsp dried or 1 tbsp chopped fresh
basil
freshly ground black pepper
to taste
2 eggs, beaten
1 tsp lemon juice
90 g (3 oz) Cheddar cheese,
grated

Cook pasta according to instructions on packet and drain well. Mix together tomatoes, onion, Worcestershire sauce, basil, pepper, eggs and lemon juice. Layer meat, pasta, tomato and onion mixture and cheese in a greased oven-proof dish, ending with cheese. Bake at 180 °C (350 °F/gas 4) for approximately 20 minutes or until heated through.
(8 servings)

VARIATIONS
☆ Substitute Viennas, corned beef or cooked meat for the meat roll.
☆ Substitute spinach pasta for shell pasta for added flavour.
☆ Add 1 tsp dried or 1 tbsp chopped fresh oregano.

HINTS
☆ Add 1 tsp cooking oil to boiling water to prevent pasta boiling over.
☆ Garnish the dish with black olives.

SUGGESTED SIDE DISHES
Marinated courgettes
Mixed salad

PANCAKES WITH HAM AND CREAM CHEESE FILLING

FILLING
250 g (8 oz) ham, cut into strips
250 g (8 oz) cream cheese
1 tsp salt
freshly ground black pepper
to taste
1 onion, chopped
2 tsp dried or 2 tbsp chopped fresh
parsley
3 tbsp mayonnaise

Pancakes with ham and cream cheese filling

PANCAKE BATTER

125 g (4 oz) plain flour
pinch salt
2 eggs
250 ml (8 fl oz) milk
125 ml (4 fl oz) water
1 tbsp brandy or lemon juice
2 tbsp melted butter

First prepare the pancake batter. Sift flour and salt together. Beat the eggs and half the milk together and stir into flour mixture. Add remaining milk and water and beat to the consistency of thin cream. Add brandy or lemon juice and melted butter and allow to stand for at least 30 minutes before frying the pancakes.

Prepare the filling by mixing all the ingredients together. Place some filling on each pancake and roll up. Serve the pancakes warm.

(6 servings)

VARIATIONS
☆ *Cook pancakes in a crêpe pan. For individual servings, spread 3 crêpes with filling and stack them one on top of the other.*
☆ *Spoon filling onto one quarter of each pancake, fold pancake in half and then in half again.*
☆ *Substitute smoked beef or leftover roast meat for the ham.*
☆ *Substitute 1 leek for the onion.*

HINT
☆ *Pancakes may be prepared in advance and frozen. Thaw on a plate placed over boiling water or defrost on 30% for approximately 5 to 8 minutes in the microwave oven.*

SUGGESTED SIDE DISH
Avocado salad

MEAT AND POTATO CAKES

125 g (4 oz) meat roll, finely chopped
2 potatoes, peeled
1 egg, beaten
5 tsp milk
1 tsp dry mustard
$\frac{1}{2}$ tsp salt
freshly ground black pepper to taste
$\frac{1}{2}$ tsp grated lemon rind
$\frac{1}{2}$ tsp baking powder
cooking oil for shallow-frying

Grate potatoes coarsely, then combine with meat and remaining ingredients except baking powder. Mix well, then stir in baking powder. Fry spoonfuls of mixture in heated cooking oil until golden brown on both sides. Drain on paper towels.

(Makes 12 to 15)

HINTS
☆ *As potatoes discolour when peeled and exposed to air, grate them just before use.*
☆ *When a 2.5 cm (1 inch) cube of bread turns brown within 40 seconds, the cooking oil has reached the correct temperature for shallow-frying.*

SUGGESTED SIDE DISH
Summer salad

ASPARAGUS AND BACON QUICHE

250 g (8 oz) rindless bacon, chopped
410 g (13 oz) canned asparagus tips, drained
4 eggs
500 ml (16 fl oz) single cream
125 g (4 oz) Cheddar cheese, grated
3 spring onions, chopped
1 tsp dry mustard
freshly ground black pepper to taste

BUTTERMILK PASTRY
185 g (6 oz) plain flour
1 tsp salt
125 g (4 oz) butter, grated
125 ml (4 fl oz) buttermilk

Prepare the pastry: sift dry ingredients, then rub in butter until mixture resembles dried breadcrumbs. Stir in buttermilk and mix to a soft dough. Place in a plastic bag and chill for 20 minutes. Roll pastry out 5 mm ($\frac{1}{4}$ inch) thick and line a large quiche dish. Bake blind (page 153) at 200 °C (400 °F/gas 6) for 15 minutes or until golden brown. Cool.

To prepare the filling, fry bacon until crisp. Drain, then crumble and sprinkle over crust. Arrange asparagus on the pastry. Beat eggs well, add remaining ingredients, mix and pour over pastry. Bake at 160 °C (325 °F/gas 3) for 35 minutes or until set. Leave to cool slightly, then serve.

(6 servings)

VARIATIONS
☆ *Substitute smoked beef for bacon.*
☆ *Substitute cream cheese pastry (page 51) for the buttermilk pastry.*

HINT
☆ *Use asparagus liquid to prepare soups or stews.*

SUGGESTED SIDE DISH
Greek salad

HAM-AND-TONGUE CROQUETTES

155 g (5 oz) cooked ham
155 g (5 oz) cooked tongue
1 leek
$\frac{1}{2}$ green pepper, seeded
15 g ($\frac{1}{2}$ oz) butter
2 tsp cooking oil
2 tbsp plain flour
150 ml ($\frac{1}{4}$ pint) milk
pinch cayenne pepper
good pinch salt
3 tbsp plain flour
1 egg, beaten
60 g (2 oz) dried breadcrumbs
cooking oil for deep-frying

Finely chop ham, tongue, meat, leek and green pepper in a food processor. Fry in heated butter and cooking oil, then add 2 tbsp flour and stir for 1 minute. Add heated milk and seasoning, stirring until thick and smooth. Leave to cool, then shape into long croquettes. Roll croquettes in flour, then in egg and finally in breadcrumbs. Place in refrigerator for 20 to 30 minutes to allow crumbs to set. Deep-fry until golden brown, drain on paper towels and serve immediately.

(4 servings)

VARIATIONS
☆ *Low-fat variation: Cook croquettes under a pre-heated grill for 5 minutes per side.*
☆ *Substitute seasoned breadcrumbs for plain dried breadcrumbs.*

HINT
☆ *Croquettes may be frozen for up to 3 weeks. Roll in breadcrumbs again before frying.*

SUGGESTED SIDE DISHES
Lettuce with vinaigrette dressing
Tomato and onion salad

flour and salt in a bowl. Add vinegar and water and mix well. Microwave on 100% for 2 minutes or until the mixture comes to the boil, stirring once during the cooking time. Beat egg and stir in some of the hot sauce. Add egg mixture to remaining sauce in bowl and microwave on 50% for another 2 minutes until thick, stirring at 30 second intervals. Leave to cool slightly, then stir in the yoghurt and black pepper.

Hot potato salad with frankfurters

HOT POTATO SALAD WITH FRANKFURTERS

125 g (4 oz) frankfurters, sliced
2 potatoes, cooked, peeled and sliced
2 courgettes, cooked and sliced
60 g (2 oz) Cheddar cheese, grated

MUSTARD DRESSING
5 tsp sugar
1 tbsp dry mustard
$\frac{1}{2}$ tsp plain flour
good pinch salt
4 tsp vinegar
4 tbsp water
1 egg
3 tbsp plain yoghurt
freshly ground black pepper to taste

First prepare the mustard dressing. Mix sugar, mustard, flour and salt in a small saucepan. Add vinegar and water and mix well. Bring slowly to the boil. Beat egg and stir in some of the hot sauce. Add egg mixture to remaining sauce and stir over medium heat until thickened and smooth – do not boil. Leave to cool slightly, then stir in yoghurt and pepper.

Heat frankfurters in a saucepan with boiling water. Layer potato, courgettes and frankfurters in a greased ovenproof dish, ending with frankfurters. Cover with mustard dressing and sprinkle with cheese. Place under a pre-heated grill until cheese has melted.
(1 to 2 servings)

VARIATION
☆ Prepare mustard dressing in a microwave oven: Mix sugar, mustard,

KEBABS WITH HONEY GLAZE

315 g (10 oz) cocktail sausages
2 bananas
15 g ($\frac{1}{2}$ oz) butter
8 rashers rindless streaky bacon, halved
1 green or red pepper, seeded and cut into large cubes

HONEY GLAZE
5 tsp clear honey
1 tsp chopped ginger root
2 tsp lemon juice

To prepare the kebabs, cut bananas into 2.5 cm (1 inch) pieces and fry in heated butter for 1 minute. Wrap bacon around each piece of banana. Thread banana, sausages and red or green pepper alternately onto skewers.

Prepare the glaze by mixing all the ingredients together. Cook kebabs for 10 to 15 minutes under a pre-heated grill, turning regularly and basting with glaze.
(2 servings)

VARIATION
☆ Substitute 6 pitted prunes soaked in sherry for the bananas. The prunes can be stuffed with either smoked oysters or cottage cheese and chives.

HINTS
☆ To prevent bananas from discolouring, immerse in boiling water for 1 minute, then peel and use.
☆ Thread ingredients either onto cocktail sticks and serve as a snack or onto bamboo skewers and serve as a main dish.

SUGGESTED SIDE DISH
Carrot mould

QUICK AND EASY PIZZA

TOPPING
90 g (3 oz) salami, sliced and quartered
1 green pepper, seeded and cut into julienne strips
black olives (optional)
125 g (4 oz) mozzarella cheese, grated

TOMATO BASE
1 onion, chopped
1 clove garlic, crushed
125 g (4 oz) button mushrooms, coarsely chopped
1 tsp butter
3 tomatoes, skinned and chopped
$\frac{1}{2}$ tsp dried or 1 tsp chopped fresh basil
1 tsp sugar
good pinch salt
freshly ground black pepper to taste

SCONE DOUGH
125 g (4 oz) plain flour
$\frac{1}{2}$ tsp cream of tartar
good pinch bicarbonate of soda
good pinch salt
good pinch dried or $\frac{1}{2}$ tsp chopped fresh oregano
30 g (1 oz) butter
5 tbsp milk

First prepare the tomato base. Fry onion, garlic and mushrooms in melted butter in a heavy-based saucepan until onion is translucent. Add tomato, basil, sugar, salt and black pepper. Cover with lid, reduce heat and simmer for 10 to 15 minutes or until thick.

To prepare the dough, sift dry ingredients and add oregano. Rub in butter until mixture resembles fine breadcrumbs, then add milk and mix to a soft dough. Press dough into a greased 20 cm (8 inch) pizza plate. Cover with tomato base, followed by topping ingredients and ending with cheese. Bake at 180 °C (350 °F/gas 4) for 15 to 20 minutes.
(4 servings)

VARIATION
☆ Substitute 410 g (13 oz) canned tomatoes for the 3 tomatoes. Add remaining ingredients and simmer for 2 to 5 minutes. Substitute pizza dough (page 130) for the scone dough.

Smoked beef topping: *Spread tomato base over pizza and top with 90 g (3 oz) smoked beef slices, cut into strips, 1 green pepper, seeded and cut into julienne strips, 410 g (13 oz) canned artichoke hearts, drained, and 125 g (4 oz) Gruyère cheese, grated.*

SUGGESTED SIDE DISH
Italian salad

Quick and easy pizza

LEFTOVERS

No matter how carefully you plan, there is often meat left over after a meal. To balance your food budget, use this leftover meat to prepare an interesting meal to serve a few days later.

HINTS

☆ *Allow leftover meat to cool completely before freezing in an airtight container for not more than a month, or storing in the refrigerator for a day or two.*

☆ *Leftover meat should not be cooked again. Heat until just hot to prevent overcooking and serve immediately.*

☆ *Dishes using leftover meat should be well seasoned with, for example, fresh herbs, sautéed onion, green pepper and garlic.*

☆ *Use leftover meat to make croquettes, fillings for puffs and fritters.*

☆ *Marinate strips of leftover meat and create a meat salad or use as a filling for pitta bread.*

☆ *Mix chopped leftover beef with sufficient Béarnaise sauce and use as a filling for vol-au-vent, omelettes, pancakes or baked potatoes.*

☆ *Place a slice of ham and cheese on a croissant for breakfast.*

☆ *Mix chopped ham and soured cream and use to fill baked potatoes.*

☆ *Add 60 g (2 oz) finely chopped ham to the ingredients of your favourite mushroom or pasta sauce.*

☆ *Add cubed ham or sliced sausage to soup for added flavour.*

Opposite clockwise from top: Meat and carrot tart (page 130); Pizza (page 130); and Meat surprise (this page)

MEAT SURPRISE

FILLING
185 g (6 oz) cooked meat (beef, pork or lamb), coarsely chopped
$\frac{1}{2}$ red pepper, seeded and chopped
1 tsp butter
1 tsp cooking oil
5 tsp medium cream sherry
$1\frac{1}{2}$ tsp dried or 4 tsp chopped fresh parsley

POTATOES
5 spring onions, chopped
30 g (1 oz) butter
2 tsp cooking oil
4 medium potatoes, cooked and mashed
$\frac{1}{2}$ tsp salt
pinch cayenne pepper
125 g (4 oz) Cheddar cheese, grated
45 g ($1\frac{1}{2}$ oz) plain flour
2 eggs
125 ml (4 fl oz) milk
$\frac{1}{2}$ tsp baking powder

First prepare the filling. Fry red pepper in heated butter and cooking oil. Mix with meat, sherry and parsley.

To prepare the potatoes, sauté spring onion in heated butter and cooking oil. Add to potato with salt, pepper, cheese and flour. Beat eggs and milk together and stir in. Sprinkle baking powder over and mix well. Spoon potato mixture into ramekins and make a hollow in the centre. Bake at 180 °C (350 °F/gas 4) for 10 minutes. Spoon in filling and bake for another 10 minutes.

(6 servings)

VARIATION

☆ *Add 60 g (2 oz) mushrooms to filling.*

SUGGESTED SIDE DISH
Green beans with nutmeg

MOCK SOUFFLE

315 g (10 oz) cooked savoury mince (page 90)
60 g (2 oz) butter
3 tbsp plain flour
$\frac{1}{2}$ tsp dry mustard
pinch cayenne pepper
$\frac{1}{2}$ tsp salt
250 ml (8 fl oz) milk
60 g (2 oz) Cheddar cheese, grated
1 tsp dried or 2 tsp chopped fresh parsley
1 tbsp medium cream sherry
4 eggs, separated

Melt butter in a heavy-based saucepan, add flour, mustard, pepper and salt. Fry for 1 minute, then add heated milk, stirring continuously until mixture is thick and smooth. Stir in mince, cheese, parsley and sherry. Beat egg yolks and slowly add to meat mixture. Whisk egg whites until stiff but not dry and fold into mixture. Pour into a greased soufflé dish and bake at 180 °C (350 °F/gas 4) for 35 to 40 minutes in a *bain-marie* (page 153). Turn off oven and leave soufflé in oven for another 5 minutes.

(4 servings)

VARIATION

☆ *Substitute any leftover or cold meat for the mince.*

HINTS

☆ *The soufflé should be golden brown and puffed when ready. Test by inserting a skewer. if it comes out clean, the soufflé is cooked.*

☆ *Beaten egg whites are the correct consistency when they are snow white, fine textured and form soft peaks.*

SUGGESTED SIDE DISHES
Buttered baby carrots and green peas
Green salad

French omelettes with meat fillings

FRENCH OMELETTES WITH MEAT FILLINGS

OMELETTES
12 eggs
125 ml (4 fl oz) water
30 g (1 oz) butter

FILLING 1
250 g (8 oz) cooked meat, chopped
1 onion, chopped
1 clove garlic, crushed
2 tsp butter
125 g (4 oz) button mushrooms, quartered
1 tomato, skinned and chopped
$\frac{1}{2}$ tsp salt
freshly ground black pepper to taste

FILLING 2
125 g (4 oz) cooked meat, coarsely chopped
75 g ($2\frac{1}{2}$ oz) butter
75 g ($2\frac{1}{2}$ oz) plain flour
$\frac{1}{2}$ tsp salt
freshly ground black pepper to taste
375 ml (12 fl oz) milk
3 spring onions, chopped
125 g (4 oz) Cheddar cheese, grated

FILLING 3
250 g (8 oz) cooked sausage, sliced
2 spring onions, chopped
1 tsp butter
freshly ground black pepper to taste
5 tbsp soured cream
$\frac{1}{2}$ tsp dried or 2 tsp chopped fresh tarragon
60 g (2 oz) Cheddar cheese, grated

First prepare the fillings.

Filling 1: Sauté onion and garlic in heated butter in a heavy-based saucepan until onion is translucent. Add mushrooms and fry lightly. Add remaining ingredients and heat thoroughly.

Filling 2: Melt butter in a saucepan. Add flour, salt and pepper and fry for 1 minute. Add heated milk and stir until thick and smooth. Stir in meat, spring onion and cheese.

Filling 3: Sauté spring onions in heated butter in a heavy-based frying pan until translucent. Add sausage and heat through. Stir in the remaining ingredients.

To prepare the omelettes, beat eggs and add water. Heat butter in a heavy-based frying pan. Pour sufficient egg mixture into pan to cover base and cook over moderate heat, lifting edges with a spatula to allow uncooked egg to run underneath. Do not turn it over. Spoon filling of your choice onto one half of the omelette, fold omelette over and turn out onto a warm plate. Serve immediately. Repeat the process with remaining egg mixture.

(10 servings)

HINTS

☆ *Instead of preparing individual omelettes, make one large omelette in a large pan. Spoon filling on top and slice omelette into portions.*

☆ *Do not add salt and pepper to the omelette mixture as it may cause discoloration. Rather add the seasoning to the filling.*

☆ *For one omelette you will need: 2 eggs, 5 tsp water and 1 tsp butter.*

HAM AND RICE CAKES

155 g (5 oz) leftover ham, chopped
125 g (4 oz) plain flour
1 tsp baking powder
good pinch salt
125 g (4 oz) cooked rice
150 ml ($\frac{1}{4}$ pint) soured cream
200 ml ($6\frac{1}{2}$ fl oz) milk
2 eggs, separated
1 tbsp melted butter
1 tsp dried or 1 tbsp chopped
fresh dill
cooking oil for shallow-frying

Sift flour, baking powder and salt together. Add ham and rice and mix lightly. Mix soured cream, milk and egg yolks together and add to meat mixture. Add butter and dill. Beat egg whites until stiff, then fold lightly into mixture. Spoon serving portions into heated cooking oil and fry until cooked and golden brown. Drain on paper towels.

(8 servings)

VARIATIONS

☆ *Substitute any leftover meat for the ham.*

☆ *Substitute whole kernel corn for the cooked rice.*

SUGGESTED SIDE DISH
Salad platter with blue cheese salad dressing

Breakfast muffins

MEAT FRITTERS

500 g (1 lb) cooked meat, cut into
long, narrow strips
1 tsp prepared mustard
cooking oil for shallow-frying

BATTER
125 g (4 oz) plain flour
1 tsp baking powder
good pinch salt
1 banana, mashed
2 eggs, beaten
90 ml (3 fl oz) milk

First prepare the batter. Sift dry ingredients together. Mix banana, eggs and milk and beat into dry ingredients.

To prepare the meat, spread each strip with mustard and dip into batter. Shallow-fry until golden brown, drain on paper towels and serve immediately.

(4 servings)

VARIATION

☆ *Serve as part of a fondue: Dip cubed meat in the prepared batter and deep-fry in a fondue pot.*

SUGGESTED SIDE DISH
Mixed salad

BREAKFAST MUFFINS

200 g ($6\frac{1}{2}$ oz) cooked beef, minced or
coarsely chopped
250 g (8 oz) plain flour
2 tsp baking powder
pinch cayenne pepper
$\frac{1}{2}$ tsp salt
4 eggs, beaten
315 ml ($\frac{1}{2}$ pint) meat stock
(page 133)
60 g (2 oz) Cheddar cheese,
grated
4 tsp dried or 3 tbsp chopped
fresh parsley
2 courgettes, grated

Sift flour, baking powder, pepper and salt together. Mix remaining ingredients and add to dry ingredients. Mix lightly but thoroughly. Spoon into greased muffin tins, filling them two-thirds full. Bake at 180 °C (350 °F/gas 4) for 12 to 15 minutes.

(6 servings)

HINT

☆ *Bake tiny muffins and serve them as a snack.*

SUGGESTED SIDE DISH
Fresh fruit

MEAT AND CARROT TART

4 carrots, grated
good pinch aniseed
60 g (2 oz) melted butter
60 g (2 oz) plain flour
1 egg, beaten
2 tbsp orange juice

FILLING

200 g (6½ oz) cooked meat, coarsely
minced
2 leeks, sliced
2 tsp cooking oil
2 courgettes, grated
good pinch dried or ½ tsp chopped
fresh mint
125 ml (4 fl oz) soured cream
1 egg, beaten
60 g (2 oz) Cheddar cheese,
grated

Boil carrots in a little salted water for 3 minutes. Drain and mix with remaining ingredients. Spread over base and sides of the pie dish.

To prepare the filling, sauté leeks in heated cooking oil for 2 minutes. Mix with remaining ingredients except cheese. Spoon filling into pie dish and sprinkle with cheese. Bake at 180 °C (350 °F/gas 4) for 30 to 45 minutes or until set.

(4 servings)

HINT

☆ Substitute 345 g (11 oz) mashed potatoes for the carrots.

SUGGESTED SIDE DISH

Lettuce with cucumber

APPLE AND CORNED BEEF PIES

410 g (13 oz) frozen shortcrust
pastry, thawed

FILLING

410 g (13 oz) minced corned beef
2 tsp lemon juice
4 tsp dry white wine
2 cooking apples, cored and
coarsely grated
1 onion, chopped
good pinch dried or ½ tsp chopped
fresh marjoram
1 tsp French mustard
½ tsp salt

First prepare the filling. sprinkle lemon juice and wine over apples to prevent discoloration. Add remaining ingredients and mix well.

To assemble the pies, roll out pastry thinly and cut into 30 x 4 cm (1¾ inch) squares. Place 10 squares on a greased baking sheet and spread with half the filling. Top each with another pastry square and spread with remaining filling. Top with remaining pastry squares. Brush pastry with milk and bake at 200 °C (400 °F/gas 6) for 12 to 15 minutes or until golden brown.

(Makes 10 pies)

VARIATIONS

☆ Use a 7.5 cm (3 inch) fluted pastry cutter to stamp out 20 rounds. Top each with a heaped tablespoon of filling, moisten edges, fold over and press with a fork to seal. Bake as above.
☆ Sprinkle sesame or poppy seeds over pastry before baking.

SUGGESTED SIDE DISH

Three bean salad

PIZZA

TOPPING

250 g (8 oz) cooked meat, cubed
1 onion, chopped
2 tsp cooking oil
2 large tomatoes, skinned and
chopped
2 tsp dried or 2 tbsp chopped
fresh parsley
½ tsp salt
freshly ground black pepper
to taste
½ tsp dried or 2 tsp chopped fresh
oregano
155 g (5 oz) Cheddar cheese,
grated

DOUGH

½ tsp dried yeast
125 ml (4 fl oz) lukewarm milk
1 tsp sugar
15 g (½ oz) melted butter
2 eggs, beaten
250 g (8 oz) plain flour
1 tsp salt

Apple and corned beef pies

First prepare the dough. Combine yeast, milk and sugar in a small bowl and set aside until foamy. Stir in butter and eggs. Sift flour and salt, make a well in the centre and add yeast mixture. Mix to a soft dough. Knead until elastic, then place in a greased bowl, turning dough to grease it all over. Leave in a warm place for 25 minutes to rise. Punch dough down and knead briefly on a floured wooden board. Roll out dough into two 5 mm ($\frac{1}{4}$ inch) thick rounds. Place on a greased baking sheet, cover and leave to rise for about 15 minutes.

Meanwhile prepare the topping. Sauté onion in heated cooking oil until translucent. Add tomato and seasoning and simmer for 5 minutes. Cool slightly, then spread over dough and top with meat and cheese. Bake at 200 °C (400 °F/gas 6) for 15 to 20 minutes.

(6 servings)

VARIATION

☆ *Add one or more of the following ingredients to the topping: Slices of mushroom, red or green pepper, black olives, anchovies, pineapple chunks, bacon, salami, ham or grated Parmesan cheese.*

HINT

☆ *To save time use fast-action dried yeast instead of standard dried yeast, stirring it into the flour before adding the remaining ingredients.*

SUGGESTED SIDE DISH
Italian salad

MEAT ROULADE

ROULADE
1 small onion, grated
75 g (2$\frac{1}{2}$ oz) butter
60 g (2 oz) plain flour
good pinch salt
500 ml (16 fl oz) milk
4 eggs, separated

FILLING
250 g (8 oz) cooked meat, cubed
1 avocado, peeled and cubed
$\frac{1}{2}$ tsp lemon juice
4 tsp mayonnaise
3 gherkins, finely chopped
4 drops Tabasco
good pinch salt
freshly ground black pepper to taste

Meat roulade

To prepare the roulade, sauté onion in heated butter. Stir in flour and salt and stir for 1 minute. Add heated milk gradually and stir until thick and smooth. Leave to cool, then stir in egg yolks. Beat egg whites to soft-peak stage and fold into mixture. Pour mixture into a greased Swiss roll tin and bake at 180 °C (350 °F/gas 4) for 30 to 35 minutes. Leave to cool, then turn out onto a damp tea-towel.

To prepare the filling, mix ingredients together and spread over roulade. Roll up like a Swiss roll, using the tea-towel as an aid.

Place roulade on a serving dish, cut into slices and serve cold.

(6 servings)

SUGGESTED SIDE DISHES
Grapefruit and watercress salad
Macaroni and vegetable salad

SOUPS

Always popular and versatile, soup may be served as a starter or as the main course. During the cold winter months in particular, hearty and nourishing soup is always welcome. Soup that has been prepared and frozen in advance makes an ideal convenience food when unexpected guests arrive.

MEAT STOCK
Brown meat stock, prepared from marrowbones and shin of beef, and white meat stock, usually prepared from veal, are normally used as a base for tasty, nourishing soups.

STORING AND FREEZING MEAT STOCK
Meat stock can be stored in a refrigerator for two to three days and can be frozen successfully for up to two months.

BROWN MEAT STOCK

2 kg (4 lb) shin of beef, sliced
6 baby carrots
2 onions, with skin
1 celery stalk, cut into chunks
1 bouquet garni (page 17)
1 tbsp vinegar
3 litres (5 pints) cold water

Place meat in a large roasting tin and roast at 160 °C (325 °F/gas 3) for 30 minutes. Transfer to a large heavy-based saucepan and add remaining ingredients. Bring to the boil and skim. Cover with lid, reduce heat and simmer for 4 hours. Skim frequently and replenish with boiling water if necessary. Strain, skim off fat, then strain again.
Makes 2 litres (3$\frac{1}{2}$ pints)

Opposite clockwise from top: Bean soup (page 135); Vegetable soup with meat strips (page 136); and Pumpkin soup (this page)

HINTS
☆ *To remove fat from meat stock: Tie a few ice cubes in a piece of muslin and pull it carefully over the surface of the stock.*
☆ *Allow the stock to cool. The congealed fat layer can then be lifted off easily.*
☆ *Do not omit vinegar when preparing stock. It encourages the extraction of meat juices.*
☆ *To clarify stock: Remove fat from cold stock. Pour stock into a saucepan with two lightly beaten egg whites and 2 crushed egg shells. Bring slowly to the boil, whisking occasionally. Boil for 2 minutes and strain.*

GARNISHING OF SOUP

- ☐ crisply fried bacon
- ☐ croûtons
- ☐ cream or soured cream
- ☐ grated Cheddar cheese or Parmesan cheese
- ☐ a sprig of herbs
- ☐ chopped fresh herbs
- ☐ blanched vegetables, cut into julienne strips
- ☐ sautéed mushrooms
- ☐ thin slices lemon
- ☐ sliced smoked sausage
- ☐ toasted almonds
- ☐ egg custard shapes
- ☐ potato croûtons
- ☐ finely chopped hard-boiled egg

ACCOMPANIMENTS

- ☐ Melba toast
- ☐ herb butter toast
- ☐ warm herb scones
- ☐ garlic bread
- ☐ wholemeal rolls or home-made bread
- ☐ cheese puffs
- ☐ cheese straws
- ☐ cheese croûtons
- ☐ savoury biscuits
- ☐ pretzels

WHITE MEAT STOCK

2 kg (4 lb) of veal, sliced
6 small carrots
3 leeks, cut into chunks
1 celery stalk, cut into chunks
1 bouquet garni
3 litres (5 pints) cold water

Place all the ingredients in a heavy-based saucepan. Bring to the boil and skim. Cover, reduce heat and simmer for approximately 4 hours. Skim frequently and replenish with boiling water if necessary. Strain, skim off fat, then strain again. Adjust seasoning if necessary.
Makes 2 litres (3$\frac{1}{2}$ pints)

PUMPKIN SOUP

1 onion, chopped
1 clove garlic, crushed
2 tsp cooking oil
2 tsp butter
1 kg (2 lb) pumpkin, peeled and cubed
1 litre (1$\frac{3}{4}$ pints) white meat stock (see above)
1 cinnamon stick
1 tsp salt
freshly ground black pepper to taste
125 ml (4 fl oz) double cream

Sauté onion and garlic in heated cooking oil and butter until translucent. Add remaining ingredients except cream and simmer until pumpkin is tender. Remove cinnamon. Liquidize soup, then reheat. Stir in cream.
(4 servings)

HINT
☆ *Add more stock if soup is too thick.*
☆ *Serve soup hot or cold.*

SUGGESTED SIDE DISH
Melba toast with apple butter

TOMATO SOUP WITH DUMPLINGS

500 g (1 lb) boned thick rib of
mutton, cut into cubes
2 tbsp cooking oil
2 onions, sliced
3 carrots, sliced
$\frac{1}{2}$ tsp dried or 1 tsp chopped fresh
basil
1 tsp salt
freshly ground black pepper to taste
410 g (13 oz) canned whole
tomatoes, chopped
1 litre ($1\frac{3}{4}$ pints) meat stock (page
133)

DUMPLINGS

250 g (8 oz) plain flour
4 tsp baking powder
good pinch salt
60 g (2 oz) butter
250 ml (8 fl oz) tomato purée
5 tbsp water
2 tsp dried or 2 tbsp chopped fresh
parsley

To prepare the soup, brown meat in
heated cooking oil in a heavy-based
saucepan. Add onion and carrot and
fry until onion is translucent. Add seasoning, tomato and meat stock. Bring
to the boil, cover with lid, reduce heat
and simmer until meat is tender.

To prepare the dumplings, sift flour,
baking powder and salt. Rub in butter,
then add tomato purée, water and
parsley and mix lightly to a soft
dough. Drop teaspoonfuls of dough
into soup, cover with lid and simmer
for 30 minutes without removing lid.
(6 servings)

VARIATION

☆ *Substitute rissoles (see below) for
the thick rib of mutton and dumplings.
Simmer the basic tomato soup for 15
minutes, then carefully add rissoles and
simmer for 30 minutes or until cooked
through.*

*Rissoles: Mix together 315 g (10 oz)
minced beef, 1 onion, chopped, 1 slice
wholemeal bread, crumbed, $\frac{1}{2}$ tsp dried
or 1 tsp chopped fresh oregano, 1 tsp
salt and freshly ground black pepper to
taste. Lightly fold in 1 stiffly beaten egg
white, then shape into small rissoles.*

Left to right: Bean soup (page 135); Mixed
vegetable soup; and Tomato soup with
dumplings

MIXED VEGETABLE SOUP

250 g (8 oz) shank of mutton, sliced
2 litres ($3\frac{1}{2}$ pints) meat stock
(page 133)
3 tbsp rice
3 tomatoes, skinned and chopped
125 g (4 oz) spinach, stalks removed
and shredded
2 celery stalks, chopped
125 g (4 oz) green beans, thinly
sliced
2 carrots, peeled and grated
2 tsp salt
freshly ground black pepper to taste
good pinch dried or $\frac{1}{2}$ tsp chopped
fresh thyme

Place all ingredients in a heavy-based saucepan and bring to the boil. Cover with lid, reduce heat and simmer for 2 hours.

(4 servings)

VARIATIONS
☆ *Substitute 410 g (13 oz) canned whole tomatoes for the 3 tomatoes.*
☆ *Substitute courgettes for the green beans.*

SUGGESTED SIDE DISH
Garlic cheese bread

BEAN SOUP

250 g (8 oz) shin of beef, sliced
200 g (6½ oz) uncooked kidney beans
1 litre (1¾ pints) meat stock
(page 133)
1 onion, chopped
3 tomatoes, skinned and chopped
1 large potato, peeled and grated
½ tsp paprika
2 tsp salt
freshly ground black pepper
to taste
2 to 3 rashers rindless bacon,
chopped
4 tsp dried or 3 tbsp chopped
fresh parsley

First prepare the beans by rinsing them under cold running water and soaking them in cold water to cover overnight. Drain and rinse under cold water.

To prepare the soup, place meat and soaked beans in a large saucepan. Add stock, bring to the boil and boil rapidly for 10 minutes. Then simmer for 2 hours or until meat is tender. Replenish liquid with stock if necessary. Remove meat and cut into cubes. Purée half the beans in a liquidizer or rub through a sieve. Return meat cubes and puréed beans to soup. Add remaining ingredients except bacon and parsley and simmer for 30 minutes. Fry bacon until crisp. Sprinkle bacon and parsley over soup just before serving.

(4 servings)

VARIATION
☆ *Substitute cubes of ham or smoked beef for the bacon.*

HINT
☆ *To reduce soaking time of beans, boil rapidly for 5 minutes, then cover and allow to soak for 1 hour in the same water. Drain and use as directed.*

SUGGESTED SIDE DISH
Wholemeal rolls with herb butter

CURRY SOUP

500 g (1 lb) minced beef
2 onions, chopped
2 cloves garlic, crushed
4 tsp chopped ginger root
1 tbsp cooking oil
4 tsp mild curry powder
4 carrots, sliced
1 cooking apple, cored and grated
2 tsp salt
good pinch grated nutmeg
1 cinnamon stick
1 bay leaf
1.5 litres (2¾ pints) meat stock (page 133)
3 tbsp medium cream sherry
125 ml (4 fl oz) single cream

Fry onion, garlic and ginger in heated cooking oil until onion is translucent. Add curry powder and fry for 1 minute. Add mince and fry until it turns colour. Add remaining ingredients except sherry and cream. Simmer for 30 to 45 minutes. Remove cinnnamon and bay leaf and stir in sherry and cream.
(6 servings)

HINTS
☆ To prevent a floury taste, always fry curry powder for 1 minute before adding further ingredients.
☆ Don't allow the soup to boil as boiling will curdle the cream.

SUGGESTED SIDE DISH
Savoury muffins

VEGETABLE SOUP WITH MEAT STRIPS

1 kg (2 lb) topside
3 litres (5 pints) meat stock (page 133)
2 large carrots, grated
1 turnip, quartered
3 leeks, sliced
2 tsp salt
freshly ground black pepper to taste
1 celery stalk, coarsely chopped
1 small cabbage, coarsely shredded

Place meat and stock in a deep heavy-based saucepan. Cover and bring slowly to the boil. Add all vegetables except cabbage and simmer for 2 hours. Add cabbage and simmer for another 15 to 20 minutes or until cabbage is tender. Remove meat from soup, cut into strips, then return to soup.
(8 to 10 servings)

VARIATION
☆ Substitute thick flank (round) for the topside.

HINT
☆ Tie meat with string in order to keep its shape.

SUGGESTED SIDE DISH
Hot French bread

DUTCH PEA SOUP

1 smoked shank of pork, approximately 500 g (1 lb)
500 g (1 lb) split peas
4 leeks, chopped
3 celery stalks, chopped
2 onions, chopped
1 tbsp cooking oil
1.5 litres (2¾ pints) meat stock (page 133)
1 bay leaf
freshly ground black pepper to taste
125 g (4 oz) smoked sausages
1 tbsp lemon juice
2 tsp dried or 2 tbsp chopped fresh parsley

To prepare the peas, rinse well, cover with water and bring to the boil. Boil for 5 minutes, then soak for 1 hour. Drain and rinse under cold running water.
To prepare the soup, fry leeks, celery

Dutch pea soup

and onion in heated cooking oil until onion is translucent. Add remaining ingredients except sausage, lemon juice and parsley. Simmer for 2 hours or until meat is tender. Remove meat and bay leaf, cut meat from bone and cube. Strain soup and purée vegetables. Return meat, vegetable purée and liquid to saucepan and reheat. Cut sausages into slices, add to soup and heat through. Stir in lemon juice, sprinkle with parsley and serve.
(6 to 8 servings)

VARIATION

☆ Substitute bacon for the smoked sausage.

HINTS

☆ Add more meat stock if soup is too thick.
☆ Stir in a little cream just before serving.
☆ Add avocado for extra flavour.

SUGGESTED SIDE DISH
Cheese and bacon twists

CHILLED COURGETTE SOUP

1 small onion, chopped
2 leeks, sliced
1 green pepper, seeded and chopped
1 tbsp cooking oil
15 g ($\frac{1}{2}$ oz) butter
500 g (1 lb) courgettes, sliced
1 bay leaf
750 ml (1$\frac{1}{4}$ pints) white meat stock (page 133)
$\frac{1}{2}$ tsp salt
250 ml (8 fl oz) single cream
3 tbsp chopped fresh mint

Sauté onion, leeks and green pepper in heated cooking oil and butter. Add courgettes and stir-fry gently. Add bay leaf, meat stock and salt. Cover with lid and simmer for about 20 minutes until vegetables are tender. Remove bay leaf. Purée mixture in food processor. Stir in cream and adjust seasoning if necessary. Chill in refrigerator, then serve garnished with slices of courgette and chopped mint.
(4 to 6 servings)

SUGGESTED SIDE DISH
Garlic rolls

Left: Consommé. Right: Chilled courgette soup

CONSOMME

2 litres (3$\frac{1}{2}$ pints) rich clarified stock (page 133)
2 carrots, cut into julienne strips
1 leek, thinly sliced
$\frac{1}{2}$ green pepper, cut into julienne strips
bouquet garni (page 17)

Place all ingredients in a large saucepan. Heat slowly without bringing to the boil. Season with salt if necessary, then serve.
(6 servings)

VARIATION

☆ Substitute red or yellow pepper for the green pepper.

SNACKS

When preparing snacks we tend to be unimaginative yet cold meats offer numerous exciting possibilities. Other recipes supplied in this book, such as rissoles and pizzas, can also be used to prepare interesting savoury snacks.

FILO SPIRALS

250 g (8 oz) rindless back bacon, chopped
250 g (8 oz) frozen spinach
1 onion, chopped
2 cloves garlic, crushed
75 g ($2\frac{1}{2}$ oz) dried breadcrumbs
30 g (1 oz) butter
60 g (2 oz) Gruyère cheese, grated
1 red pepper, seeded and chopped
8 sheets filo pastry
60 g (2 oz) butter, melted

Thaw spinach and drain thoroughly. Fry bacon in a heated heavy-based saucepan. Remove from saucepan and drain on kitchen paper. Sauté onion and garlic in rendered bacon fat until onion is translucent. Combine onion, garlic and bacon with 3 tbsp dried breadcrumbs in a bowl. Fry spinach lightly in heated butter, drain and squeeze out excess moisture. Combine spinach, 3 tbsp breadcrumbs and cheese in a separate bowl. Combine red pepper and remaining breadcrumbs in a bowl. Layer 4 sheets of pastry, brushing each with the melted butter. Spread half the bacon mixture across one-third of the pastry and half the spinach mixture across the next third of the pastry.

Sprinkle half the red pepper mixture over remaining pastry, leaving a 4 cm ($1\frac{1}{2}$ inch) border at the end. Roll pastry up tightly from the bacon end, place on a tray, cover with cling film and refrigerate for 30 minutes. Repeat process with remaining pastry and ingredients and refrigerate. Cut rolls into 1 cm ($\frac{1}{2}$ inch) slices and place on a greased baking sheet. Bake at 180 °C (350 °F/ gas 4) for about 15 minutes or until golden brown. Cool spirals on the baking sheet and serve slightly warm.
Makes about 50

VARIATION
☆ *Substitute puff pastry for the filo pastry, but remember not to roll up the pastry too tightly.*

SALTED SILVERSIDE AND CHEESE TOAST

75 g ($2\frac{1}{2}$ oz) salted silverside, grated (page 87)
2 tsp dried or 5 tsp chopped fresh parsley
5 tsp snipped chives
3 tbsp mayonnaise
1 tsp prepared mustard
60 g (2 oz) Cheddar cheese, grated
freshly ground black pepper to taste
10 slices white bread

Combine all ingredients except bread. Remove crusts from bread. Spread meat mixture on bread, cut diagonally into quarters and place on an ungreased baking sheet. Place under a pre-heated grill for approximately 5 to 7 minutes or until lightly toasted.
Makes 40 triangles

VARIATION
☆ *Substitute 200 g ($6\frac{1}{2}$ oz) ham, smoked beef or leftover cooked meat, finely chopped, for the silverside.*

MINCE ON A SKEWER WITH YOGHURT DIP

500 g (1 lb) minced lean beef
1 onion, finely chopped
1 clove garlic, crushed
1 small cooking apple, cored and grated
1 egg, beaten
1 tsp salt
freshly ground black pepper to taste
1 tsp dried or 1 tbsp chopped mixed fresh herbs

YOGHURT DIP
$\frac{1}{2}$ cucumber, seeded, grated and well drained
250 ml (8 fl oz) plain yoghurt
5 tsp chopped fresh mint
$\frac{1}{2}$ tsp salt
white pepper to taste

First prepare the dip by combining all the ingredients and mixing well.

Mince minced meat again and mix with remaining ingredients, kneading lightly. Mould mixture into a small sausage around one end of each skewer. Place on the rack of a grill pan and cook 10 cm (4 inches) under a pre-heated grill until golden brown and cooked. Serve hot or cold with the dip.
Makes 15

VARIATIONS
☆ *Substitute chopped gherkins for the cucumber.*
☆ *Substitute cream cheese for the plain yoghurt.*
☆ *Substitute 1 tsp dried mint for the fresh mint if fresh is not available.*

HINTS
☆ *If wooden skewers are used, soak them in water before use to prevent scorching.*
☆ *Cook over moderate coals and serve as a starter at a barbecue.*

Opposite top left: Steak spirals with pepper sauce (page 140). Top right: Salt beef and cheese straws (page 143). Bottom from left: Curry triangles (page 141); Mini-burgers (page 143) and Salted silverside and cheese toast (this page)

STEAK SPIRALS WITH PEPPER SAUCE

1 rump steak
$\frac{1}{2}$ tsp salt
2 tsp coarsely ground dried green peppercorns

SAUCE
2 tbsp drained green peppercorns, crushed
1 tsp French mustard
250 ml (8 fl oz) double cream
2 tbsp brandy

First prepare the sauce by combining ingredients and mixing well.

To prepare the meat, slash fat edges at 2.5 cm (1 inch) intervals to prevent curling during cooking. Heat a ridged pan to smoking hot and cook steak for 5 to 7 minutes in total (rare) or 7 to 10 minutes in total (medium). Remove from pan and allow to stand for at least 10 minutes before slicing thinly. Season with salt and pepper, thread concertinawise onto a cocktail stick or long thin bamboo skewer and serve with pepper sauce.
Makes 20

VARIATIONS
☆ Low-fat variation: Substitute low-fat plain yoghurt for the cream.
☆ Substitute 2 tbsp capers for the peppercorns in the sauce.

CRUMBED PORK BITES

5 thin pork slices, cut from leg
prepared mustard
3 tbsp plain flour
1 egg, lightly beaten
90 g (3 oz) dried breadcrumbs
2 tbsp sesame seeds
cooking oil for deep-frying
$\frac{1}{2}$ tsp salt
freshly ground black pepper to taste

Place meat between two layers of cling film and flatten slightly with palm of hand. Cut meat into 2 cm ($\frac{3}{4}$ inch) strips and spread thinly with prepared mustard. Coat lightly with flour, shake off excess and dip into egg. Coat well with breadcrumbs mixed with sesame seeds. Thread concertinawise onto small skewers, then refrigerate for 20 to 30 minutes to allow breadcrumbs to set. Deep-fry for about 3 minutes or until golden brown and cooked. Drain on paper towels and season with salt and pepper to taste.
Makes about 20

HINTS
☆ Pork bites may be prepared several hours ahead and kept covered with paper towels in the refrigerator. Fry just before serving.
☆ Serve the pork bites with a variety of prepared mustards, such as garlic mustard, ginger mustard and cider mustard.

LAMB KEBABS

750 g (1$\frac{1}{2}$ lb) boned leg or shoulder of lamb, cut into cubes
15 g ($\frac{1}{2}$ oz) butter
1 tbsp cooking oil
500 g (1 lb) dried apricots
250 g (8 oz) dried apple rings
1$\frac{1}{2}$ tsp salt
freshly ground black pepper to taste

MARINADE
4 tbsp cooking oil
200 ml (6$\frac{1}{2}$ fl oz) dry white wine
2 tbsp lemon juice
2 tbsp clear honey
2 tsp dried or 2 tbsp chopped fresh mint
2 cloves garlic, crushed

Brown meat in heated butter and cooking oil in a heavy-based saucepan. Mix marinade ingredients and marinate meat for 1 hour. Add apricots and apple and marinate for another 30 minutes. Thread meats, apricots and apple rings alternately onto cocktail sticks or small skewers and cook 10 cm (4 inches) under a pre-heated grill for 10 minutes or until cooked, turning and basting regularly with marinade. Season with salt and pepper and serve at once.
Makes 15

VARIATION
☆ Substitute 1 tsp dried or 1 tbsp chopped fresh rosemary for the mint.

HINTS
☆ Dried fruit burns easily so turn kebabs regularly while grilling.
☆ Bamboo or wooden skewers may be passed through a clove of garlic for added flavour.
☆ For added flavour, use sprigs of fresh herbs to apply the baste when grilling the kebabs.

MUFFINS WITH A FILLING

315 g (10 oz) minced lean beef
1 onion, chopped
1 clove garlic, crushed
1 tbsp cooking oil
1 tomato, skinned and chopped
$\frac{1}{2}$ tsp salt
freshly ground black pepper to taste
good pinch dried or $\frac{1}{2}$ tsp chopped mixed fresh herbs
2 eggs, beaten
90 ml (3 fl oz) milk
60 g (2 oz) grated Cheddar cheese
2 tsp dried or 5 tsp chopped fresh parsley

BATTER
2 eggs
125 ml (4 fl oz) cooking oil
125 ml (4 fl oz) milk
125 g (4 oz) plain flour
2 tsp baking powder
$\frac{1}{2}$ tsp salt

To prepare the filling, sauté onion and garlic in heated cooking oil in a heavy-based saucepan until onion is translucent. Add meat and fry until it turns colour. Add tomato, salt, pepper and herbs and simmer for 5 minutes. Mix eggs, milk and cheese and stir into meat mixture.

To prepare the batter, beat eggs, oil and milk together. Sift flour, baking powder and salt in a mixing bowl. Make a hollow in flour, stir in liquid and mix lightly. Spoon mixture into greased muffin tins, leaving them half full. Spoon a heaped tablespoon of meat mixture on top, followed by 2 tsp batter. Bake at 180 °C (350 °F/gas 4) for 15 to 20 minutes. Sprinkle with parsley and serve lukewarm.
Makes 12

VARIATION
☆ Substitute any savoury mince for the meat mixture.

HINT
☆ Microwave on 70% for 8 minutes.

CURRY TRIANGLES

750 g (1½ lb) frozen puff pastry,
thawed
sesame seeds

FILLING
500 g (1 lb) minced lean beef
2 onions, chopped
1 tbsp chopped ginger root
2 cloves garlic, crushed
1 tbsp cooking oil
1 tsp mild curry powder
1 dried chilli, crushed
2 tbsp medium cream sherry
1½ tsp salt
freshly ground black pepper
to taste
5 tsp vinegar
3 to 4 gingernuts, crumbed

To prepare the filling, fry onion, ginger and garlic in heated cooking oil until onion is translucent. Add curry powder and chilli and fry for 1 minute. Add mince and fry until it turns colour. Add sherry, salt, pepper, vinegar and gingernuts and stir over low heat until thick. Leave to cool.

Roll pastry out very thinly on a lightly floured surface. Cut pastry into 7.5 cm (3 inch) squares and dampen edges with milk. Spoon a heaped tablespoon of mince mixture in the centre of each square and fold into a triangle. Brush lightly with milk and sprinkle with sesame seeds. Place triangles on a baking sheet and bake at 220 °C (425 °F/gas 7) for approximately 15 minutes or until golden brown and well puffed.

Makes about 20

VARIATIONS
☆ Substitute thin slices of bread for the pastry and toast the curry triangles in a sandwich toaster. Omit the sesame seeds.

HINT
☆ If dried chillies are not available, increase quantity of curry powder to 4 tsp.

Curry triangles

HAM AND CHEESE PUFFS

125 g (4 oz) butter
250 ml (8 fl oz) water
125 g (4 oz) plain flour
good pinch salt
4 eggs

FILLING
155 g (5 oz) ham, finely chopped
250 g (8 oz) cottage cheese
3 tbsp mayonnaise
freshly ground black pepper
to taste
3 tbsp snipped chives
paprika

To prepare the puffs, combine butter and water in a saucepan and bring to the boil. Add flour and salt all at once and stir vigorously until mixture leaves the sides of the saucepan and forms a smooth ball. Remove from heat and cool slightly. Add eggs one at a time, beating well after each addition. Spoon mixture into a piping bag fitted with a star tube and pipe 5 cm (2 inch) lengths about 2 cm ($\frac{3}{4}$ inch) apart onto a very lightly greased baking sheet. Bake at 220 °C (425 °F/gas 67) for 15 minutes, then lower temperature to 180 °C (350 °F/gas 4) and bake for another 10 to 15 minutes. Prick puffs with a sharp knife and cool on a wire rack.

To prepare the filling, combine all the ingredients except paprika and mix well.

Just before serving, cut puffs in half and pipe or spoon filling into centres. Sprinkle with paprika.
Makes 12 to 15

VARIATIONS
☆ Combine chopped leftover roast meat with béchamel sauce.
☆ Substitute corned beef for the ham.
☆ Substitute herb or cream cheese for the cottage cheese.

HINTS
☆ Cottage cheese tends to gather liquid so drain it well in a piece of muslin before combining it with the other ingredients.
☆ To ensure crisp puffs, return the pricked puffs to the turned-off oven and leave them for 30 minutes to dry out with the door ajar.
☆ If puffs brown too much before they feel firm and light, cover them loosely with a sheet of foil.

Ham and cheese puffs

MINI-BURGERS

12 small bread rolls or a French loaf,
sliced into rounds
90 g (3 oz) butter, melted

PATTIES
500 g (1 lb) minced lean beef
1 onion, chopped
1 cooking apple, cored and grated
$\frac{1}{2}$ tsp salt
freshly ground black pepper
to taste
1 tsp dried or 1 tbsp chopped mixed
fresh herbs
2 tbsp cooking oil
60 g (2 oz) Cheddar cheese, grated
snipped chives to garnish

First prepare the bread. Brush rounds of
bread on both sides with butter and
place on a baking sheet. Bake at
180 °C (350 °F/gas 4) for about 15
minutes or until lightly browned and
crisp.

To prepare the patties, combine
meat, onion, apple, salt, pepper and
herbs. Shape mixture into small balls
and flatten to form thick patties. Fry
patties in heated cooking oil in a heavy-
based frying pan until golden brown.
Place a patty on each crisp bread round
and top with cheese. Just before serving, cook burgers 10 cm (4 inches)
under a pre-heated grill until cheese
has melted. Garnish with fresh chives.

Makes 24

VARIATIONS
☆ Add one of the following to the
meat mixture: a dash of Tabasco,
Worcestershire sauce, prepared
mustard or chutney.
☆ Omit the mixed herbs and add a
pinch of paprika, chilli powder, ground
coriander or curry powder.

Front: Mini-burgers. Back: Salt beef and cheese straws

SALT BEEF AND CHEESE STRAWS

75 g (2$\frac{1}{2}$ oz) salted silverside (beef
jerky), (page 87)
60 g (2 oz) mature Cheddar cheese,
grated
3 tbsp snipped chives
pinch cayenne pepper
750 g (1$\frac{1}{2}$ lb) frozen puff pastry,
thawed
5 tsp coarse salt

Combine silverside, cheese, chives and
cayenne pepper. Roll out half the pastry
very thinly on a lightly floured surface
and spread meat mixture evenly over
surface. Roll out remaining pastry and
place on top of filling. Press lightly
together. Cut pastry into 15 x 1.5 cm
(6 x $\frac{1}{2}$ inch) wide strips. Twist strips and
place on a greased baking sheet.
Sprinkle with coarse salt and bake at
220 °C (425 °F/gas 7) for 10 minutes or
until golden brown. Cool on baking
sheet, then transfer to a wire rack.

Makes about 20

VARIATION
☆ Substitute chopped pastrami for the
salted silverside.

HINTS
☆ Salt beef and cheese straws are at
their best freshly baked and served
slightly cooled.
☆ Uncooked, prepared cheese straws
may be kept in the refrigerator for a
few hours.
☆ Uncooked cheese straws may be
frozen for up to one month. Bake just
before serving for 12 to 15 minutes.

SAUCES

It is the complementary sauce which often provides the finishing touch as it can be used to great effect to add colour to the plate, ginger up a dish or moisten the food. Take care, however, that the sauce complements and does not overwhelm the natural flavour of the food.

STORING SAUCES

Store sauces with a roux (page 156) base in the refrigerator for 2 to 3 days. Allow the sauce to cool completely before placing it in the refrigerator. To prevent a skin forming on the surface, cover the container with cling film. Home-made mayonnaise may be kept in a sealed container in the refrigerator for 2 to 3 weeks.

APPLE SAUCE

3 large cooking apples (about 500 g/ 1 lb), peeled, cored and sliced
125 ml (4 fl oz) water
4 tsp sugar
1 whole clove
1 cinnamon stick
15 g ($\frac{1}{2}$ oz) butter

Place apple, water, sugar, clove and cinnamon into a saucepan. Bring to the boil, cover with lid and reduce heat. Simmer for 5 minutes or until fruit is soft. Remove clove and cinnamon. Sieve or liquidize until smooth, then return pulp to saucepan. Heat slowly and stir in butter.
Makes about 250 ml (8 fl oz)

Opposite clockwise from top: Redcurrant sauce, Peri-peri sauce and Apple sauce (all this page). Front: Oven-roasted kasseler rib roll (page 57)

REDCURRANT SAUCE

315 g (10 oz) redcurrant jelly
pinch ground ginger
1 tsp grated lemon rind
2 tbsp lemon juice
3 tbsp port

Mix all ingredients thoroughly in a saucepan over low heat with a whisk.
Makes about 250 ml (8 fl oz)

VARIATIONS
☆ Stir in 1 tsp prepared mustard.
☆ Substitute quince jelly for redcurrant jelly.

ESPAGNOLE SAUCE

30 g (1 oz) butter
2 rashers rindless bacon, chopped
2 leeks, chopped
$\frac{1}{2}$ celery stalk, chopped
1 carrot, peeled and grated
5 tsp plain flour
500 ml (16 fl oz) meat stock (page 133)
bouquet garni (page 17)
4 tsp tomato purée
salt and freshly ground black pepper to taste

Melt butter in a heavy-based saucepan, add bacon, leeks, celery and carrot and fry until onion is translucent. Stir in flour and fry for about a minute or until roux (page 156) turns a walnut colour. Simmer for 1 minute, then remove from heat and add stock gradually, stirring continuously until sauce has thickened. Reduce heat, add bouquet garni, cover with lid and simmer for 20 minutes. Stir in tomato purée, then purée the mixture in a food processor. Return to saucepan and reheat. Season to taste.
Makes about 500 ml (16 fl oz)

VARIATION
☆ Add 3 tbsp muscadel or port or 125 ml (4 fl oz) red wine together with the stock and boil, stirring constantly, until the sauce is reduced and thickened.

HINT
☆ Stir the roux continuously over low heat to prevent it from burning.

PAN GRAVY

If a roast has been prepared, pour off the excess fat in the pan, leaving about 2 tbsp. Add about 5 tsp plain flour, depending on the thickness of gravy required, and stir over low heat until golden brown. Add about 250 ml (8 fl oz) heated meat stock (page 133) and stir until gravy thickens. Season with salt and freshly ground black pepper to taste. If desired, stir in 3 tbsp single cream or soured cream, heat through, then strain.

VARIATIONS
☆ Substitute dry white wine for half the meat stock.
☆ Substitute crème fraîche or soured cream for the cream.

PERI-PERI SAUCE

2 onions, finely chopped
3 cloves garlic, crushed
1 tbsp cooking oil
75 g (2$\frac{1}{2}$ oz) melted butter
1$\frac{1}{2}$ tsp peri-peri powder
2 tbsp lemon juice

Sauté onion and garlic in heated cooking oil until onion is translucent. Add melted butter and peri-peri according to taste. Stir in lemon juice and heat through.
Makes about 150 ml ($\frac{1}{4}$ pint)

WHITE SAUCE CONSISTENCIES

CONSISTENCY	BUTTER	PLAIN FLOUR	MILK	SALT	METHOD	USES
Thin sauce	15 g (½ oz)	15 g (½ oz)	250 ml (8 fl oz)	½ tsp	Melt butter in a heavy-based saucepan. Add flour and stir with a wooden spoon for 3 minutes over low heat. Remove from heat and add milk slowly while stirring continuously. Return to heat and bring to the boil, stirring until sauce is smooth. Reduce heat and simmer for 2 minutes, stirring occasionally. Remove from heat and season with salt and white pepper.	Base for soups
Medium-thick sauce (pouring)	25 g (¾ oz)	25 g (¾ oz)	250 ml (8 fl oz)	½ tsp		For accompanying sauces
Medium-thick sauce (coating)	30 g (1 oz)	30 g (1 oz)	250 ml (8 fl oz)	½ tsp		For coating sauces
Thick sauce (panada)	60 g (2 oz)	60 g (2 oz)	250 ml (8 fl oz)	½ tsp		Binding agent for croquettes and as a basis for soufflés

VARIATIONS FOR WHITE SAUCES

SAUCE	MEDIUM-AND THICK WHITE SAUCE	OTHER INGREDIENTS	METHOD	SERVING SUGGESTIONS
Caper sauce	300 ml (½ pint) basic white sauce (use half milk and half meat stock)	1 tbsp lemon juice 1 tbsp capers, coarsely chopped	Add lemon juice to meat stock before preparing the sauce. Add capers to white sauce just before serving.	Lamb Beef Tongue
Cheese sauce	300 ml (½ pint) basic white sauce	60 g (2 oz) Cheddar cheese, grated ½ tsp dry mustard pinch cayenne pepper	Add cheese to white sauce. Mix until smooth, then season with mustard and cayenne pepper.	Pasta dishes Minced meat dishes Réchauffés (page 156)
Mushroom sauce	300 ml (½ pint) basic white sauce	125 g (4 oz) mushrooms, chopped 1 tbsp medium cream sherry	Sauté mushrooms in melted butter. Proceed as for white sauce method. Add sherry just before serving.	Steaks or chops Minced meat dishes Hamburgers
Onion sauce	300 ml (½ pint) basic white sauce	1 onion, finely chopped pinch nutmeg	Sauté onion in melted butter until translucent. Proceed as for white sauce method. Season with nutmeg.	Lamb Offal Steaks or chops Minced meat dishes Hamburgers
Parsley sauce	300 ml (½ pint) basic white sauce	2 tsp dried or 2 tbsp chopped fresh parsley	Add parsley to white sauce just before serving.	Réchauffés (page 156) Minced meat dishes
Béchamel sauce	Slice of onion 1 small carrot 5 whole peppercorns 1 bay leaf		Add onion, carrot, peppercorns and bay leaf to milk in basic recipe and bring to the boil. Cover and infuse for 10 minutes, then strain. Proceed as for basic white sauce.	

Stir a little cream into any of the above sauces for a richer flavour.

SWEET AND SOUR SAUCE

1 onion, chopped
1 green pepper, seeded and cut into julienne strips
1 carrot, cut into julienne strips
15 g ($\frac{1}{2}$ oz) butter
410 g (13 oz) canned pineapple chunks,
drained and juice reserved
$\frac{1}{2}$ tsp ground ginger
1 tbsp soy sauce
2 tbsp wine vinegar
4 tsp soft brown sugar
2 tbsp cornflour

Fry onion, green pepper and carrot in heated butter in a heavy-based saucepan until onion is translucent. Mix pineapple juice, ginger, soy sauce, wine vinegar, brown sugar and cornflour thoroughly. Add together with pineapple chunks to onion mixture and heat, stirring, until thickened.

Makes about 500 ml (16 fl oz)

MAYONNAISE

1 whole egg
$\frac{1}{2}$ tsp salt
pinch dry mustard
$\frac{1}{2}$ tsp sugar
pinch white pepper
2 tbsp lemon juice
250 ml (8 fl oz) light olive oil

Place all the ingredients, except cooking oil, in a food processor or liquidizer and blend until well mixed. With motor running, pour in oil very slowly until mixture is thick and smooth. Adjust seasoning if necessary.

Makes about 300 ml ($\frac{1}{2}$ pint)

HINT

☆ Substitute wine vinegar or herb vinegar for the lemon juice.

VARIATIONS

☆ Mayonnaise may also be made by hand. Place 2 egg yolks, $\frac{1}{2}$ tsp salt, pinch dry mustard, $\frac{1}{2}$ tsp sugar and a pinch white pepper in a mixing bowl and beat until smooth. Add 125 ml (4 fl oz) light olive oil while beating continuously. Stir in 1 tbsp lemon juice. Beat in another 125 ml (4 fl oz) light olive oil, drop by drop, until mixture is thick and smooth. Stir in another 1 tbsp lemon juice. Adjust seasoning if necessary.

☆ Add any of the following to the basic mayonnaise:

Lemon mayonnaise: Add the finely grated rind of 1 small lemon.

Garlic mayonnaise: Add 1 clove garlic, crushed.

Herb mayonnaise: Add 2 tsp finely chopped spring onion or 2 tsp each chopped fresh parsley and basil or any combination of fresh herbs.

GARLIC SAUCE

3 tbsp snipped chives
5 cloves garlic, crushed
15 g ($\frac{1}{2}$ oz) butter
125 ml (4 fl oz) dry white wine
250 ml (8 fl oz) single cream

Sauté chives and garlic in heated butter in a heavy-based saucepan. Add wine and boil until sauce thickens. Stir in cream and heat through.

Makes about 300 ml ($\frac{1}{2}$ pint)

Clockwise from top: Espagnole sauce (page 145). Herb mayonnaise and Sweet and sour sauce (both this page)

MARINADES, BASTES AND BUTTERS

Marinades were once used to preserve meat but today they are used to give meat extra flavour as well as to tenderize and make it more succulent.

TO PREPARE A MARINADE

Always use a little cooking or olive oil (or other flavoursome oils such as peanut and walnut oil) in the marinade as this prevents the meat from drying out. The addition of an acid, such as white or red wine, chopped tomato, lemon juice and herb vinegar, helps to soften the meat to a certain extent. As a general rule, use one part oil to three parts liquid when making a marinade, although this may vary according to the meat cut being marinated.

For a delicate flavour, pineapple juice and sherry may be used and supplemented with meat stock.

Flavourings such as spring onion, garlic, ginger root, sprigs of fresh herbs such as thyme and marjoram, mustard seeds, juniper berries and black pepper may also be added. Marinades are classified as follows:

Cooked marinades are usually prepared by heating whole spices and other flavourings together. The flavour of whole spices such as cloves and mustard seeds is enhanced by heating.

Uncooked marinades on the other hand are quick to prepare as heating is not necessary to release the flavour. The ingredients are merely mixed together. Sprigs of fresh herbs are popular as flavourings in uncooked marinades.

Opposite clockwise from top right: Caper butter and Blue cheese butter (both page 152); Honey marinade (page 151); and Soured cream basting mixture (page 152)

MEAT CUTS SUITABLE FOR MARINATING

Grill: Chops, steaks, ribs and kebabs.
Oven-roasts: Fillet, leg of lamb, pork rib roll, prime rib and so on.
Pot-roasts, stews, braised dishes: Cuts with a small amount of fat such as beef topside, silverside and thick flank are suitable for marinating.

HINTS ON MARINATING MEAT

☆ *Use glass, ceramic or plastic containers when marinating meat.*
☆ *Avoid using chipped enamel or metal containers – the acid in the marinade reacts with the metal.*
☆ *Marinate meat in a container just large enough to ensure that the meat is covered by the marinade. Turn meat regularly.*
☆ *Be careful not to marinate meat for too long since its own flavour can be overpowered by the strong flavour of the herbs and spices.*
☆ *Large meat cuts can be marinated for 4 to 6 hours or overnight, while steaks, chops and kebabs need only be left in the marinade for 2 to 3 hours.*
☆ *Meat can be marinated at room temperature to hasten the process but remember that higher temperatures also hasten bacterial growth. It is preferable therefore to marinate meat in the refrigerator.*
☆ *Meat flavoured with marinade containing sugary ingredients such as honey and apricot jam should be grilled very slowly to prevent the meat from burning and acquiring a bitter taste.*
☆ *Baste meat regularly with marinade while cooking to increase the flavour absorption and succulence.*

USES FOR LEFTOVER MARINADE

☐ *Marinades can be used as a cooking liquid for pot-roasts, stews and braised dishes as follows:*

1. Remove meat from marinade and dry thoroughly with kitchen paper.
2. Skim the oil from the marinade.
3. Brown meat rapidly in heated butter and cooking oil. The oil removed from the marinade can be used for this purpose.
4. Bring marinade to the boil, add to the meat and simmer until meat is cooked.

☐ *A marinade can be re-used later. Bring marinade to the boil, leave to cool, then store in the refrigerator.*
☐ *Use leftover marinade to baste a dry oven-roast.*
☐ *A marinade can also be used to baste a marinated oven-roast or grilled meat while it is cooking.*
☐ *Add a little marinade to gravy for extra flavour.*

BASTING MIXTURES

Most marinades can be used to baste meat and should be applied frequently by brushing the mixture over the meat while it is cooking. When cooking lean meat cuts, add cooking oil or melted butter to the basting mixture to enhance the flavour and to ensure that the meat remains succulent.

HINTS

☆ *Use sprigs of herbs as basting brushes for added flavour.*
☆ *Mixtures containing sugary ingredients should be brushed over the meat only towards the end of the cooking time as they burn easily.*

COOKED MARINADE

2 tbsp cooking oil
1 onion, chopped
1 celery stalk, chopped
$\frac{1}{2}$ carrot, chopped
5 tsp dried or 5 tbsp chopped fresh
parsley
2 cloves garlic, crushed
500 ml (16 fl oz) wine vinegar or
cider
500 ml (16 fl oz) meat stock
(page 133)
2 bay leaves
1 tsp dried or 1 tbsp chopped fresh
thyme
$\frac{1}{2}$ tsp dried or 1 tsp chopped fresh
rosemary
5 black peppercorns, crushed
1 tsp juniper berries, crushed

Heat oil in a deep saucepan. Add onion, celery, carrot, parsley and garlic and fry over moderate heat for 5 minutes but do not allow to brown since this imparts a bitter flavour. Add remaining ingredients and simmer, covered, for 45 minutes, stirring occasionally. Strain and leave to cool completely before using.
Makes about 1 litre (1$\frac{3}{4}$ pints)

VARIATIONS

Pineapple marinade: *Replace vinegar with 500 ml (16 fl oz) pineapple juice.*
Sherry marinade: *Replace vinegar with 250 ml (8 fl oz) dry sherry and 250 ml (8 fl oz) meat stock (page 133).*
Wine marinade: *Replace vinegar with 500 ml (16 fl oz) white or red wine.*

HINT

☆ *Any remaining marinade may be used at a later stage. Simply strain the marinade, reheat it and leave it to cool. Store in an airtight container in the refrigerator.*

UNCOOKED MARINADE

500 ml (16 fl oz) dry white wine
90 ml (3 fl oz) cooking oil
3 tbsp herb or wine vinegar
1 tbsp lemon juice
1 tsp grated lemon rind
1 bay leaf
1 sprig of parsley

Mix ingredients together and store in an airtight container in the refrigerator.
Makes about 690 ml (22 fl oz)

MINT YOGHURT MARINADE

4 tbsp chopped fresh mint
250 ml (8 fl oz) plain low-fat yoghurt
3 tbsp cooking oil
2 cloves garlic, crushed
1 tbsp lemon juice
1 tsp salt

Mix ingredients together in a glass or plastic container.
Makes about 300 ml ($\frac{1}{2}$ pint)

HONEY MARINADE

2 tbsp lemon juice
2 tbsp olive or cooking oil
1 tbsp chopped spring onion or 1 tsp dried or 1 tbsp chopped fresh rosemary or thyme
1 tsp salt
freshly ground black pepper to taste
1 clove garlic, crushed
1 tbsp clear honey

Mix ingredients together in a glass or plastic container.
Makes about 90 ml (3 fl oz)

BASIC BASTING MIXTURE

125 ml (4 fl oz) cooking or olive oil
375 ml (12 fl oz) red or dry white wine
1 clove garlic, crushed
1 small onion, sliced
freshly ground black pepper to taste

Mix ingredients together thoroughly. The flavour will improve if the mixture is left to stand for a few hours before basting the meat while it is cooking.
Makes 500 ml (16 fl oz)

BEER BASTING MIXTURE

90 ml (3 fl oz) beer
1 tbsp prepared mustard
1 tbsp vinegar
1 tbsp chutney

Mix ingredients together and baste the meat regularly while it is cooking.
Makes about 125 ml (4 fl oz)

HERB AND OIL BASTING MIXTURE

125 ml (4 fl oz) cooking or olive oil
1 tbsp lemon juice
1 clove garlic, crushed
½ tsp each dried or 1 tsp each
chopped fresh rosemary, marjoram
and parsley

Mix ingredients together. Using a crushed rosemary sprig, baste the meat regularly while grilling. The basting mixture can be prepared in advance and left in the refrigerator until needed.
Makes about 150 ml (¼ pint)

SOURED CREAM BASTING MIXTURE

125 ml (4 fl oz) soured cream
1 clove garlic, crushed
2 tbsp chopped spring onion
1 tsp paprika
good pinch freshly ground black
pepper
2 tbsp lemon juice
1 tsp grated lemon rind

Mix the ingredients together and baste the meat while it is cooking.
Makes about 150 ml (¼ pint)

VARIATION
☆ *Substitute 125 ml (4 fl oz) buttermilk for the soured cream.*

SAVOURY BUTTERS

Plain grilled meat can be made more interesting by serving it topped with a pat of savoury butter. Serve the butter sliced into 5 mm (¼ inch) thick slices or cast in small individual moulds.

TARRAGON BUTTER

90 g (3 oz) butter
1 tsp dried or 1 tbsp chopped fresh
tarragon
1 tbsp chopped spring onion
½ tsp lemon juice
½ tsp salt
freshly ground black pepper
to taste

APPLE BUTTER

125 g (4 oz) butter
90 ml (3 fl oz) apple sauce
(page 145)

TABASCO BUTTER

90 g (3 oz) butter
½ tsp Tabasco
½ tsp salt
freshly ground black pepper
to taste

PEPPER BUTTER

125 g (4 oz) butter
2 tsp drained green peppercorns
1 tsp freshly ground black pepper
1 tsp freshly ground dried green
peppercorns

MAITRE D'HOTEL BUTTER (Parsley butter)

125 g (4 oz) butter
4 tsp dried or 3 tbsp chopped fresh
parsley
2 tsp lemon juice
½ tsp salt
freshly ground black pepper

CAPER BUTTER

90 g (3 oz) butter
2 tsp capers, chopped
1 tsp lemon juice
1 tsp grated lemon rind
1 clove garlic, crushed
½ tsp prepared mustard
freshly ground black pepper
to taste

CHIVE AND GARLIC BUTTER

90 g (3 oz) butter
1 tbsp lemon juice
2 cloves garlic, crushed
2 tbsp snipped chives
½ tsp salt

MUSTARD BUTTER

90 g (3 oz) butter
4 tsp prepared mustard
2 tsp lemon juice
½ tsp salt
freshly ground black pepper
to taste

GARLIC BUTTER

125 g (4 oz) butter
3 cloves garlic, crushed
salt and freshly ground black pepper
to taste

MINT AND SPRING ONION BUTTER

90 g (3 oz) butter
1 tsp dried or 1 tbsp chopped fresh
mint
1 tbsp chopped spring onion
1 tsp lemon juice

GINGER BUTTER

125 g (4 oz) butter
2 tbsp chopped preserved ginger

ANCHOVY BUTTER

90 g (3 oz) butter
1 tsp lemon juice
5 anchovy fillets, drained and finely
chopped

BLUE CHEESE BUTTER

90 g (3 oz) butter
60 g (2 oz) blue cheese
2 tsp lemon juice
½ tsp salt
freshly ground black pepper to taste

To prepare savoury butter, cream butter, add remaining ingredients and mix thoroughly. Place butter on a sheet of foil, cling film or waxed paper and shape into a sausage. Wrap and roll it lightly, then refrigerate until firm.

GLOSSARY

Al dente: An Italian word to describe when pasta is cooked: tender but firm to the bite.

Atjar: A seasoned relish made of sliced fruits or mixed vegetables. These ingredients are mixed with chillies and other spices and are canned or bottled in vinegar oil. Atjar must mature in a cool place for 1 to 3 months.

Aspic: A clear jelly used to cover or glaze foods to prevent them from drying out and to enhance the appearance of the dish. The basis of aspic is a concentrated meat or fish stock which sets naturally.

QUICK ASPIC
4 tbsp cold water
4 tsp gelatine
440 g (14 oz) canned consommé or 410 ml (13 fl oz) savoury meat stock
5 tsp port, sherry or Madeira

Pour cold water over gelatine and leave until spongy. Heat over hot water or in the microwave oven until dissolved. Heat consommé or stock and stir in gelatine and port, sherry or Madeira. Strain.

Au gratin: A dish that is covered with a sauce. Breadcrumbs (and sometimes grated cheese) are sprinkled over the sauce and the dish is then placed under a pre-heated grill until golden brown or until cheese has melted. These dishes are served in the dish in which they are baked.

Bacon: Thinly sliced cured and smoked pork with or without the rind. When cured but not smoked, it is referred to as green bacon.

HOW TO COOK BACON
Fry: Place bacon in a cold frying pan without extra fat. Cook over low heat, turning frequently. For crisp bacon, pour off fat as it accumulates.
Grill: To grill large quantities of bacon, place bacon on the rack of a grill pan and cook 10 cm (4 inches) under a pre-heated grill for 2 to 3 minutes.

Bain-marie: A baking tin half filled with hot water in which soufflés, baked custards and terrines are cooked.

Bake blind: To bake a pie crust without a filling. Line the crust with waxed paper and fill with dried beans. Bake at 200 °C (400 °F/gas 6) for 15 minutes or until pastry is lightly browned. Remove paper and beans and return to oven for another 5 minutes.

Barding: To cover lean meat cuts with a layer of speck or bacon to prevent them from drying out during the cooking process.

Baste: To brush or spoon pan juices, rendered fat or a special basting mixture over meat while oven-roasting or grilling to prevent it from drying out. A spoon, basting brush, baster or even a few sprigs of fresh herbs, tied together and lightly crushed, may be used.

Batter: A rather thin, creamy mixture consisting mainly of eggs, plain flour and milk. Seasoning may also be added. When frying or baking, some meat cuts and other foods are dipped into a batter, breadcrumbs or flour to protect them from the high temperature of the cooking oil.

BATTER
125 g (4 oz) plain flour
1 tsp baking powder
good pinch salt
125 ml (4 fl oz) milk
2 eggs, beaten
125 ml (4 fl oz) water
2 tbsp melted butter

Sift dry ingredients together and add remaining ingredients. Allow to stand for 30 minutes before using.

Beef olives: Meat is cut across the grain into thin slices measuring approximately 7.5 x 10 cm (3 x 4 inches). Topside and thick flank are most commonly used. A filling is placed on top, the meat is rolled and secured with string or cocktail sticks. Beef olives are browned and then simmered until cooked, in a flavoursome liquid such as meat stock, fruit juice or wine.

Beurre manié: A thickening agent for sauces where equal amounts of soft butter and plain flour are mixed to a paste and added bit by bit to a hot liquid while stirring continuously. Sauces, soups and stews are usually thickened this way. A wire whisk may be used to ensure a smooth end result.

Blanch: Vegetables are placed in boiling water for a few minutes (the exact time depends on the type of vegetable) and are then drained and dipped in iced water. The vegetables are now ready for freezing. Green vegetables prepared this way retain their colour during cooking.

Boeuf: Beef.

Bouchée: A little puff pastry case, slightly larger than a vol-au-vent, baked blind and filled with a sweet or savoury filling. A pastry lid may be placed on top.

Bouquet garni: See page 17.

Bredie: A traditional South African stew prepared only with mutton or lamb, usually the breast. This is because the dish is Malay in origin and as Moslems the Malays do not eat pork. The sauce of a bredie is rich and thick and is obtained by using meat with a fair amount of bone and fat, rolling it in flour and browning it before the vegetables are added. The ingredients are simmered slowly in small quantities of liquid to allow the flavours to intermingle. The flavour of a bredie is determined by the type of vegetable added.

Brown: To fry meat in a mixture of cooking oil and butter until brown, before cooking it using one of the moist-heat cooking methods. Browning improves the flavour and appearance of the meat.

Cast-iron pot: Round- and flat-bottomed pots used for cooking a variety of foods, usually over an open fire. A new cast-iron pot is almost always coated with a layer of lacquer or paint which must be removed completely before it can be used. Always dry your pot well after cleaning it and rub it down with cooking oil before storing it in a dry place. Should traces of rust appear, remove them by rubbing with fine-grained sandpaper or coarse salt. Rinse, then coat with oil.

TO PREPARE A NEW CAST-IRON POT
Place a few hot coals in the pot, cover with a lid and leave over a hot fire for 30 minutes. Remove the coals and allow pot to cool. Using sandpaper, scour its inner surface and lid. Rinse off all loose dust. Fill the pot three-quarters with water, add 500 ml (16 fl oz) vinegar and 500 g (1 lb) salt. Bring to the boil over the fire and boil for 30 minutes. Pour out vinegar mixture, allow pot to cool, then scour again until the surface is shiny and smooth. Rinse again and half fill pot with water. Add 250 ml (8 fl oz) vinegar, 250 g (8 oz) salt and any available vegetable waste and peelings. Simmer over fire for 1 hour, then discard the contents and allow the pot to cool. Melt cubes of speck or mutton or beef fat in the pot over hot coals, then rub the fat into all the scoured surfaces of the pot and the lid, using paper towels.

Casserole: An ovenproof dish with a tightly fitting lid, made from earthenware, glass or metal. The word 'casserole' also refers to the meat dish itself which is prepared in the oven in this dish. The food is usually served from the casserole.

Caul: The lacy membrane or fat layer which surrounds the stomach of animals. Caul from pork is most commonly used for preparing liver in caul as well as for barding.

Chill: To place food in the refrigerator until very cold but not frozen.

Chine: To remove the triangular bone of the backbone to facilitate carving. Ask your butcher to do this for you.

Chipolata: A small pork sausage of Italian origin, often served as an hors d'oeuvre.

Chop: To cut food into small pieces on a chopping board or with a food processor.

Chorizo: A spicy, smoked pork sausage of Spanish origin.

Clarify: To remove impurities from salted butter by heating it. Clarified butter is often used for browning meat and to cover pâtés.

TO CLARIFY BUTTER

Melt the butter over low heat. Skim the froth from the surface, then remove and allow to stand. Pour off and use the clear yellow liquid and discard the milky residue left behind.

Coat: To dip meat in plain flour, beaten egg and breadcrumbs or a batter to protect it from the high temperature of the cooking oil when frying. It can also mean to spoon a sauce, aspic or mayonnaise over meat.

Coconut milk: Pour 250 ml (8 fl oz) boiling water over 90 g (3 oz) desiccated coconut. Allow to stand for 30 minutes, then strain through a piece of muslin. Use liquid to flavour stews and sauces.

Collagen: Collagen is the white connective tissue found in meat. Low heat, liquid and long, slow cooking process convert the connective tissue into gelatine. It is this process which tenderizes the meat.

Consommé: A clear soup made from a hearty meat stock which has been reduced and clarified. It can be served cold or hot.

Corned (salted) beef: Any cut of beef that has been cured. Brisket and silverside are the most popular choices.

Crème fraîche: This can be used instead of cream or soured cream.

CREME FRAICHE
250 ml (8 fl oz) single cream
1 tbsp plain yoghurt or buttermilk

Mix cream and yoghurt or buttermilk in a jar. Cover and keep warm overnight or for at least 8 hours at room temperature. Chill well. The mixture will thicken as it cools.

Crêpes: Delicate, light and lacy pancakes of French origin.

Croquette: Chopped meat or mashed potato bound with a thick white sauce (panada) and shaped into a cylinder or round shape. It is then dipped in beaten egg and breadcrumbs and shallow- or deep-fried.

Croûte: A toasted or fried circle of bread on which a savoury mixture is served. Certain meat cuts such as tournedos are usually served on a croûte to absorb the meat juices.

Croûtons: Tiny toasted or fried cubes of bread used as garnish or to accompany soups.

Crudités: Slices or sticks of raw vegetables which can be served plain or with a dipping sauce.

Cushion: The thick rib of lamb, mutton or pork which has been boned and stuffed. Cushion of lamb and pork are oven-roasted, whereas cushion of mutton is pot-roasted or cooked in a cooking bag or foil.

Cutlet: 2 to 2.5 cm ($\frac{3}{4}$ to 1 inch) thick chops cut from the pork or lamb rib after the backbone has been removed. The tips of the ribs are usually frenched.

Duchess potatoes: A rich mixture of mashed potatoes and egg seasoned with salt, white pepper and grated nutmeg is piped into rosettes on a greased baking sheet and browned in a pre-heated oven at 220 °C (425 °F/gas 7) or under a pre-heated grill. Duchess potatoes are one of the few potato dishes that can be prepared in advance. They are usually served as a vegetable side dish or piped into decorative borders around heatproof platters.

DUCHESS POTATOES
1 kg (2 lb) potatoes, peeled and quartered
60 g (2 oz) butter
1 tsp salt
pinch white pepper
pinch grated nutmeg
2 eggs, lightly beaten
2 egg yolks

Cook potatoes in salted water until tender. Drain well, mash potatoes and beat until very smooth. Add butter, salt, pepper, nutmeg, eggs and egg yolks and mix thoroughly. Pipe mixture through a piping tube into rosettes on a greased baking sheet or as a border around heatproof platter and brown in a pre-heated oven at 220 °C (425 °F/gas 7).

Eisbein: A term of German origin used when referring to a fresh or cured and smoked shank of pork which is boiled in water until tender. Eisbein is traditionally served with sauerkraut or boiled whole potatoes.

Elastin: Elastin is the yellow connective tissue found in meat. Only a small amount of elastin is found in muscle fibres and is always accompanied by large quantities of collagen. Elastin is tough and must be removed before cooking as it is not broken down when cooked using a moist-heat cooking method.

Escalope: A thin slice of meat, usually veal, cut from the topside. Usually it is covered with egg and breadcrumbs before being shallow- or deep-fried.

Filo pastry: This paper-thin pastry is available from supermarkets and delicatessens. Sheets are brushed with melted butter and used in sweet and savoury dishes. When baked, this pastry is very crisp.

Flambé: Alcohol, e.g. brandy, is warmed and poured over a dish and then set alight. This process adds flavour to the dish and, in the case of fatty foods, burns off fat.

French roast lamb: Meat, fat and connective tissue are removed from the tips of the rib bones. Carefully cut through and remove all the connective tissue, meat and fat from the first 2.5 cm (1 inch) of the rib ends.

Garnish: To arrange edible decorations such as lemon slices, sprigs of herbs, olives or carrot curls around or on top of a dish to make it more attractive.

Ghee: An Indian word for clarified butter.

Glaze: To brush egg and milk over pastry to give the surface a shiny appearance. Syrup, jam or other sweet ingredients may be used to glaze ham (page 58).

Green peppercorns: These unripe pepper berries from Madagascar are preserved in brine and are usually available in small jars or cans. The flavour of green peppercorns is much milder than that of black peppercorns and they are soft enough to be ground or mashed. Green peppercorns are also available in dried form.

Hors d'oeuvre: Small appetizers (starters) which are served before a meal or as the first course of a meal.

Julienne: To cut vegetables and/or fruit into very thin strips.

Kasseler rib: A term of German origin used when referring to a cured and smoked pork rib, either left whole or sawn into chops. The whole rib is oven-roasted or cooked in foil while chops are cooked over coals or under a pre-heated grill.

Kebab: Cubes or strips of meat threaded onto a skewer with or without vegetables and/or fruit. Sometimes a kebab is marinated before it is grilled.

Larding: The process whereby thin strips of speck, or other fat are inserted into lean meat to make it more succulent and to add flavour. The fat is inserted with the grain of the meat, usually with a larding needle.

Luncheon meat: Prepared from an emulsion of pork cubes and sometimes seasoned according to trade name, e.g. peppercorns, red or green pepper. It is usually rectangular in shape and is cut into thin slices for salads and sandwiches.

Maître d'hôtel butter: Parsley and lemon butter served on meat.

Marbling: Term used for fat deposits within the muscles. Unlike intramuscular or subcutaneous fat, this fat forms part of the edible meat and cannot be removed.

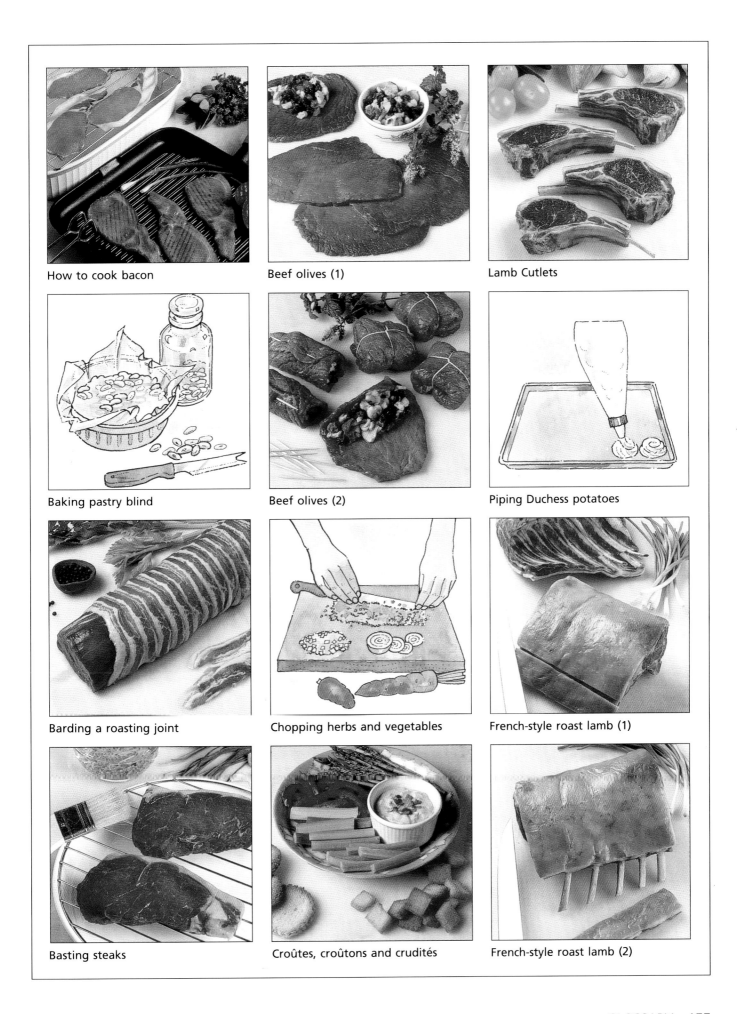

How to cook bacon

Beef olives (1)

Lamb Cutlets

Baking pastry blind

Beef olives (2)

Piping Duchess potatoes

Barding a roasting joint

Chopping herbs and vegetables

French-style roast lamb (1)

Basting steaks

Croûtes, croûtons and crudités

French-style roast lamb (2)

Marinade: A mixture of oil, vinegar, herbs and spices in which meat is marinated for a few hours to give it extra flavour and succulence and to tenderize it slightly.

Noisettes: Boned lamb, mutton or pork rib and loin, which is rolled and tied with string before being cut into 2.5 cm (1 inch) thick slices. The eye muscle of the rib and loin of lamb or pork is also known as a noisette.

Offal: All edible parts removed during the dressing (slaughtering) of a carcase are regarded as offal. These include the heart, liver, brains and tongue.

Omasum: The third compartment of the stomach of a ruminant animal.

Parma ham: Leg of pork which has been treated with salt and spices before being matured for a few months under special temperature- and moisture-controlled conditions. Unlike other hams, Parma ham is never cooked or smoked. Also known as prosciutto, Parma ham is Italian in origin and is traditionally served thinly sliced with fresh fruit (especially figs and melon).

Pastrami: Usually prepared from the brisket, pastrami is well-seasoned pickled beef and gets its name from the Romanian word, *pastra*, to preserve. After the meat has been cured, it is rolled in a special mixture, obtainable commercially from spice merchants, and then smoked. Pastrami is then cooked in a cooking bag at 160 °C (350 °F/gas 3) for 20 to 30 minutes per 500 g (1 lb). An alternative method is to cure the meat and simmer it until almost cooked. Rub the pastrami mixture into the meat and roast at 160 °C (325 °F/gas 3) for approximately 1 hour, then allow to cool before slicing thinly.

Pastry funnel: If the filling of a pie is not firm enough to mound, support the pastry by placing a pastry funnel in the centre of the dish before putting in the filling. After placing the pastry on top of the filling, cut a few small slits in the pastry or a cross on top of the pie funnel to allow the steam to escape.

Pilaff: A dish of savoury rice to which meat, fish or chicken may be added.

Pitta: A Middle Eastern bread which puffs up when cooked, and when split forms a convenient pocket for stuffings. White and wholemeal varieties are available from delicatessens and supermarkets.

Poach: To cook food in an open pan with just enough liquid to cover the food. The liquid is kept just below boiling point.

Poppadom (Poppadum): A thin, lentil-flour round which when fried swells dramatically into a crunchy golden wafer. They are available at health food stores, supermarkets and delicatessens and are eaten with or crumbled over curries and other Indian dishes.

Porterhouse steak: 2.5 cm (1 inch) slices which are cut from Scotch fillet (British/Australian porterhouse); 5 cm (2 inch) slices with bone and fillet which are cut from the loin in the section nearest to the rump and are usually roasted (American porterhouse).

Purée: A smooth thick pulp of cooked and sieved fruit, vegetables, meat or fish.

Quenelles: A finely sieved mixture of cooked meat, fish or poultry which is shaped into dumplings and poached. Quenelles are served as an entrée or as a garnish in soups.

Quiche: A savoury tart with a custard filling to which a variety of ingredients is added.

Ramekins: Small ovenproof bowls made of earthenware, porcelain or metal which are used for individual soufflés, mousses or egg dishes.

Réchauffé: A dish prepared from leftover food.

Reduce: To concentrate or thicken a liquid by boiling it rapidly, without a lid.

Ridged pan: A cast-iron pan for cooking meat. New pans should be seasoned before use.

TO SEASON A RIDGED PAN

Heat the pan for a few minutes with rendered fat until smoking hot, then wipe off excess fat with paper towels. It should not then be necessary to use any fat or oil when cooking steaks or chops.

Risotto: A rice-based dish from the northern provinces of Italy. It can be served plain, flavoured with butter and cheese or more elaborately with, for instance, mushrooms, tomatoes and meat. Risotto is usually served as a dish on its own with grated Parmesan cheese. One exception to this rule is Risotto alla Milanese, which is served as an accompaniment to Osso bucco.

Rissoles: Round minced meat patties rolled in crumbs and fried.

Rösti: This thick crispy golden brown cake is a traditional Swiss potato dish. Parboiled and grated potatoes are spread in a frying pan to form a thick cake which is cooked on both sides, cut into ample wedges and served with all meat dishes or with eggs for breakfast. Sometimes rösti is flavoured with crisp bacon or onion.

Roulade: This French word for 'roll' applies to slices of meat rolled around a filling. It also refers to a soufflé-type mixture that is cooked in a Swiss roll tin and spread with either a sweet or savoury filling before being rolled and served hot or cold.

Roux: Equal amounts of butter and plain flour stirred together over low heat and used as a base for sauces or to thicken stews.

Saddle: The whole lamb, mutton or pork loin (before the carcase is halved).

Salami: Spicy sausages made from pork and pork fat and sometimes beef. Salami is available fresh or smoked.

Sambal: A side dish served with Indian, Indonesian and Malayan food. A sambal is served in small portions, or in a small bowl, with the main dish.

Sauté: To cook onion and garlic in a small amount of fat until soft and glazed.

Schnitzels: Thin slices of veal or pork 3 to 5 mm ($\frac{1}{8}$ to $\frac{1}{4}$ inch) thick dipped in flour, egg and finally dried breadcrumbs. The meat is refrigerated to allow the crumbs to set before being shallow-fried.

Score: To make a shallow diamond-shaped pattern or parallel incisions in the outer fat layer of lamb or mutton or the rind of pork to improve the appearance and to facilitate carving.

Simmer: To cook in gently bubbling liquid kept just below boiling point.

Skim: To remove the fat or scum that floats on top of a liquid during the cooking process. A metal skimmer, kitchen paper, absorbent paper or ice cubes can be used.

Soufflé: A light, well-puffed egg dish which may be either sweet or savoury.

Speck: Pork fat. Also a name for German streaky bacon.

Steak tartare: Raw, finely chopped seasoned beef, traditionally served topped with a raw egg yolk and accompanied by small bowls of chopped onions and capers.

Stock: The liquid obtained after water, meat, bones, vegetables, herbs and seasoning have been simmered together for a few hours to extract flavour. Stock is used instead of water as a basis for sauces and soups, and in stews, casseroles and other dishes.

Sweetbreads: The thymus gland of a young animal, usually a calf, although sometimes the pancreatic gland is sold instead. Cooked sweetbreads are light pink in colour.

Tacos: Mexican corn pancakes fried until crisp and then filled with a savoury filling. Crisp taco shells are available at most health food shops and supermarkets.

Timbale: A cup-shaped mould made of earthenware or metal. The name also applies to the dish prepared in the mould, for example tomato timbales.

Trim: To cut off any excess fat or rind, for example from bacon.

Vinaigrette: Vinaigrette or French dressing is the basic oil-and-vinegar salad dressing of France. Vinaigrette consists of a mixture of olive oil, wine vinegar (the usual proportion of oil to vinegar is three parts to one, but this can be varied to suit your own taste), salt and freshly ground black pepper. Herbs, mustard and garlic may also be added.

Vol-au-vent: A small puff pastry case filled with a savoury filling to which cubes of meat or fish have been added. The cases are often served as hors d'oeuvre or snacks.

Zester: An instrument used to remove thin strips of rind from citrus fruit, leaving the white pith behind.

Kebabs

Pittas, poppadums and tacos

Schnitzels

Larding a beef roast

Scotch fillets and T-bone

Scoring a pork roast

Noisettes of lamb

Ridged steak pans

Vol-au-vent and bouchées

Using a pastry funnel

Saddle of lamb

Zester for citrus fruit

INDEX